Public History

Public History

An Introduction from Theory to Application

Jennifer Lisa Koslow

Florida State University, Tallahassee, FL, USA

Registered Office
John Wiley & Sons, Inc., 111 River Street, Hoboken, NJ 07030, USA

Editorial Office
111 River Street, Hoboken, NJ 07030, USA

For details of our global editorial offices, customer services, and more information about Wiley products visit us at www.wiley.com.

Wiley also publishes its books in a variety of electronic formats and by print-on-demand. Some content that appears in standard print versions of this book may not be available in other formats.

Library of Congress Cataloging-in-Publication Data

Name: Koslow, Jennifer Lisa, 1970– author. | Wiley-Blackwell (Firm), publisher.
Title: Public history : an introduction from theory to application / Jennifer L. Koslow, Florida State University, Tallahassee, USA.
Description: Hoboken, NJ : Wiley-Blackwell, 2021. | Includes bibliographical references and index.
Identifiers: LCCN 2020038918 (print) | LCCN 2020038919 (ebook) | ISBN 9781119146742 (paperback) | ISBN 9781119146780 (adobe pdf) | ISBN 9781119146797 (epub)
Subjects: LCSH: Public history.
Classification: LCC D16.163 .K67 2021 (print) | LCC D16.163 (ebook) | DDC 900–dc23
LC record available at https://lccn.loc.gov/2020038918

Cover Design: Wiley
Cover Image: © Heidi Besen/Shutterstock.com

Set in 9.5/12.5pt STIXTwoText by SPi Global, Pondicherry, India

10 9 8 7 6 5 4 3 2 1

Contents

Preface

Purpose of the Book

History departments across the United States increasingly offer classes to undergraduates on the ways and means of collecting, preserving, and interpreting history with and for public audiences. These courses are categorized as public history. Undergraduate history majors view the subject with interest as they contemplate what to do with their degree upon graduation. In addition, public history classes often serve as foundations for students interested in pursuing experiential or service-learning components with a cultural organization as part of their educational experience.

In recent years, the National Council on Public History (NCPH) has given attention to undergraduate curriculums. The NCPH put together a "Best Practices" for introducing undergraduates to public history in 2016. This document discusses the need to provide students with basic training in historical methods as well as introducing them to the various genres wherein public history is most often constructed and practiced: museums, archives, historic preservation, heritage tourism, media, oral history, and cultural resources management. What I have found in my years of teaching public history is that while students are excited about the prospect of working in historic sites and spaces, and with historical material, they often know very little about the history of the institutions within which they hope to seek employment. As a result, I structure my public history courses to provide students with a foundation of historical knowledge about the types of places they might work in when they graduate. In addition, I discuss contemporary theories and methods.

The goal of *Public History: An Introduction from Theory to Application* is to offer undergraduates a synthetic analysis of the past with exercises in the fundamentals of practice. After using this textbook, students will be able to identify significant individuals and events associated with the history of museums, historic preservation, archives, and oral history. Also, students will be able to critically evaluate how, why, where, and who produces history in public settings. Central to these inquiries will be investigations into four major themes in the practice of public history: uncovering hidden histories, constructing interpretations, creating a sense of place, and negotiating contested memories. Although there are some global references and comparisons made throughout the text, this book is focused explicitly on developments within the United States.

Structure of the Book

Public History: An Introduction from Theory to Application provides students with a background in the history, principles, and practices of the field of public history. Each chapter, except for Chapter 8 Practicing Ethical Public History, is divided into four sections: History, Theory, Practice, and Further Resources. Each section begins with an introductory narrative that sets out the history of that particular genre of public history. (The length varies by topic.) The next narrative section discusses current theories of best practices related to collecting, preserving, and interpreting history concerning the specific genre. The third part of each chapter is a series of exercises that ask students to take the history and theory of what they have studied for that genre and put it into practice. The final section of each chapter is a bibliography of further resources.

The text follows the outline I most typically use to teach undergraduates. I start with the history of public history and then move on to the subject of museums because people are most familiar with this type of location. However, instructors are not beholden to my outline and should feel free to assign the chapters in any order that works for their course. Also, I often spend more time on some topics than others. As a result, I spread some material (museums is a prime example) over two or three weeks. Instructors should assign the content in a way that supports their course design and timetables.

1

Defining Public History

One of the most common questions Public Historians get asked is, "what is Public History?" This chapter will provide you with a historical background on the history of professional historians working with and for public audiences since the early twentieth century in the United States. It will also cover late twentieth-century developments such as the establishment of the *Public Historian* and the formation of the National Council on Public History (NCPH). The section on theory will explain how public historians consider sharing inquiry and authority in collecting, preserving, and interpreting history for general audiences. You will also learn the basics of historical practice: distinguishing primary from secondary sources, analyzing primary and secondary sources, and constructing a reasonable argument based on evidence.

History

In some ways, public history is an old profession; in other ways, it is a newly defined specialty within the broader discipline of history. This section examines who created the term "Public History" and why. It also provides a background on the many instances of professional historians – those with academic degrees in history – working in what has come to be known as public history. I use capitalization (Public History) to distinguish the formalization of a profession within the discipline of history. I use lower case (public history) to describe a larger world of history as public service, which is accomplished by a variety of people who may or may not have formal academic credentials in history. Considering these two histories helps explain what historians mean when they say they study, teach, and practice public history.

Robert Kelley coined the term "Public History" in 1975. Kelley was born in 1925 in Santa Barbara, California. After serving in World War II, he earned a BA from

Public History: An Introduction from Theory to Application, First Edition. Jennifer Lisa Koslow.
© 2021 by John Wiley & Sons, Inc. Published 2021 by John Wiley & Sons, Inc.

what would become the University of California, Santa Barbara, and then a PhD in history from Stanford University. The University of California, Santa Barbara's History Department then hired him as a faculty member. His original focus of study was the politics of water and mining in California. His research brought him to the attention of the California Attorney General, who hired Kelley to produce reports and serve as an expert witness on behalf of the state on the subject of the history of hydraulic mining and its environmental consequences. Twenty years later, Kelley attempted to take the valuable skill set that he had learned through that experience and translate it into a formal curriculum for graduate students in history.

Kelley's interest in developing a new program in what he termed "Public History," was more than a theoretical dalliance. In the 1970s, undergraduate interest in majoring in history declined, but graduate programs were slow to catch up.[1] Consequently, programs produced more PhDs than there were openings for teaching history at four-year colleges and universities. As a result, job opportunities for graduate students in history precipitously declined. Graduate students had been trained to teach in institutions of higher education. Now what?

Robert Kelley advocated a new type of graduate training. Based on his own experience, he believed historians could and should play a critical role in policy making. In his seminal piece, "Public History: Its Origins, Nature, and Prospects," Kelley defined Public History as "the employment of historians and historical method outside of academia; in government, private corporations, the media, historical societies and museums, even in private practice." Although Kelley's definition might seem place-based, he viewed these as spaces of "public process." His goal was to prompt graduate students, and the broader historical profession, to recognize that the traditional skills graduate students learned ("narrative communication in concise clear form; an appetite for extended research; an interest in problem solving; and the power of conceptualization") married well with public concerns.[2]

Still, in preparing History majors to work in the public sector, Kelley understood that a new curriculum was needed to address a different set of questions public servants faced. How do you work as a team? How do you approach projects that are assigned to you versus projects that you have constructed of your volition? Last, what types of administrative skills must you acquire to be successful in non-academic environments? These questions were not just about creating alternative forms of work but were about articulating a new field of study within the discipline of history.

After founding a program in 1975, Kelley worked with his colleague G. Wesley Johnson to establish a journal, the *Public Historian*, in 1978. They arrived at this decision after hosting several conferences that brought together historians working in a variety of positions and places for the public's benefit and those who hoped to create graduate programs. A journal, Kelley and Johnson reasoned, could serve as a platform for communication across this very diverse universe. After yet another round of meetings, it became clear that a national organization was needed and, in 1979, the NCPH was born. Shortly after, the two entities became connected. Upon joining NCPH, members received the *Public Historian*. Combined, the two offered practitioners of public history space to present original research, offer advice from the field, and disseminate reviews of relevant literature. The NCPH and *Public Historian* continue to provide an essential space for Public Historians to converse.

Kelley can be credited with coining the term "Public History" and for articulating the demand for a distinct curriculum within history degrees. However, as scholars who study the development of the historical profession will tell you, historians in the United States had a long history of public engagement before the 1970s, especially with the federal government. In the early twentieth century, they worked with the federal government as consultants, as staff of federal departments, and as employees of the National Park Service (NPS). By recognizing when, how, and why historians participated in public engagement during the twentieth century teaches us about the meaning of "history practiced as public service."[3]

World War I, for instance, provided a prime opportunity for historians to engage in public outreach.[4] When war broke out in Europe in June of 1914 residents of the United States were divided as to which side to support and the government took an official stance of neutrality. Woodrow Wilson created the Committee on Public Information (CPI) to promote favorable opinions for government actions when the United States officially entered the war in April 1917 on the side of the Allied Powers (Great Britain, France, Italy, Japan, and Russia). The CPI printed numerous materials in newspapers and magazines. In addition, it hired several hundred men to give four-minute speeches at community events across the nation.

The CPI also hired leading historical scholars to create materials to distribute to public schools to explain the causes of the war and the character of the belligerents. For instance, Charles Beard and John Franklin Jameson participated in writing *The War Cyclopedia: A Handbook for Ready Reference on the Great War*. (In 1882, Jameson received the first PhD in history granted by Johns Hopkins University.[5] Charles Beard received his PhD from Columbia University in 1904 and was known for his provocative texts that proposed a relationship between economic interests and the nation's founding institutions.[6]) As is the case with most encyclopedias, individual names did not appear on the entries. Taken as a whole, however, the encyclopedia demonstrates that historians desired engagement in public projects. It is also an example that challenges a widespread belief that historians only became political in the late twentieth century.

Although the historical profession prided itself in the early twentieth century on using objectivity to reach conclusions about the past, the *War Cyclopedia* was a piece of propaganda. It argued that the Germans were entirely at fault for present predicaments. The entry "frightfulness" offers an example. It read in part:

> The name given to the German method of warfare whereby they make war terrible in the hope of winning victory through fear. . . . it does not mean the occasional and incidental horrors attached to warfare, but deliberate, systematic, and calculated terror conceived and ordered for the purpose of striking mortal fear into the hearts of foemen. . . . the German military authorities, unwilling to face like men the dangers of the situation they had themselves created, with studied design shot and hanged hundreds of Belgians, those innocent of all offense as well as those who had threatened or injured German soldiers."[7]

The *War Cyclopedia* was meant to clarify to those living in the United States why they should support the Allies. It did not invite debate over the reasons for the actions of the various participants. By today's standards of best practices within the discipline of history, the *War Cyclopedia* did not provide reasonable arguments based on evidence. However, it serves as an essential reminder that historians can have considerable sway over public perceptions of the past.

In the early twentieth century, historians also engaged in the creation of public policy. The United States Department of Agriculture (USDA), for instance, established a Division of Statistical and Historical Research in the 1910s. In 1919, a group of historians formed the Agricultural History Society (AHS) "to promote the interest, study and research in the history of agriculture."[8] The two entities worked together to provide government officials with perspectives on the past related to the production and consumption of agricultural products. In 1927, the AHS began publishing a journal, *Agricultural History*, to which USDA employees became regular contributors. This relationship continued until the 1960s when the research interests of scholars and the USDA diverged from each other.[9]

The 1930s was a critical period for the development of public history. In response to the financial crisis known as the Great Depression, Franklin D. Roosevelt's New Deal sponsored numerous employment programs for all different categories of skilled and unskilled labor. A series of programs provided funding for projects to collect and preserve historical records. For instance, the Federal Writers' Project (FWP) collected narratives of African Americans to preserve the history of slavery. The FWP also produced a series of guidebooks for each of America's 48 states to promote domestic heritage tourism. The Works Project Administration (WPA) conducted a historical records survey that inventoried the whereabouts of local government records by county. The federal government also funded a study of historic structures through NPS and Library of Congress. The 1930s also witnessed the creation of the National Archives.[10] The most significant legacy for the development of public history was the federal government's investment in NPS during this period.

NPS was established in 1916. Its mission was "to conserve the scenery and the natural and historic objects and the wildlife therein and to provide for the enjoyment of the same in such manner and by such means as will leave them unimpaired for the enjoyment of future generations."[11] However, it was not until the 1930s that NPS began to regularly employ historians and what scholar Ian Tyrell has referred to as "historical workers."[12] The unprecedented economic downturn known as the Great Depression transformed NPS in several ways. For one, the parks became sites for work relief programs. The Civilian Conservation Corps provided hundreds of young men employment constructing park amenities that marked history on the landscape and built structures to house and display material culture.[13] Perhaps most importantly, Verne Chatelain became NPS's first chief historian. Scholar Denise Meringolo argues that under his tenure a new field arose: history as public service.[14]

Horace Albright, director of NPS from 1929 to 1933, hired Chatelain to head the historical division within the newly created Branch of Research and Education.[15] Chatelain received a doctoral degree in the history of policy at the University of Minnesota and was teaching history at Peru State Teachers College in Nebraska when Albright asked him to take on the position at NPS. Chatelain made it his goal to create a coherent policy for managing historic resources within and between all of the nation's federal parks.

In attempting to develop a strategy for history management, Chatelain drew upon examples of public outreach from outside of academia. After the Civil War in the United States, several organizations used grassroots efforts to preserve historical resources at the local and state level. These preservationists came from a variety of backgrounds and often did not possess an academic degree. In particular, patriotic organizations expressed considerable enthusiasm for creating public engagements with history. In addition, some states created historical societies to collect and preserve their histories. In Minnesota, a model that Chatelain studied, the Minnesota Historical Society successfully worked together with the Daughters of the American Revolution on preservation projects.[16] The members of these organizations were, in a sense, public historians. They fostered opportunities for the public to connect the past with the present. Even today, public history continues to attract practitioners from a variety of fields including artists, information scientists, architects, and archaeologists, to name a few.

At NPS, Chatelain found that traditional historical training – the analysis of textual documents to draw conclusions about the past – did not prepare students very well for working in the parks. Traditional historical training did not include information on how to analyze material culture, how to work across disciplines with scientists, and how to make connections with public audiences. Working at a historic site, however, park service employees of history needed to explain how material artifacts worked to shape societies of the past. Grist mills and spinning wheels were just two examples that Chatelain gave of objects that stymied history workers.[17] He needed to turn traditionally trained historians into "real Park Service men;" historians who could engage in interdisciplinary conversations with scientists, preservation organizations, and public audiences.[18] In doing so, they would learn to construct interpretations that created a sense of historical place.

Chatelain's tenure overlapped with the start of the Great Depression and the subsequent election of Franklin D. Roosevelt to the office of president in 1932. Roosevelt's New Deal programs had a direct positive impact on NPS. The territory it managed was enlarged, its programmatic capability was enhanced, and its financial support was greatly expanded. The passage of the Historic Sites Act of 1935 further improved Chatelain's abilities. Through it, he was able to develop a set of standards by which historic sites could be evaluated and included in a program for managing the nation's historic resources. He established a national policy that articulated a coherent narrative to join together different sites and stories. His push for an overarching interpretive framework guided NPS long after he had left his position. Public history, as historian Denise Meringolo demonstrates, owes a debt to Chatelain for developing history as a government job in the early 1930s. Here, she argues, is the origin of the notion of history as public service.[19]

During the 1940s, more positions opened up in government for historians.[20] The war prompted agencies to hire historians to identify records of permanent historical value and manage their preservation. Every service of the armed forces employed historians. The American Historical Association (AHA, the largest professional organization for historians working in the United States) also found itself in an interesting position. The War Department desired a series of pamphlets to provide a historical perspective on the conflict and the issues that communities would likely face in a postwar period. For example, Herbert Heaton and A.L. Burt, both historians at the University of Minnesota, wrote "Shall I go into Business for Myself?" and "Canada: Our Oldest Good Neighbor."[21]

Despite periods of cooperation, by the mid-twentieth century, the working domains of government history workers and academic historians functioned as separate entities. In the very early part of the twentieth century, for instance, members of local preservation societies and the staff of the few existing state historical societies (state entities that collected research materials and that sometimes also housed a library or museum) began meeting at the annual conference of the AHA. In 1940, however, these interests spun off from the AHA to form the American Association for State and Local History (AASLH).[22] The AASLH's mission was to work with NPS, local private historical organizations, and state agencies. It also began publishing a magazine of history for widespread consumption, *American Heritage*. In 1979, historians working within the federal government founded the

Society for History in the Federal Government to address their own unique professional needs. As Jack M. Holl argues, federal historians work for the public sector, but not all of them necessarily work for or with general audiences.[23]

As government history workers established their own identities in the postwar period, universities began to grow. The GI Bill (1944) girded that development. The tremendous expansion of access to higher education opened up traditional teaching job opportunities for graduate students until the 1970s.

The elaboration of the "new social history" in the 1960s and 1970s also informed the development of public history. In the immediate post-World War II period, many historians of US history studied aspects that unified people together as one nation. In response to, and as a part of civil rights activism, historians changed the direction of their analysis to examine the institutional factors that divide Americans. In addition, instead of focusing on the actions and beliefs of political and economic leaders, historians evaluated historical events from the bottom-up. In new social history, scholars studied the historical role of women, minorities, and other marginalized groups in shaping social, political, and economic environments around the world. A number of these new social historians wanted "to democratize not just the content of history (adding the stories of African Americans, industrial workers, immigrants, women, and gays) but also its practice."[24] The idea of co-creation was embraced and, perhaps, best actualized in the emergence of oral history (which will be discussed in Chapter 6). Thus, overall there was a synergy between the development of Public History and new social history as complimentary perspectives and mechanisms by which to foster engagement with the past and encourage inclusivity.

As the twentieth century became the twenty-first, Public History as a distinct field within history grew. Currently, there are over 100 graduate programs listed on the NCPH's website.[25] In addition to the development of opportunities for academic training, the notion that history can be a public service has also grown. The NCPH's annual conference attracts hundreds of history workers from both the private and public sectors. Filmmakers, preservationists, museum curators, and academics (to name a few) meet to discuss theories and practices for engaging in history with and for public audiences. The meeting provides useful information for those beginning their careers and for those looking for continuing professional development. The conference's diversity is its strength. While the environments within which people practice might be different, there is a consensus that public history should be useful, interdisciplinary, and collaborative.

These conversations also extend beyond national borders. In 2010, the International Federation for Public History (IFPH) was established. It was then "designated as an Internal Commission of the International Congress of Historical Sciences, a non-governmental organization created to promote the historical sciences through international cooperation."[26] Its goal is to create international conversations about best practices in teaching, researching, and evaluating public history. It does this through its blog, website, and an annual (sometimes biannual) conference.

The IFPH is also a reminder that the lexicon of public history differs depending on national contexts. In the United States, the creation of formalized degree programs calcified the term Public History to describe a common curriculum centered on community engagement. In other nations, however, there are different origin stories and different descriptors are used.[27] In a global context, heritage studies, memory studies, museum studies, and public history often serve as analogous preparation for conceptualizing the use of history as public service. This particular textbook focuses on these developments with a US context but refers to global developments when they played a critical role in influencing ideas and discourses in the United States.

Public history, while often an unfamiliar term to many at first, is a profession with a long history. In the twentieth century, historians have developed materials and programs to engage public audiences. While historians working in government, cultural organizations, and academia might work in different locations, the idea of history as a public service provides common ground. Another aspect that offers common ground is the appreciation and application of historical methods to decode the past and understand the future.

So, what is Public History? Public History is an academic credential that signifies that a person has mastered the art of historical methods in combination with how to collect, preserve, and interpret history for and with public audiences. Public history is also a process by which history is used to serve the public in making the past relevant to the present.

Theory

In this world, we often ask, "how do we know?" A historian will tell you to "think historically." What does that mean? In its most basic form, thinking historically means to gather and analyze evidence from the past to form a reasonable conclusion as to how and why something happened.

Historians begin their projects with questions, not answers. For example, why did women, as opposed to the government, take the lead in saving George Washington's house in the 1850s? Or, how did veteran organizations change how the National Air and Space Museum displayed the *Enola Gay* in the 1990s? There is no set of preordained questions for historians to ask. Instead, individual curiosity drives research agendas.

Once historians have a question they then pose a hypothesis and then conduct research in an attempt to find an answer. In their years of schooling, historians are trained to construct reasonable explanations to their questions based on their evaluation of evidence. Sometimes this means that a historian needs to change their question when they cannot find evidence or the evidence points them in a different direction.

The process of historical research and analysis involves engaging with what we call secondary and primary sources. Secondary sources are scholarly assessments of a historical topic. All good historians consult with other scholars in composing questions. Historical scholarship (be it articles, books, exhibits, or discussions at conferences) is a conversation. In creating a question, historians want to know what other people have asked as well as how they have answered that question. This often leads to new questions or revisiting old questions with a fresh eye.

Primary sources are materials that situate the question within the context of its time. They are the evidence. Examples of primary sources are letters, newspapers, government documents, photographs, and other creations of material culture (clothing, utensils, tools, structures, etc.). Primary sources can be texts (i.e. written documents), images, or artifacts. Historians read secondary works as they examine primary sources and vice versa while they construct a reasoned interpretation of the past.

Historians ask several questions while they work with primary sources. First, what is the nature of the source? For example, is a private diary for oneself? Or is it a letter to be shared with family members? Is it a photograph taken by a journalist for a newspaper? Is it a previously classified email between two government officials? In analyzing the source, historians ask who created it, when and where was the source created, and why was it created? Once a historian determines the answers to those questions, they turn their attention to the source's subject matter. A historian looks at keywords, focal points, and key phrases. Once a historian completes that analysis they can assess the significance of the source for their question. Does it contradict the historian's hypothesis, or does it support it? How does it compare and contrast to the other sources the historian has analyzed? Does the historian need to come up with a new theory as to why something happened?

Once a historian has completed their examination of the past about a particular historical question, they disseminate this new knowledge. The historian might convey their findings in an article, book, class, lecture, conference, exhibit, blog, and website. As they share their conclusions new historical questions arise, and the process begins all over again! This is why history is not "fixed." Instead, it is an evolving interpretation of past events.

In addition to historical methods, Public Historians employ two additional tenets: sharing authority and sharing inquiry. However, they are not always easy to achieve. How do you work with general audiences to formulate intellectual content and deliverable products? Public historians aspire to collaborate as they work to collect, preserve, and interpret history for and with public audiences.

In 1990, historian Michael Frisch gave voice to the idea that public history was particularly helpful for this type of methodology. In his experience, especially in conducting oral histories, public history had "a capacity to redefine and redistribute intellectual authority."[28] Instead of viewing audiences as empty vessels within whom to fill knowledge, audiences become central to the interpretive process. Public audiences can and should participate in determining how to construct the historical narratives that become history: the stories we read in books, exhibits, and other displays of the past. Although cultural politics can make this methodological approach challenging to implement, it is nonetheless the goal.

In 2006, scholars Katharine T. Corbett and Howard S. Miller offered a self-reflection on their ability to actualize this methodology in their long careers as Public Historians. Their summary judgment about the benefits and limits of sharing inquiry and authority offer public historians sage advice on collaborative actions. They reminded practitioners "the buck stops with the historian."[29] The role of the scholar is to implement the best practices of the historian's craft. Cooperation does not constitute an abdication of that fundamental responsibility.

In sum, Public Historians use some of the same tools as their colleagues working in institutions of higher learning. They make reasonable arguments based on primary evidence. They evaluate their arguments with other historical arguments. They reconsider their arguments as new primary evidence appears, or they approach the topic from a new angle. At the same time, Public Historians work to include a diversity of audiences in constructing historical questions and evaluating the evidence. In doing so, Public Historians often aim to involve otherwise marginalized groups in the production of historical narratives. However, this is not always as easy at it seems. A variety of impediments, from legacies of mistrust to the dearth of material artifacts, can inhibit inclusion.

There is no one set topic from the past that Public Historians pursue to collect, preserve, and interpret. However, four themes often recur in the work of public historians. They are (i) public history can uncover hidden histories, (ii) public history allows for the construction of multiple interpretations, (iii) public history can create a sense of place, and (iv) public historians often grapple with negotiating contested memories. People encounter history in their everyday experiences, usually when they are least expecting it. Individuals create meaning about the pasts they meet, and that interpretation can change. A person's encounter with the past can shape how they interact with a location. Last, fierce debates sometimes occur about the meaning of the past. Throughout this text, we will come back to these four themes as we investigate the history of who, when, where, and why history is collected, preserved, and interpreted with public audiences.

Practice

1) Analyze two different primary sources about the same event and develop an argument about them. (Try the digital collections at the Library of Congress or the National Archives.[30]) As you analyze the documents figure out what is the nature of each source (diary? photograph? letter? government document?). If you can, figure out who created each source and when and where each source was created. Can you determine why each source was created? Once you identify the basics, can you figure out the subject matter of each source? Are there any keywords, focal points, or key phrases that drew your attention? Create a summary and assess the significance of each source. Last, do the sources leave some questions unanswered? What are the limits of the two sources you analyzed?

2) Read one of the earliest articles from the *Public Historian* and analyze it in the context of when it was published. What was the reason for the article? What types of historical questions or problems was the author responding to when they wrote it?

3) Take an article from the *Public Historian* and divide the sources into primary and secondary and locate at least one of each.

4) Attend a public history event (a talk for a general audience, walking tour, etc. where a historian guides the discussion). Summarize the content of what you learned from your experience. Did you find the delivery method compelling? Why or why not?

5) Interview a Public Historian about their job. How do they include public audiences in collecting, preserving, and interpreting history? How do they work with colleagues in other disciplines?

Further Resources

- Alderson, Jr, William T. "The American Association for State and Local History." *Western Historical Quarterly* 1, no. 2 (April 1970): 175–182.
- American Association of Local and State History: www.aaslh.org.
- American Historical Association: www.historians.org.
- Ashton, Paul, and Alex Trapeznik. *What is Public History Globally? Working with the Past in the Present.* London, UK: Bloomsbury Academic, 2019.
- Corbett, Katharine T., and Howard S. Miller. "A Shared Inquiry into Shared Inquiry." *The Public Historian* 28, no. 1 (Winter, 2006): 15–38.
- Davis, Terry L. "For History's Sake, Associations Advance the Field." *The Public Historian* 22, no. 2 (Spring, 2000): 51–60.

- Frisch, Michael. *A Shared Authority: Essays on the Craft and Meaning of Oral and Public History.* Albany, NY: State University of New York Press, 1990.
- Graham, Otis L. Jr. "Robert Kelley and the Pursuit of Useful History." *The Journal of Policy History* 23, no. 3 (2011): 429–437.
- Holl, Jack M. "Cultures in Conflict: An Argument Against 'Common Ground' Between Practicing Professional Historians and Academics." *The Public Historian* 30, no. 2 (Spring, 2008): 29–50.
- Johnson, G. Wesley. "The Origins of 'The Public Historian,' and the National Council on Public History." *The Public Historian* 21, no. 3 (Summer, 1999): 167–179.
- Kelley, Robert. "Public History: Its Origins, Nature, and Prospects." *The Public Historian* 1, no. 1 (Autumn 1978): 16–28.
- Meringolo, Denise D. *Museums, Monuments, and National Parks: Toward a New Genealogy of Public History.* Amherst, MA: University of Massachusetts Press, 2012.
- National Council on Public History: https://ncph.org
- Rosenzweig, Roy, and David Thelen. *The Presence of the Past: Popular Uses of History in American Life.* New York, NY: Columbia University Press, 1998.
- Society for History in the Federal Government: http://shfg.org/shfg.
- Townsend, Robert B. "History in Those Hard Times: Looking for Jobs in the 1970s." *Perspectives on History* (September 2009).
- Tyrell, Ian. *Historians in Public: The Practice of American History, 1890–1970.* Chicago, IL: University of Chicago Press, 2005.

References

1 Robert B. Townsend, "History in Those Hard Times: Looking for Jobs in the 1970s," *Perspectives on History* (September 2009).
2 Robert Kelley, "Public History: Its Origins, Nature, and Prospects," *The Public Historian* 1, no. 1 (Autumn 1978): 16 and 23.
3 Denise M. Meringolo, *Museums, Monuments, and National Parks: Toward a New Genealogy of Public History* (Amherst, MA: University of Massachusetts Press, 2012), xxxi–xxxii.
4 Ian Tyrell, *Historians in Public: The Practice of American History, 1890–1970* (Chicago, IL: University of Chicago Press, 2005), 162–164.
5 "J. Franklin Jameson Biography," www.historians.org/about-aha-and-membership/aha-history-and-archives/presidential-addresses/j-franklin-jameson/j-franklin-jameson-biography; http://americanarchivist.org/doi/pdf/10.17723/aarc.19.3.007767111482qu14?code=same-site.

6 "Charles A. Beard Biography," www.historians.org/about-aha-and-membership/
aha-history-and-archives/presidential-addresses/charles-a-beard/
charles-a-beard-biography.

7 *War Cyclopedia* (Washington DC: Government Printing Office, 1918), 104–105.

8 "Agricultural History Society," http://aghistorysociety.org/society.

9 Tyrell, *Historians in Public*, 166–168.

10 Ibid., 175–180.

11 "Organic Act of 1916," www.nps.gov/grba/learn/management/organic-
act-of-1916.htm.

12 Tyrell, *Historians in Public*, 173.

13 Ibid., 173–174.

14 Meringolo, *Museums, Monuments, and National Parks*, xiii–xiv and xxxii.

15 Ibid., 98.

16 Ibid., 104.

17 Ibid., 107.

18 Ibid., 108.

19 Ibid., 155.

20 Tyrell, *Historians in Public*, 185–191.

21 "GI Roundtable Series, Pamphlets," www.historians.org/about-aha-and-
membership/aha-history-and-archives/gi-roundtable-series/pamphlets.

22 William T. Alderson, Jr. "The American Association for State and Local History,"
Western Historical Quarterly 1, no. 2 (April 1970): 175–178. Terry L. Davis, "For
History's Sake, Associations Advance the Field," *The Public Historian* 22, no. 2
(Spring, 2000): 51–53.

23 Jack M. Holl, "Cultures in Conflict: An Argument Against 'Common Ground'
Between Practicing Professional Historians and Academics," *The Public Historian*
30, No. 2 (Spring, 2008): 30–32.

24 Roy Rosenzweig and David Thelen, *The Presence of the Past: Popular Uses of
History in American Life* (New York, NY: Columbia University Press, 1998): 4.

25 "Guide to Public History Programs," https://ncph.org/program-guide.

26 "IFPH-FIHP Bylaws," http://ifph.hypotheses.org/sample-page/
ifph-bylaws-fihp-statuts.

27 Paul Ashton and Alex Trapeznik, *What is Public History Globally? Working with
the Past in the Present* (London, UK: Bloomsbury Academic, 2019), 2–3, German
context, 70; Indian context, 79; and Scandinavian context, 121.

28 Michael Frisch, *A Shared Authority: Essays on the Craft and Meaning of Oral and
Public History* (Albany, NY: State University of New York Press, 1990), xx–xxi.

29 Katharine T. Corbett and Howard S. Miller "A Shared Inquiry into Shared
Inquiry," *The Public Historian* 28, no. 1 (Winter, 2006): 21.

30 "Library of Congress, Digital Collections," www.loc.gov/collections; "National
Archives Catalog," https://catalog.archives.gov.

2

Exhibiting History

In 2007, the International Council of Museums (ICOM) defined a "Museum" as "a non-profit, permanent institution in the service of society and its development, open to the public, which acquires, conserves, researches, communicates and exhibits the tangible and intangible heritage of humanity and its environment for the purposes of education, study and enjoyment."[1] This modern definition was centuries in the making. However, sometimes the word "museum" is employed in less formal arrangements. Sometimes museums are not permanent. Sometimes they are focused on only providing entertainment. Sometimes they are for-profit organizations. Sometimes they are not interested in research. Public Historians must acknowledge that not all museums fit the ICOM's definition. Still, studying those institutions that either fit within the rubric above or aspire to meet it is essential. These are the places with which most Public Historians will either work in or work with to collect, preserve, and interpret history with and for general audiences.

Museums are places of public trust. The evidence that supports this point is more than anecdotal. In the late 1980s and early 1990s, historians Roy Rosenzweig and David Thelen studied the various ways Americans engaged with the past. They knew from social movements of the 1960s and 1970s that people's engagement with history could be empowering.[2] Using social science techniques in 1994, Rosenzweig and Thelen supervised a survey of 808 Americans, of whom they made sure there was diversity represented. Rosenzweig and Thelen learned that except for Native Americans, interviewees identified museums as the most "trustworthy source of information about the past."[3] The reason being is that, for most people, they could see the material artifact for themselves. Also, most people believed that the collaborative nature of museum work made museum workers honest in displaying material culture to the public.[4] As a result, the infrastructure of the museum made it trustworthy.

Public History: An Introduction from Theory to Application, First Edition. Jennifer Lisa Koslow.
© 2021 by John Wiley & Sons, Inc. Published 2021 by John Wiley & Sons, Inc.

This chapter begins with some significant examples that help historicize the development of institutions known as museums, with a focus on the United States. In particular, the emphasis is on those institutions that presented history (including natural history) as a major aspect of its work and those that grabbed public attention. What might be hidden to you at first but should become clear are the continuities between the motivations of museum visitors and museum makers. "How do I know?" was a fundamental question that audiences sought to answer in museums. Nothing about answering this question necessarily was at odds with the desire to be entertained. Individuals who built museums in the United States did not often see a contradiction between the goals of providing entertainment and education. Also, the term "museum" is a malleable one. At different moments, it has meant different things: a place of objects, a place of research, a place of education, a place of experience, a place of identity formation, and a place of power. How and why people have created museums is at the crux of this story.

In the theory section, we will look at how museum professionals approach their institutions in the twenty-first century. Museums started as temples and, in many ways, they still are. However, in the late twentieth century ideas about democratic participation transformed expectations. Museums are now expected to be participatory spaces. In the theory section, we will look at the meaning of those changes for Public Historians. In addition, museums are places of interpretation. We will examine what this concept means for storytellers of history.

History

Americans were not the first to create a specific structure devoted to collecting objects believed to have historical significance.[5] In the seventeenth century, wealthy Europeans began to collect material objects and put them into "cabinets of curiosities." A cabinet of curiosity reflected the interests of its collector. In the Age of Enlightenment, these spaces functioned as a place to accumulate and disseminate knowledge. They often consisted of geological substances and zoological specimens. Cultural artifacts from around the globe also often found their way into these accumulations. As Katy Barrett, Curator of Art at the Royal Museums Greenwich, argues, examining the objects evoked a sense of awe-inspiring educational wonder.[6] Through this assemblage, the collector believed that they could obtain universal knowledge. Collectors also designed their cabinets to be shared among their peers.

A significant development in the history of public museums was the establishment of the British Museum in the mid-eighteenth century. Sir Hans Sloane, a British physician, collected almost 80,000 objects throughout his lifetime.[7] He wrote into his will that upon his death the collection should be offered to King George II on behalf of the British nation. If that offer was declined, Sloane stipulated that it should be made available for purchase to the Royal Academies of Science in Paris, St. Petersburg, Berlin, and, last, Madrid. However, the donation came at a cost. Sloane had two daughters, and he stipulated that the proceeds of the purchase, 40,000 pounds, be split between them.[8]

Parliament held a public lottery to raise funds in 1753 to afford the purchase price of what amounted to approximately seven million US dollars in today's relative wealth. After securing the funds, Parliament then found a suitable space to house the vast collection: Montagu House. Six years later, in 1759, the British Museum opened its doors and collections to "all studious and curious persons."[9] The mission of the institution was to preserve the collections. Its administration was less concerned with disseminating that knowledge to the public.

"Studious and curious persons" needed to apply for entry. It often took several months for a request to be processed while references were checked. Once issued, tickets were only valid for a specific appointment and, once inside, for a very limited time. A German visitor described his disappointingly rushed experience in 1782:

So rapid a passage through a vast suite of rooms in little more than one hour of time, with opportunity to cast but one poor longing look of astonishment on all the vast treasures of nature, antiquity and literature, in the examination of which one might profitably spend years, confuses, stuns and overpowers the visitor."[10]

On Easter Monday 1837, this changed. The British Museum opened its doors to the general public and attracted almost 24,000 visitors that day. Fears that the "public" would destroy the collections, perhaps in a drunken haze, proved unfounded. The museum kept holding open days and slowly increased access. Over the course of the nineteenth century, museums and libraries became understood as places to foster an educated and moral citizenry. The passage of the Museums Act of 1845 and the Public Libraries Act of 1850 led to the widespread establishment of these cultural institutions across the United Kingdom. However, this level of local government support to create similar ventures was not replicated in the United States.

Museums were not always successful ventures. Pierre Eugène Du Simitière's American Museum is a case in point. Originally from Geneva, Du Simitière spent his young adulthood traveling in the West Indies. In his travels, Du Simitière collected varieties of specimens of the natural world. He also drew images of the flora and fauna he encountered. He came to colonial America in the mid-1760s, settling in Philadelphia in 1769 at the age of 33. There he became a member of the American Philosophical Society (APS), which had been founded by Benjamin

Franklin in 1743 to promote "useful knowledge." Du Simitière turned to painting to support himself. His portraits of revolutionary leaders led to some fame. He also designed images that appeared on official coins, seals, and medals. However, neither activity amounted to financial success.

Among intellectual circles of Du Simitière's time, he was known for his collecting acumen. Historian of science Martin Levey argues that Du Simitière always intended to create a museum.[11] Posting advertisements in Philadelphia's papers, Du Simitière opened up his house to "Gentlemen and Ladies" who wished to view "the curiosities it contains" in the summer of 1782. However, he charged 50 cents for admission, and only opened it three days a week. In addition, just eight people could view the material at one time, and they had to stay with the tour. As a result, opening the museum did not resolve Du Simitière's financial problems and he died a pauper just two years later. His collection was sold at public auction. To contrast Du Simitière's failure we will turn our attention to an example of success.

Charles Willson Peale created the most influential American museum in the history of the Early Republic. His motivation did not come from precedent. First, while Peale and Du Simitière lived within a few blocks of each other in Philadelphia, there is no archival evidence that Peale drew direct inspiration from Du Simitière's experience.[12] Second, although it is possible that Peale was familiar with the Charleston Library Society's attempt to create a museum in the 1770s, the American Revolution had interrupted its effort.[13] Moreover, Peale desired something that neither of these other ventures attempted. Peale wanted to combine amusement and education into one institution and open it to the masses. However, despite its popularity, Peale's museum did not last long past his death, and by the late nineteenth century his model for museum making was forgotten.

Born in 1741, Peale began his adult life as a saddlemaker. However, painting turned out to be his talent. In the 1760s, Peale secured the support from some wealthy benefactors in Maryland to pay for his training in London. Upon his return in 1769, he moved his family to Philadelphia and painted portraits of leaders of the American Revolution. Peale became known for his contributions to shaping public memory of the Revolution through his luminary pictures. These were depictions of allegorical stories of America's victories painted on a thin fabric, which he placed in the windows of his house and backlit with candles to be viewed at night.[14]

It appears that Peale's first contemplation of a museum began with a conversation with his brother-in-law. Colonel Nathaniel Ramsay had come to visit the family in 1784. Peale, as did many artists of his day, had a small studio gallery affixed to the house to display his work. As Ramsay looked at the various pieces, he noticed a set of huge bones set out on a table. They were fossils from a variety of animals from a region in the Ohio country (present-day Kentucky) known as Big Bone Lick. The bones belonged to a physician, John Morgan. Peale was drawing them for a German army surgeon who wished to bring them back for study in his native land. Peale's brother-in-law suggested that people might pay to see the fossils more then they would pay Peale for his artistry.[15]

Peale was not poor, but support for his growing family was a concern. (Peale had 17 children. He was married and widowed several times.) Peale wrote to two different scientists to see what they thought about the idea of creating a natural history museum for general audiences. He received divided advice. The only other models were European, and they were state-supported. As a result, Peale turned his attention for a few years to create "moving pictures" (illuminated backlit scenes that changed before the viewer). However, his curiosity about creating a museum never completely disappeared, and in 1786 he began this venture in earnest.

Peale needed objects. He placed an advertisement in the *Pennsylvania Packet* from July 7 until November 12, 1786, seeking donations of "many Wonderful Works of Nature which are now closeted but seldom seen" to become part of his "Repository for Natural Curiosities." He would mark each item's origin and, unless the donor objected, publicly credit the donor. He used his house, which had a room for display. He charged 25 cents, which was a modest admission fee. He desired to create a place that was a "school of useful knowledge" and to "diffuse its usefulness to every class in our country." Moreover, it was to be open to "the adult of each sex and age." Lastly, he believed that amusement was essential to instruction. Here then was a museum that was open to all citizens regardless of their sex, age, or class.[16]

The Age of the Enlightenment informed Peale's ideas of institution building. He embraced the idea that knowledge could and should be obtained through systematic observation and description of phenomena. He wanted his museum to serve as a visual encyclopedia of the world. In pursuit of this goal, he became a member of the APS. Peale also corresponded with scientists in Europe hoping to secure artifacts. However, they were more interested in acquiring American items than exchanging objects.

Peale's opening of his museum was fortuitous. In the late eighteenth century, Philadelphia was the seat of political power and knowledge production. Besides being home to the APS, it was also the site of the University of Pennsylvania. Philadelphia also served as the nation's capital from 1790 to 1800, while facilities in Washington DC were being built. Peale secured the support of leading officials. For instance, when Peale began offering subscription tickets in 1796 George Washington and John Adams were the first two on the list of purchasers. Peale also corresponded with Secretary of State Thomas Jefferson about the idea of a national museum. Although generally supportive of the concept, Jefferson explained that most Congressmen viewed their power as limited when it came to spending public money on materials not enumerated in the Constitution.

Although Peale's museum did not succeed in becoming the nation's official museum it benefited in other ways from these associations. For instance, Jefferson would later place animal skins and skeletons from Meriwether Lewis and William Clark's expedition in the museum.[17]

Between his contacts at the APS, government, and his advertisements in the newspaper, Peale acquired more than a thousand objects. In 1794, space opened up in Philosophical Hall, which bordered a major public park (now known as Independence Square). The APS leased the building from the state and promptly offered it to Peale as a residence and as a museum space. In 1802, the city granted Peale space in the adjacent State House (today it is known as Independence Hall),

Figure 2.1 Charles Willson Peale's self-portrait of him and his museum. *Source:* Gift of Mrs. Sarah Harrison (The Joseph Harrison, Jr. Collection).

including the Assembly Room and the room wherein the Declaration of Independence had been signed. Unlike a traditional cabinet of curiosity, which was a display of a collector's wealth, Peale viewed his museum as a public service. He believed that moving into these quasi-public spaces moved him one step closer to his ultimate goal, which was to turn his privately funded museum into a nationally funded public one. However, this goal was never realized.[18]

Peale used a Linnaean classification system to order knowledge in his museum. (Carl Linnaeus, a Swedish physician, botanist, and zoologist, delineated a system in 1735 for categorizing the natural world.) Peale was unique in placing birds into landscapes to display them in the context of their natural habitats. He also acquired and showed live animals: especially snakes. His most famous addition was a mastodon skeleton, a distant relative of the elephant, which he obtained in 1801 from a farmer in the Hudson River Valley in New York. While bones had been found and displayed in various forms before, Peale secured enough remnants to reconstruct two complete skeletons. He presented one at the museum, for which he charged a separate 50-cent admission and had his sons take the other on tour in Europe and then through the southern United States. Described in the popular press as the "mammoth," the word soon became an adjectival fad to describe people and events.[19]

In 1810, Peale's son, Rubens, took over daily management of the museum. Rubens Peale added nighttime attractions. Enjoying an evening in a "brightly lighted room," visitors could listen to an organ concert or watch demonstrations of chemistry experiments. In 1816, Rubens replaced the oil lamps with gas lighting, which was a first in the United States for a large public space. While this was a considerable expense ($5,000, which is almost $88,000 today), Rubens was able to recoup the cost within a few months. In 1814, Peale's son Rembrandt opened a museum in Baltimore. This was the first time a structure was built explicitly to be a museum, but it was not as large as the original in Philadelphia or as devoted to science. Rubens created the third iteration in New York City in 1825.[20]

Two years later, in 1827, Charles Willson Peale died. He was 86. His museum and its spin-offs did not last. The same year as his death, the Philadelphia museum moved into a new building because the statehouse was sold to the city. However, the latest building quickly developed leaks and other structural issues appeared. Financial problems in the 1830s became exacerbated by the Panic of 1837. As a way out of debt, the Baltimore, New York, and eventually the Philadelphia collections were sold to an up-and-coming entrepreneur in museum making, Phineas Taylor Barnum.

Peale's museum was the first successful effort to create an institution dedicated to collecting, preserving, and interpreting the history of natural sciences for public audiences in the United States. It had an "educational function, [was] open to all, administered by experts, offere[d] lectures, [and] issue[d] publications."[21]

However, Peale's museum faded from memory once the objects were deaccessioned and the museum closed. When museum makers began to build educational institutions again in the late nineteenth century, they did not know that there was an American tradition to draw from for a model. Instead, they would attempt to draw a contrast to the world of cheap amusements that became popularized by Barnum and his likes.

In the nineteenth century, museum making was tied to other demographic changes. The rise of cities and the development of working- and middle-classes opened up new opportunities for leisure. Institutions known as "dime museums" began to appear. One marker of distinction between allegedly reputable and dissolute spaces was whether the museum promoted itself as a space for both "ladies and gentleman" as opposed to just the male gaze. The most famous and most financially successful dime museum was Phineas Taylor Barnum's American Museum.

Barnum was born in 1810 in Bethel, Connecticut (a rural town approximately 70 miles north of New York City). Although a small town, it did have a common school and there was a private academy in a nearby town. Consequently, Barnum received a well-rounded education growing up. He was the oldest of five children. His father, who had kept an inn and was a tailor, died when Barnum was 16. His father's passing could have been tragic for the family because he died with debts. However, the family was able to stay in the house and keep most of their personal property. Moreover, Barnum's grandfather was one of Bethel's wealthiest citizens.[22]

As a young man, Barnum worked at a country store and then attempted to open two different grocery stores of his own. He also married and began to have children. He was known as someone who liked a good practical joke. He was also interested in politics, and when the local paper rejected his letters to the editor for publication, he started a newspaper. In 1834, Barnum decided to try his luck in New York City. About a year after his resettlement, a friend, Coley Bartram, showed him a business opportunity in the paper that would change Barnum's fortunes. A touring exhibition of Joice Heth was for sale.

Joice Heth was an elderly African American woman. Her managers claimed that she had been George Washington's nanny. Hence, in 1835, this put her at 161 years of age. For a fee, persons could stand in her presence as she sat and sang hymns. Barnum secured a contract to exhibit Heth, and then he obtained space for her presentation on lower Broadway Avenue. The location he rented had become a known spot for popular entertainment; people went to see illuminated moving panorama paintings at the same hall. Also, within walking distance was John Scudder's American Museum.[23] In a period when minstrel shows were rising in popularity, Heth's was not the only African American body on display. Nor was this only an American phenomenon.[24] However, Heth's alleged connection to the nation's founding father made Heth a particularly enticing performance to attend.

After a stint in New York City, Barnum took Heth out on tour through New England. Scholar James Cook argues that Barnum's genius was in knowing how to market Heth with other popular amusements.[25] In Boston, Barnum acquired a room next door to Johann Maelzel's automaton chess-player, which was dressed in Turkish attire. Barnum's juxtaposition begged the question, was Heth a real person or a machine? Heth left space for imagination in the way in which she presented herself. She sat in silence as people gawked. She chose when to speak and sing. Barnum invited audience members to participate in determining for themselves whether what they were viewing was real or fake.

Determining authenticity was a democratic experience.[26] Barnum's manipulations took place when the boundaries of democracy in the United States were expanded: for example, voting rights were extended to white men who did not own property. As people moved to cities, the personal relations between producers and consumers became more tenuous. The rise of a consumer culture meant that people no longer necessarily knew the origins of the goods they were buying. Individuals in the nineteenth century had to determine for themselves whether what they purchased was genuine.

After several months of touring, Heth became ill and died in February of 1836. An autopsy (which Barnum charged interested parties 50 cents to attend) suggested that she was closer to 80 years at her death, not 161 years. What is unknown is why she allowed herself to be on display. As an elderly African American woman without dependents to help her, allowing herself to become a public curiosity would have been a means of support.[27] Exhibition offered people with disabilities a viable income and a chance to see the world.[28]

Barnum's experience with Heth confirmed for him that he had a future in producing spectacles. In 1841, John Scudder's American Museum (just the collection, not the building within which it was housed) became available for purchase. Barnum did not have enough capital to buy the collection. However, he convinced the wealthy merchant who owned the building to do so and allow Barnum to pay him for it in installments. This time he was as successful financially as he was in marketing. In the next twenty-three and a half years, Barnum sold almost 38 million admission tickets. To help put the enormity of Barnum's success in perspective, the entire population of the United States in 1865 was estimated at around 35 million.[29]

In the twenty-some-odd years that Barnum's American Museum was opened, Barnum figured out ways to combine popular entertainment with education. The original Scudder collection was concentrated on natural history objects. Barnum acquired the Peale museums' collections, which were also focused on science. He added wax figures and live entertainment to the mix, including the creation of the nation's first public aquarium. After visiting a zoo in London, Barnum hired members of its staff to build glass tanks within which he put sharks, dolphins, and native and exotic fish. In 1861, he added to this by capturing a few beluga whales.

Figure 2.2 A promotion for Barnum's American Museum. *Source:* Library of Congress, Rare Book and Special Collections Division. Barnum, P. T. Barnum's American Museum illustrated. [New York: William Van Norden and Frank Leslie?, 1850] Pdf. https://www.loc.gov/item/10034181

To provide the necessary saltwater for these ventures, Barnum laid pipes to the New York Bay and installed a steam engine to pump the water.[30]

In his museum, Barnum continued to encourage audience participation in debating the authenticity of the objects presented. Often they were frauds. His Fejee Mermaid exhibit was a prime example. The importance of the displays was not their prospective ability to deceive, however. It was in providing a place wherein audience members were willing to participate in the possibility of being tricked. Discussions about the evolutionary relationship between living things were also heightened during this period (for instance, Darwin published *On the Origin of Species* in 1859). Barnum's exhibits opened a space wherein audience members could debate the veracity of the claim. Nineteenth-century culture both produced Barnum's museum and influenced it.

Barnum did not close his museum by choice. Instead, it burned to the ground on July 13, 1865. He opened a second site in New York, but two years later, it too burned to the ground. After this second catastrophe Barnum took his show on the road. However, his interest in natural history continued. Until his death in 1891, Barnum donated a significant number of zoological specimens to the Smithsonian, the American Museum of Natural History in New York, and helped establish a natural history museum at Tufts University.[31]

While Barnum's American Museum represents the epitome of leveraging mid-nineteenth-century popular culture into a successful venture in museum making, another important institution also saw its birth in the mid-nineteenth century: the Smithsonian Institution. The Smithsonian owes its existence to the bequest of James Smithson, a British citizen. Smithson was born into wealth but with a caveat. His father, Hugh Smithson, was the Duke of Northumberland. However, his mother was not married to Smithson. Elizabeth Hungerford Keate Macie was a widow, wealthy, and a cousin of Smithson's wife. James Smithson (whose original name was James Lewis Macie) was born in Paris in 1765. His mother took this action to hide her pregnancy. Eight years later, Macie brought her son back to London where he lived with a guardian named Joseph Gape. In 1773, Gape petitioned the House of Lords to have Smithson naturalized, which made him a British citizen but with limited rights. After the death of Smithson's mother in 1800 (his father had died in 1786), he petitioned to change his name, which was legally granted in 1801.[32]

Although Smithson could not assume a noble title because of the circumstances of his birth, he was provided with a gentleman's education. He graduated from Pembroke College, Oxford University, in 1786 and pursued a life of scientific

Figure 2.3   James Smithson.
Source: Smithsonian Institution Archives, MAH 14574 or MAH14574, Created by De la Batut, George Henry, "James Smithson Engraving", MAH-14574-000002, Retrieved on 2020-09-25.

inquiry. To that end, he became a fellow of the Royal Society and published numerous works, especially related to new fields of chemistry and mineralogy. Living in London, he participated in a newly developing culture of public science. He and his peers took a democratic approach to the production and dissemination of knowledge. The late eighteenth century was an Age of Revolution, and Smithson viewed the collapse of the French monarchy with optimism. Throughout his life, Smithson moved between England and the European continent both for research purposes and health reasons. He also managed to make very wise financial investments in canals and railroads, which amounted to a significant fortune. One thing he did not do, however, was ever travel to the United States.[33]

Upon his death, Smithson bequeathed his fortune to his nephew. However, in the 1820s, a few years before Smithson's death, he added a contingency plan to his will. If his nephew were to die without heirs, Smithson directed his fortune to be distributed to the United States to found "at Washington, under the name of the Smithsonian Institution, an establishment for the increase & diffusion of knowledge among men." Why did Smithson add this clause? Unfortunately, a fire destroyed the types of documentation – personal papers and effects – that might definitively explain Smithson's motivations. Scholar Heather Ewing sees the gift as part of the larger story of Smithson's life. He struggled with personal and professional insecurities. While he was published, he never secured fame. While living the life of a gentleman, he never achieved aristocratic legal status. The Smithsonian Institution provided a permanent honored status in a country founded, Smithson believed, on democratic ideals.[34]

Smithson died in 1829 in Genoa, Italy, and his nephew died in 1835 in Pisa. The first question for the United States was whether to accept the funds. The second was if it did, what would a Smithsonian Institution consist of exactly? It took almost a decade for Congress to settle those questions. Congress, while acknowledging that there was no precedent for accepting this type of philanthropic gift, did move forward in July of 1836 with the necessary legal procedures to receive the money (Benjamin Rush was sent to represent the United States in settling these affairs in London[35]). The final amount placed into the US Treasury from settling the will was $515,169, which is roughly equivalent to 14 million US dollars in relative price today.[36] While Rush worked on the logistics of securing the gift, former president and US Representative John Quincy Adams argued that the money should be used to found a national observatory for the development of astronomy.[37] Others proposed establishing a national university. In 1846, Congress passed a compromise that legislated the Smithsonian into being.

The Act to establish the Smithsonian Institution was vague, which has allowed the institution to develop over time instead of remaining a static fixture. The statute established a board of regents whose task was to supervise the "business" of the institution. The board was charged with finding a site to construct a building, oversee its construction, and ensure that it included "suitable rooms or halls for the reception and arrangement upon a liberal scale, of objects of natural history, including a geological and mineralogical cabinet; also a chemical laboratory, a library, a gallery of art, and the necessary lecture rooms."[38] The Act directed all future "objects of art and of foreign and curious research and all objects of natural history, plants, and geological and mineralogical specimens, belonging, or hereafter to belong, to the United States" to "be delivered to such persons as may be authorized by the board of regents to receive them, and shall be arranged in such order, and so classed, as best [to] facilitate the examination and study of them." It is essential to recognize that the legislation did not specifically create a museum but instead left room open for future developments. At the start of the twenty-first century, the Smithsonian Institution consists of 19 museums, a national zoo, and promotes itself as the "world's largest museum, education, and research complex."[39] However, the mission remains the same as articulated in Smithson's will.

In terms of the Smithsonian's development of a National Museum, George Brown Goode needs a mention for his influence. Born in Indiana in 1851, Goode was an only child, and he received private tutoring. As a young man, he attended Wesleyan University from which he graduated in 1870. He was then hired to direct a new endeavor. Wesleyan had received an endowment to establish a museum of natural history.

Figure 2.4 The Smithsonian Institution's first building, often called the Castle, was constructed in 1855. *Source:* Jennifer Koslow.

During this period, Goode became a protégé of Spencer F. Baird, a leading naturalist who first worked at the United States Fish Commission and then at the Smithsonian. In 1875, Baird requested Goode's help in constructing the Smithsonian's zoological display at the Philadelphia Centennial Exhibition, which was to be held the next year. World Fairs and International Expositions served as spaces for displaying national wealth and ingenuity. They often articulated racial ideas that justified imperialism.[40] They also offered global citizens a glimpse into a possible future. Baird used the Philadelphia Exhibition as a lobbying tool to convince Congress to appropriate funds to construct a building specifically as a museum, which it did in 1878. Organizationally, the National Museum was a part of the Smithsonian Institution. Although officially the assistant secretary, Goode supervised the movement and organization of materials into the new space. In 1885, Goode became the official director of the National Museum. He served in the position until he died of pneumonia in 1896.

Figure 2.5 The National Museum sat adjacent to the Smithsonian's Castle. *Source:* Jennifer Koslow.

Goode was a scientist (his specialty was ichthyology [fish]), an early museologist, and eventually a historian of science.[41] He believed that history and science
were progressive. Collecting, preserving, and interpreting material culture was a
mechanism to demonstrate positivist developments. Within the Smithsonian's
National Museum, "Goode's mission was nothing less than the creation of 'an
illustrated encyclopedia of civilization.'"[42] To facilitate learning, Goode desired for
the items to be accompanied by "instructive labels" to truly be a "people's
museum."[43] In addition to collecting objects similar to that of his predecessors
("portraits, busts and personal items of America's heroes"), he also desired objects
that spoke to advancements in technology and the arts. Hence, "Tiffany lamps,
the Slater spinning and carding machines, and the John Bull locomotive would
find their place alongside Washington's tea service."[44] In doing so, Goode merged
science and culture. Even when he collected something ordinary, he turned
household goods (quilts, for instance) into the exceptional when displayed.

Goode offered a concept for both everyday management of museums and a
broader philosophical classification system for different types of museums. He
identified six fundamental categories of museums based upon their foundations:
art, historical, anthropological, natural history, technological, and commercial.
He identified five additional subcategories of proprietorship: national; local, pro-
vincial, or city; college and school; professional or class; and cabinets for special
research owned by societies or individuals.[45] This taxonomy is still familiar to
museum visitors and managers today.

At the turn of the twentieth century, several wealthy industrialists began invest-
ing in museums. The Art Institute of Chicago, the Metropolitan Museum of Art in
New York City, and the Cleveland Museum of Art were established and expanded
during this period. Museums were a place for industrialists to display their wealth.
Moreover, philanthropic industrialists also viewed their donations as a means to
contribute to the common good. Steel magnate Andrew Carnegie articulated this
idea an article titled "Wealth," which was published in the *North American Review*
in 1880 and reprinted as "The Gospel of Wealth." By making cultural institutions
open to the public, philanthropic industrialists believed they could elevate society.

The idea that museums should display a positive, progressive story remained a
dominant narrative in the twentieth century. Henry Ford's Greenfield Village is
an excellent example of this impulse. In 1916, Henry Ford disparaged the study of
history: "History is more or less bunk. It's tradition. We don't want tradition. We
want to live in the present and the only history that is worth a tinker's dam is the
history we make today."[46] After World War I, however, he changed his mind. He
decided that he did not like the way modern capitalism worked. He ascribed to
several conspiracy theories about who controlled Wall Street (including anti-
Semitic ones). In response, as scholar Michael Wallace explained, "Ford reformu-
lated his position on history: only history as traditionally taught in schools was

bunk. It concentrated too much on wars, politics, and great persons and not enough on the material reality of everyday life for common folk."[47] Consequently, Ford began a project. He wanted to collect, preserve, and interpret evidence of vernacular life. He sought entire structures (the remnants of Edison's Menlo Park laboratory and the Wright brothers' family home) as well as artifacts. The result was two museums: (i) an industrial museum and (ii) a display of early American life, which was titled "Greenfield Village."

Greenfield Village opened in 1929. The first time visitor numbers were recorded was 1934, and approximately 243,000 visitors attended. Six years later, in 1940, the museum counted 633,000 visitors. (It was not the first open-air museum. Artur Hazelius's Skansen in Sweden owned that distinction.[48]) Greenfield Village was also, what we now call, a "living history" museum. Interpreters dressed in seventeenth-century outfits. They did not, however, deliver their interpretation in a persona as some living history museums do today. (Living history museums decide whether to use first person or third person narratives for a variety of reasons.) Greenfield Village celebrated America's folkways. However, in doing so, it presented a static image. Greenfield Village did not mention any conflict (class, race, and gender) that had existed. Instead, it offered a nostalgic representation of the past.

Ford was not alone in creating this type of museum. John D. Rockefeller Jr. funded the creation of Colonial Williamsburg in the 1920s (its production will be discussed in greater detail in Chapter 3). Similar to Ford's museum, Colonial Williamsburg also presented the public with romanticized portrayals of history. Here white women "hostesses" donned colonial outfits, answered the door of the historic homes, and provided information.[49] Yet, that was far from seventeenth-century reality in Williamsburg. Enslaved men and women answered the doors, did the cooking, cleaning, and so forth. Colonial Williamsburg did not begin interpreting slavery as part of its story until 1979.[50] Taken together, Colonial Williamsburg and Greenfield Village offered visitors an imagined past, which supported a sense that history was progressive and positive. It left out struggle and conflict. As historians began to reshape the narratives of US history to account for discord, it should not be surprising that attempts to revamp the history told in museums led to controversy.

In the 1990s, a few museum exhibits of history became the center of public controversy, most famously the *Enola Gay* at the National Air and Space Museum in 1994. This was not the only time, however, that a museum became a site of controversy over an exhibition of history. In attempting to make museums more democratic and inclusive, misunderstandings abounded. We will examine three controversies: *Harlem on My Mind: Cultural Capital of Black America, 1900–1968* (1969); *The West as America: Reinterpreting Images of the Frontier, 1820–1920* (1991); and *The Crossroads: The End of World War II, The Atomic Bomb, and the*

Onset of the Cold War. Each was front-page news, and each had different out-comes. One went on as planned, one was edited, and one was canceled. Understanding the cultural politics of museums helps to illuminate the power and limits to that power Public Historians have in sharing authority and inquiry with various audiences.

The 1960s was a time of reexamination and reaction. For example, in the mid-1960s, Congress passed two transformative pieces of legislation – the Civil Rights Act of 1964 and the Voting Rights Act of 1965 – that declared that the federal government would no longer be a passive bystander in movements for social justice. However, these Acts did not relieve all tensions or resolve all issues. Despite activist efforts to improve conditions of inequality, police actions and the assassination of Martin Luther King Jr. led to a series of riots in African American urban neighborhoods in the mid to late 1960s. After the riots in the summer of 1967 in Newark and Detroit, President Lyndon B. Johnson created a national advisory commission to study the issue of civil disorders. Led by Illinois Governor Otto Kerner, the subsequent report that was issued in 1968 famously concluded that the nation was "moving towards two societies, one black, one white, separate and unequal."[51] The controversies over *Harlem on My Mind* were both a result and a reflection of contemporary racial tensions and conflicts.

Allon Schoener conceived *Harlem on My Mind* and was fully encouraged by the Metropolitan Museum of Art's (the Met) new director Thomas Hoving. Hoving received his PhD in art history from Princeton in 1959 after which he went to work at the Cloisters, which was a branch of the Met devoted to Medieval Art. Hoving worked at the Cloisters for the next seven years, rising from staff to curator. In 1966, New York City's mayor, John Lindsay, appointed Hoving commissioner of the city's parks. He remained in the position only a year before the Met's board of trustees selected him as the museum's new director, where he remained for the next decade.[52] In 1967, when he took the position, he was 35, charismatic, and willing to take chances. Some of his innovations are still recognizable today. For instance, he transformed parachutes into giant public promotional material. He also became associated with the idea of the blockbuster exhibit when he brought the *Treasures of Tutankhamun* from the Egyptian Museum in Cairo to New York City. In his memoir, Hoving recalled that his goal was to create a "'new' Met [that would] proclaim in a very loud voice 'Welcome.'" He "want[ed] the place to become not only a place for exhibitions, but a living forum for communication and teaching and education and celebration."[53]

Allon Schoener was an art historian by training. Working in the museum world since the early 1950s, he became interested in employing new communications technology. By the late 1960s, Schoener had produced over 100 television programs for the San Francisco Museum of Art. He conceived of *Harlem on My Mind Exhibit* as an experience of "electronic theater," which was a deliberate disruption of the

Met's traditional modes of representation. In this way, Schoener's goals sat well within the broader context of the late 1960s.[54]

Harlem on My Mind was notable for many reasons. First, it paved the way for the use of new communications technology as a legitimate form of media presentation. Second, it helped define a "blockbuster." Third, the exhibit tackled a major contemporary issue: racism. Schoener's idea was to present "a sixty-year panorama of Harlem history." Organized chronologically, Schoener envisioned an immersive experience. Photographs were enlarged to life-size proportions, music played, and voices were broadcast. Lives of everyday people, as well as celebrity figures, were displayed. Schoener's "objective was to encourage gallery visitors to project themselves into the subject of the image, thus becoming active participants in the gallery experience."[55]

The first controversy to erupt was that of the exclusion of African American painters. In the Met's initial press release, the museum stated that "paintings, prints, and drawings," would be included in the exhibit in addition to photography and sound recordings. However, Schoener has always maintained that he was never consulted about this press release. He argues that he had always been clear on what he was going to include. Paintings were not new media and, consequently, by definition, were to be excluded. Schoener's motivation was based in debates about what constituted legitimate art, not racism.[56] In the 1960s, photography was not considered an art form in conservative circles. Schoener used the Met as a platform to contest that view and to bestow legitimacy. Schoener's intentions aside, for many African American painters, Schoener's decision to exclude them from telling the story of Harlem through their chosen medium served as a source of indignity.

As scholar Bridget R. Cooks has analyzed, this exclusion prompted African American artists to organize. As historian John Henrik Clarke explained: "The basis of the trouble with [*Harlem on My Mind* was] that it never belonged to us and while a lot of people listened to our suggestions about the project. [*sic*] Very few of these suggestions were ever put into effect."[57] In response, African American artists formed the Black Emergency Cultural Coalition (BECC) to stage a boycott of the exhibit. The critical issue was the ability of Harlem's African American artists to represent Harlem artistically. Cooks argues that *Harlem on My Mind* turned out to be a pivotal moment. In organizing against their absence, African American artists changed how major museums represented them, who curated their art, and their place as staff in museums.[58] However, this occurred in the aftermath, not during the exhibit itself.

Another controversy ensued over the introduction to the exhibit catalog. In an attempt to be innovative, Hoving enlisted the help of 17-year-old Harlem resident Candice Van Ellison. She came to his attention through her participation in the New York Council on the Arts "Ghetto Arts Corps" program. Van Ellison wrote an essay for school on the history of Harlem, wherein she discussed race relations. In it, she characterized Jews as oppressors and described anti-Semitism as a normative prejudice. At a time when Jewish-African American alliances for civil rights were breaking down in the post-1964/1965 era, Ellison's work reflected and exacerbated mounting tensions. However, it turned out that not all of the characterizations were hers. In preparing Ellison's work for inclusion, Schoener asked her to remove her footnotes and her use of quotation marks. He believed those gave it an air of academic writing that would be off-putting to the public. It turned out that Ellison had been relying on two renowned white sociologists – Nathan Glazer and Daniel Patrick Moynihan – for many of the most inflammatory statements.[59] One wonders what the reception might have been if Schoener had let Ellison's work stand in its original form.[60]

Despite pickets and protests, the Met did not waver in its commitment to run the exhibit. Between January 18 and April 6, 1969, thousands of people visited it. Approximately 15% of the visitors the first day were African American, which was a significantly higher number than the number of African Americans who typically visited the Met.[61] Nor did Hoving interfere with Schoener's curatorial decisions. The only significant alteration to the exhibit in response to public pressure was related to the catalog. At first, the Met inserted an apology for any offense caused by the language in Van Ellison's essay into the paperback edition it was selling. However, under pressure from New York City Council the Met soon stopped selling the catalog altogether. Still, Random House kept selling a hardcover edition in stores into which it inserted a disclaimer about the essay.

In sum, the controversies surrounding *Harlem on My Mind* – in particular, the exclusion of African American traditional artists and the perceived inflammatory language in the catalog – came about because of contemporary cultural politics. In many ways, this was a step forward for the Met to challenge the status quo of the art world. It attempted to legitimize photography as an art form. It tried to legitimize the African American experience as a subject of examination for a major cultural institution. In those goals, it succeeded. There were also unintended consequences. Initially, African American artists from Harlem had been excited at the prospect of inclusion at one of the most venerable institutions of art in the world. Their exclusion from decision-making power over how to represent Harlem represented a breakdown in sharing authority and inquiry. They channeled their anger into a movement, which resulted in long-term change in the art world.

Harlem on My Mind displayed history as art and art as history. It was controversy amid the cultural politics of the late 1960s. Similarly, the disputes in the 1990s reflected the cultural politics of the late twentieth century. In particular, the controversies over *The West as America* and *The Crossroads* emanated from main-streaming of new social history.

The 1960s was a period of change in America. One of those changes was how history was conceived, written, and taught in institutions of higher learning.

Contemporary actions of civil rights activism inspired a new generation of historians to investigate the differences that separated Americans. As Peter Charles Hoffer has explained: "This new approach to history would also stress that historians should tell the many stories of people ignored in older histories."[62] However, the goal was never to create "me too" histories merely. Instead, social historians desired to produce new knowledge about how class, race, and gender informed the structures within which people made decisions for themselves and their families.

The National Museum of American Art (NMAA) ran *The West as America: Reinterpreting Images of the Frontier, 1820–1920* from March 15 to July 28, 1991. In a review, historian Andrew Gulliford of Middle Tennessee State University said it "raised critical and uncomfortable questions about the basic American myths and their relationships to art."[63] Here was "new Western history" (inspired by new social history) on display. New Western history examined the development of the West within the context of conquest instead of characterizing the movement of white Americans into the region as settlement. New Western history scholars contended that wording mattered. The use of the word "settlement," they argued, portrayed these developments as peaceful individual actions. Doing so, they claimed, obscured the state's use of violence to remove Native peoples and masked state support for redevelopment. For instance, the Homestead Act of 1862 provided white Americans with the opportunity to secure land. Similarly, the federal government subsidized the construction of the transnational railroad. *The West as America* interpreted artistic representations from the turn of the century of these developments through the lens of new Western history. However, some visitors might not have known that their sense of historic place was about to be disrupted. An advertisement for the Hyatt hotel in the *New York Times* recommended visiting the exhibit under its "weekend tips." It stated: "Relive the spirit of the Wild West as the National Museum of American Art presents the West as America: Reinterpreting Images of the Frontier, 1820–1920."[64]

As soon as the exhibit opened it received significant criticism. An editorial in *The Wall Street Journal*, for instance, expressed the side of disapproval: "Only in the land of the free, of course, is it possible to mount an entirely hostile ideological assault on the nation's founding and history, to recast that history in the most distorted terms—and have the taxpayers foot the bill."[65] Daniel Boorstin, a renowned historian and former Librarian of Congress, wrote in the comment book that accompanied the exhibit: "A perverse, historically inaccurate destructive exhibit!"[66] Michael Kimmelman, the *New York Times*' senior art critic, gave a similarly negative assessment: "The show preaches to visitors in wall texts laden with forced analyses and inflammatory observations."[67] Within a day, US Senator Ted Stevens and Slade Gorton raised concerns at a Senate Appropriations Committee about this exhibit and a few other projects.[68]

The exhibit also received praise. The NMAA had placed a comment book, which was an innovation in the gallery. Seven hundred and thirty-five individuals left a comment, of which 509 had something "specifically positive [to say] about some aspect of the show."[69] For example, "C.R." wrote: "excellent job. The way it was. Don't let the politicians deter you. They don't cope too well with reality, anyway." Lea Zeldin wrote: "history and vision united in the propaganda of an art invented for imperialism. The real sin is the [*sic*] in the eye of the patriot. What will the art of George Bush's gulf war be for my children and grandchildren?" The exhibit also stirred strong emotions. A. Rodriguez commented: "This exhibit has aroused a lot of anger in me. How I feel after viewing it is that all white people, and especially Spaniards, should pack up their bags in 1992 and return to Europe. Of course they won't, so I hope they just rot in hell."[70]

In response to the controversy, the museum (its director and curators of the exhibit) concluded that they had been too dogmatic in their interpretive labels. Betsy Broun, NMAA's director, had reviewed and approved of all of the labels before the show's opening. In hindsight, however, she recognized that she had read them "from the perspective of an academic" and not "with the inner ear of someone who might have come in off the street with a general background." She conceded that the labels "were heavy-handed."[71] Similarly, curator Bill Truettner reflected, "what were we thinking?"[72] Consequently, the curators came up with a solution. They modified several labels during the show's run. In many cases the new labels provided more clarity and evidence for the interpretation being argued.[73]

In the end, *The West as America* did not close early. The Smithsonian did not lose federal funds. In looking back, the curatorial staff were divided as to whether the controversy had any significant impact on their jobs.[74] Three years later, a more substantial controversy over contested memories occurred at a different Smithsonian Institution, the National Air and Space Museum, with different results.

Congress originally authorized the National Air Museum in 1946. However, authorization did not lead to immediate construction. In 1966, Congress reauthorized the museum and renamed it the National Air and Space Museum (NASM). Still, funding continued to be an issue. Barry Goldwater, a US Senator from Arizona and infamous presidential candidate in 1964, was instrumental in changing this. Speaking in Congress in 1970, Goldwater argued that "the time is at hand when the American people want to have a decent home for the National Museum where their country's exciting story in air and space can be told."[75] Goldwater successfully lobbied President Richard Nixon to lend his support. Construction began in 1972 and the museum opened in 1976.

Goldwater justified the museum on grounds more than entertainment. He felt that the museum's "true value," he believed, would be in the "inspirational feeling which the story of [America's] achievements can give." He went on to name examples of what he believed to be significant artifacts for inclusion: a Wright brothers' plane, the aircraft with which Lindbergh crossed the Atlantic, and the Apollo 11 spacecraft.[76] He also dismissed the idea of accessioning the *Enola Gay*: "what we are interested in here are the truly historic aircraft. I wouldn't consider the one that dropped the bomb on Japan as belonging to that category."[77] (As an FYI for those who wonder about the plane's name, the commander of the plane, Paul Tibbetts, chose to name the B-29 bomber for his mother, Enola Gay Tibbetts.) Goldwater's assessment of the *Enola Gay* in 1970 versus expressions of reverence about the plane in the 1990s, speaks to how values and interpretations of objects can change. At the 50th anniversary of the end of World War II, Goldwater's appraisal no longer held sway.

In the years leading up to the 50th anniversary of the end of World War II (1995), the curators of the Smithsonian's NASM asked themselves a historical question: how do we, as a society, discuss a war we won? Moreover, how do we grapple with the multiple meanings of the United States' use of atomic bombs at Hiroshima and Nagasaki? For instance, what role did these events play in ending World War II? Furthermore, what role did these events play in policies related to diplomacy during the Cold War and post-Cold War Era? In contemplating an exhibit to mark the occasion, Martin O. Harwit, the museum's director, declared "few events have had a more profound impact on our times than the creation of nuclear weapons and their employment against Hiroshima and Nagasaki."[78] He reasoned that NASM had "an opportunity and an obligation to help visitors understand this pivotal moment in the history of the United States."[79]

Was the use of the atomic bomb on Japan necessary for ending World War II? Historians had asked and attempted to answer this question within a few decades after the war ended. Their answers only became more complicated throughout the twentieth century as the government declassified its records. Historians looked at the factors that President Truman confronted and asked how they influenced his decision. There was the question of the Soviets. When and how would they enter the Pacific arena? Did Truman drop the bombs partly to impress the Soviets with the US's military might? What about the expense? The Manhattan Project cost billions of dollars. How would the American taxpayer feel about the federal government if the weapon were not used? Would the taxpayer feel that their money had been wasted? What about the human question? Would dropping the bomb shorten the war and save American lives? All of these questions about timing, personal ambition, motivations of scientific and military leaders, human costs, and beliefs about international diplomacy factored into Truman's decision. Historians disagreed on which was the most influential factor and changed their answers over time as new sources shed light on some questions but raised additional ones. In contrast to these historical debates, many Americans did not view the use of atomic weapons at the end of World War II as a historical question. NASM's attempt to mainstream this event as a contingent one came at a peak in the "culture wars" of the 1990s.

The debate over *The West as America* exhibit in 1991 was one example of how government support for the cultural arts and humanities was contested. The dispute over how to present the *Enola Gay* at NASM occurred in the swirl of two other events: debates over standards for history education and the midterm elections of 1994. As a result, historians found themselves entangled in the politics of the present.

Deliberations over the proposed National Standards for History in the Schools, which were to have guided K-12 teachers on history education, shaped the *Enola Gay* controversy.[80] Initiated under the George H.W. Bush administration in 1992, "hundreds of teachers, administrators, historians, parents, and others with a stake in the history in our schools participated in developing these standards through a national consensus-building process that involved more than 30 major professional, scholarly and public interest organizations."[81] These were not federal guidelines; however, a grant from the National Endowment for the Humanities and monies from the Department of Education undergirded the work of those involved. In October of 1994, Lynne Cheney (former second lady of the United States) criticized the proposed National History Standards in an op-ed in *The Wall Street Journal* titled "The End of History." She argued, "We are a better people than the National Standards indicate, and our children deserve to know it."[82] She accused the creators as being influenced by "political correctness" in constructing a framework for students to investigate the history of the United States. Looking at names mentioned (and their frequency) she determined that the standards focused on people she believed to be of lesser importance to the history of the United States. More grievous, in her opinion, the standards emphasized failures over positive accomplishments.

A few weeks later *The Wall Street Journal* published a response by Gary Nash and Charlotte Crabtree, the co-directors of the National Standards Project. They disputed Cheney's characterizations. They contended that the standards included the very people and concepts Cheney claimed were absent. For instance, she believed "not a single one of the 31 standards mentions the Constitution." However, Nash and Crabtree explained that there were five standards "devoted to the creation, ratification and achievements of the Constitution."[83] Cheney had noted the absence of a specific reference to Robert E. Lee. In response, Nash and Crabtree reasoned that it would be "clear" to any educator that Robert E. Lee would have to be discussed in meeting the following standard: "Students should evaluate how political, military, and diplomatic leadership affected the outcome of the Civil War." Nash and Crabtree maintained that the standards brought to students a way to analyze the nation's history by studying "men and women, named and unnamed, from all walks of life and all ethnic, racial, religious, and national backgrounds." In doing so, Nash and Crabtree argued: "this is not 'political correctness;' it is simply accurate history, for any history that ignores large parts of American society is incomplete and therefore distorted."

These debates over history education occurred during a heated midterm election. In 1994, the Republican Party won the Senate, giving Republicans complete control over Congress for the first time in 40 years. The Contract for America served as a campaign pledge by many Republican members of the House of Representatives. Although there was nothing specifically related to history education, the Republicans' goal was to "restor[e] the faith and trust of the American people in their government."[84] In the debates over how to present the *Enola Gay* at the Smithsonian asking a historical question about the government's trustworthiness became seen as unpatriotic.

Much like the history standards, proposals and plans to create an exhibit to display the *Enola Gay* began long before 1994. The initially proposed exhibition was titled "The Crossroads: The End of World War II, The Atomic Bomb, and the Onset of the Cold War." While planning, the title was edited to "The Last Act: The Atomic Bomb and the End of World War II." Martin O. Harwit, NASM's director, began conceptualizing plans for the exhibit shortly after his arrival at the museum in 1987. Harwit was born in Prague in 1931 and immigrated to the United States in 1946 when he was 15. Harwit received his BA in Physics from Oberlin and an MA from the University of Michigan. He then served in the US Army after which he received a PhD in astrophysics from Cambridge University, and after which he became a professor at Cornell University.[85]

Harwit's interest in the *Enola Gay* developed from many different angles. First, the plane required restoration. Second, Harwit wanted NASM to provide the public with the opportunity to learn about and analyze the development of strategic bombing of civilians during the twentieth century. Lastly, 1995 marked the 50th anniversary of the end of World War II.[86] As initially expressed by NASM's curator of World War II Aviation, Michael Neufeld, NASM had an "obligation and an opportunity to help visitors better understand the meaning and implications of the decisions and events [of this anniversary] that have shaped the subsequent history of the twentieth century."[87]

After the first full planning document was completed in June of 1993 it was delivered to the secretary of the Smithsonian, Robert Adams. In turn, Adams sent a memorandum to the staff. Upon receiving it, Tom Crouch, one of NASM's curators, expressed concern to Harwit about the museum's ability to tell multiple stories simultaneously during such an important anniversary. In an internal memo, Crouch asked Harwit: "Do you want to do an exhibition intended to make veterans feel good, or do you want an exhibition that will lead our visitors to think about the consequences of the atomic bombing of Japan? Frankly, I don't think we can do both."[88] Private discussions about the complicated nature of exhibiting the material, as one would expect from professionals, did not translate into radical transformations in the planning process. The standard process consisted of this early planning phase then the drafting of exhibit scripts, and then the construction of displays. Harwit budgeted two-and-a-half years for this progression; the exhibit was set to open in May of 1995.

Harwit intentionally desired to analyze these events within the context of the most current scholarship. An advisory committee composed of academic historians (those working at universities) and Air Force historians participated in reading an early exhibit script. The advisory's mostly positive critique was collected in February 1994. Harwit also wanted to include various stakeholders in these processes. As a result, the Air Force Association (AFA) was given a draft. In hindsight, this is where the exhibit began to derail.

The AFA's "mission is to promote a dominant United States Air Force and a strong national defense, and to honor Airmen and our Air Force Heritage."[89] In the wake of the end of the Cold War, the AFA sought friendly forums within which to present its arguments about the continuing need for investment in the aerospace industry. The AFA's belief that NASM, as the nation's official museum, should be one of those forums was understandable. However, the two mission statements are not synonymous. NASM's stated goals are to "commemorate[e] the past" and "to educat[e] and inspire[e] people to foster appreciation for the importance of flight to humanity."[90] Unsurprisingly, the two organizations took very different approaches to historicize the role of atomic weaponry.

Exhibit scripts are not exhibits. They provide a sense of how an exhibit's graphics, words, and objects will sit in relation to each other, but they are not immersive experiences. At 5500 square feet, the exhibition focused on the end of the war, leaving out much of the historical context that preceded the dropping of the atomic bomb. For instance, there was one textual mention of the attack at Pearl Harbor but no photographs. The advisory committee of historians overall supported how NASM approached the material. Perhaps their familiarity with the events leading up to the end of World War II made them less sensitive to what appeared to others to deemphasize the events in the Pacific War leading up to 1945.

Museum professionals and laypersons are often apt to read exhibit scripts in very different manners. Harwit believed that the "fifty-six-foot-long, brightly polished, brilliantly sparkling bomber" with "an atomic bomb casing immediately beneath its open bomb bay" conveyed an emotional power through its size, look, and placement in the exhibit that could not be expressed in an exhibit script.[91] Likewise, Harwit knew that reading the accompanying text to the 15-minute film of the surviving members of the 509th Composite Group telling their stories firsthand did not have the same emotional impact as listening to their voices. Just reading the text without contemplating the relationship of objects (in their three-dimensional aspects) lent the impression that the curators were more compassionate to the Japanese victims. For instance, the script had long captions for three objects from ground zero: a child's lunch box, scorched clothing, and a small watch. The text emotionally spoke about the civilians who lost their lives in the attack. The curators used more words to discuss these artifacts because they believed that the small mundane aspect of these objects needed greater textual context than the *Enola Gay*.[92]

In contrast to the curators' holistic ability to read the exhibit script, the AFA took a different approach. Its members focused on numbers of pictures depicting Japanese victims and American casualties, finding many more of the former versus the latter. Also, the AFA took a sentence out of context from the script, published it through their newsletter, and leaked it to the press, which then reprinted the statement ad nauseam. On its own, the sentence suggested that the United States were the aggressors in World War II: "For most Americans this war was fundamentally different from the one waged against Germany and Italy—it was a war of vengeance. For most Japanese, it was a war to defend their unique culture against Western imperialism." The sentence, however, reads very differently when it is relayed within its original context:

In 1931 the Japanese Army occupied Manchuria; six years later it invaded the rest of China. From 1937 to 1945, the Japanese Empire would be constantly at war.

Japanese expansionism was marked by naked aggression and extreme brutality. The slaughter of tens of thousands of Chinese in Nanking in 1937 shocked the world. Atrocities by Japanese troops included brutal mistreatment of civilians, forced laborers and prisoners of war, and biological experiments on human victims.

In December 1941, Japan attacked U.S. bases at Pearl Harbor, Hawaii, and launched other surprise assaults against Allied territories in the Pacific. Thus began a wider conflict marked by extreme bitterness. For most Americans this war was fundamentally different from the one waged against Germany and Italy—it was a war of vengeance. For most Japanese, it was a war to defend their unique culture against Western imperialism. As the war approached its end in 1945, it appeared to both sides that it was a fight to the finish.[93]

Although this text would later be revised, the quote out of context was repeated and repeated to argue that the curators at NASM were biased and unpatriotic. Moreover, John T. Correll, the editor in chief of *Air Force* magazine, kept insisting that there was no historical question as to why Truman decided to use the atomic bomb against Japan. He told his readers "a recurring undertone in the plan and scripts for this exhibit has been suspicion about why the United States used the atomic bomb." He argued, "museum officials have seemed reluctant to accept that it was a military action, taken to end the war and save lives." In this way, Correll articulated the dominant argument the United States put forth to its citizens in reporting on this event. (Remember, the Manhattan Project was kept secret.) Correll asserted that there was no debate. Still, he acknowledged there was at least one contemporary critic: "Some of the speculation on this point has been removed in the latest draft, but the script lingers respectfully on such individuals as nuclear scientist Leo Szilard, who protested the use of the bomb."[94] The question the curators wanted to pose was how to reconcile these two points? How to combine a perspective such as Szilard's with other sources that advocated for the use of the bomb? How did Truman weigh those different perspectives in deciding to use this weapon against noncombatants?

In the end, Harwit and the curators created numerous drafts throughout 1994. The *Enola Gay* remained the centerpiece with a portion of the fuselage on display. (The idea of showing the plane in its entirety was abandoned in the late 1980s when it was realized that it was too heavy for NASM's floor to support.) The AFA wrote about the proposed exhibit in its newsletter. It also called the attention of Congress and the American Legion to these events. In August of 1994, 23 US Representatives (18 Republicans and 6 Democrats) wrote a letter to Secretary Adams to "express [their] concern and dismay." They cited evidence of disproportion that the AFA provided to them. In September, the US Senate passed a resolution that argued that any display should not "impugn the memory of those who gave their lives for freedom." Also, in September and October, the curatorial staff sat several times with representatives of the American Legion to conduct line-by-line edits of the script. Both groups continued to find fault with NASM's script. In response, the newly appointed secretary of the Smithsonian, Michael Heyman, canceled *The Last Act* in late January 1995. In its place, he directed NASM to create a new display that would focus solely on the *Enola Gay* and its restoration. On May 1, 1995, Harwit resigned.[95]

In 2003, NASM permanently installed the *Enola Gay* at the Steven F. Udvar-Hazy Center, which is near Washington Dulles International Airport. The outcome of the events at NASM's main branch on the National Mall is apparent in the interpretive label that accompanies the plane. Ideally, the very first line of an interpretive label should tell the viewer an object's significance. The label for the *Enola Gay* begins: "Boeing's B-29 Superfortress was the most sophisticated propeller-driven bomber of World War II, and the first bomber to house its crew in pressurized compartments."[96] However, that is not why this particular plane is in the Smithsonian. The *Enola Gay* was not acquired because it is an example of a B-29 bomber. The Smithsonian accessioned it because it was the plane used to drop the first atomic bomb as an act of warfare. It takes until the second paragraph of the label for someone to learn that fact if they did not already know it. In general, the descriptive nature of the 129-word label raises more questions than it

Figure 2.6 In 1995, the Smithsonian displayed the front fuselage from the Enola Gay as part of a pared-down exhibit that hoped to avoid controversy. *Source:* Smithsonian Institution Archives, 95-4624, Created by Enola Gay (Bomber), "Enola Gay on Display", 95-4624_wk, Retrieved on 2020-09-25.

answers. The absence of analysis is a byproduct of the controversy over its exhibition in 1995.[97]

The impact of the *Enola Gay* controversy on Public Historians is still in flux almost 25 years later. On the one hand, the controversy opened the eyes of many historians working at universities to the fact that their peers at cultural institutions did not necessarily enjoy the same academic freedoms. At NASM a variety of stakeholders, including the United States Congress, weighed in on how NASM should present this history. While NASM did not lose its funding it was a threat put on the table.

The history of displaying history in museums in the United States stems back centuries. While the specifics of how, why, and where depend upon time and space there are a few continuities. First, museum formation in the United States has not been dependent upon the government. While there are public museums, private individuals have been at the forefront of museum making. Second, history has always been used as a vehicle for entertainment. Education and entertainment have been intertwined since Pierre Eugène Du Simitière's failed attempt to create a museum in Philadelphia. There is no single explanation as to who or why someone created a museum. This diversity opened up opportunities. At the same time, for most of this history, museums reflected the views of those in power. The turn of the twenty-first century has yielded changes in thinking about the power of representation. Museum makers believe that they have a responsibility to convey to their audiences an honest narrative of the past. Sorrow and barriers are as much a part of the story as joy and improvement. As hidden histories are revealed and multiple perspectives incorporated into exhibits to create new senses of place contested memories bubble up to the surface. Knowing how museum makers displayed history in the past can help public historians negotiate unsettled terrain in the future.

Theory

For most of their history, museums have been defined by the collections they held within them. As institutions of knowledge they were typically sites of research and scholarship. As universities became the dominant space for producing new knowledge, museums found new purposes. Museums became institutions of public service.[98] As Michael Spock, director of the Boston Children's Museum, articulated it, "the museum was for somebody rather than about something."[99] Still, museums have remained primary in collecting, preserving, and interpreting objects. How we think about the meaning of those objects has changed over time. In this section, we will look at how museums resemble temples in many respects. We will examine how they have also become forums and places of participation. Last, we will look at how interpretation works in history museums.

The mid-to-late twentieth century was a period of global change in thinking about the role of museums in society. In 1971, Duncan Cameron wrote a provocative piece to his peers in museology titled "The Museum, a Temple or the Forum." He described the process of collecting as a way for people to create "nonverbal reality model[s]" of their worlds that aided in helping people conceptualize relationships. He argued that the twentieth century changed peoples ideas about the purpose of a museum. Instead of being about the private collector, the rise of the public museum meant that the institution should hold meaning for the democratic masses who visited.[100]

The objects within the museum, Cameron explained, were initially those that museum makers believed "to be significant and valuable." Cameron argued that the public agreed: "The public generally accepted the idea that if it was in the museum, it was not only real but represented a standard of excellence."[101] This is what made them temples.

In the 1960s and 1970s, as democratic impulses questioned institutions of power, the social function of museums also came into question. Interrogations about how class, race, and gender shaped both collections and their interpretation came to the foreground. Some wondered whether museums should serve as forums: spaces for "confrontation, experimentation, and debate."[102] Cameron argued that temples and forums should be related but distinct entities. Each, he believed, was important, but combining them could diminish their independent social functions. He summarized his point about their interrelationship:

> In the presence of the forum the museum serves as a temple, accepting and incorporating the manifestations of change. From the chaos and conflict of today's forum, the museum must build the collections that will tell us tomorrow who we are and how we got there. After all, that's what museums are all about.[103]

Although Cameron advocated keeping the forum separate, museums have worked to incorporate aspects of the forum into their institutions. Through programming and citizen curatorial programs, museums have opened up possibilities for experimentation and debate within museums. At the same time, public forums continue to put pressure on museums to think about their collecting policies and interpretive frameworks.

Within museums, educational theories have shaped strategies of interpretation. In the 1990s, museums began to adopt interpretive strategies based on the idea of "constructivism."[104] Fundamental to this theory is the idea that "knowledge and the way it is obtained are dependent on the mind of the learner."[105] Visitors to museums "don't simply add new facts to what is known, but constantly reorganize and create both understanding and the ability to learn as they interact with the world."[106] One way in which museums began to revamp their exhibits in response to the idea of constructivism was to incorporate more interactive activities into their displays. The ultimate goal is to foster engagement. In the late twentieth century, the paradigm shift dovetailed with the rise of a new type of approach: the participatory museum.

As explained by Nina Simon, a participatory approach is more than an additive to a visitor's experience. Unlike interactives, which "supplement traditional didactic content presentation," participatory activities allow visitors to "act as content creators, distributors, consumer, critics, and collaborators." A more traditional strategy is for the "institution [to] provide content for visitors to consume." In doing so, a museum can "focus on making the content consistent and high quality, so that every visitor, regardless of her background or interests, receives a reliably good experience." In adopting a participatory strategy, the museum's staff needs to be comfortable with the idea that it will not be able to "guarantee the consistency of visitor experiences." Thus, participatory techniques are both exciting and scary.[107]

Simon advises museum makers that design is critical in implementing participatory principles. First, not everyone wishes to participate at the creator level. Second, museum makers are better off creating parameters for a participatory experience for it to have real meaning for participants. She gives the example of a

Dutch library that wanted to design a mechanism for people to provide feedback, which could be made readily available to the community. The librarians created a shelving process whereby when people returned their books they put them on a shelf that described how they felt about the book: "boring," "funny," and "great for kids" among others. Software allowed the librarians to automatically "tag" each book with the descriptor, which could then be seen in the catalog. Similarly, Simon argues that an exhibit that asks visitors to vote for their favorite object offers visitors "a better-scaffold experience than an open-ended board with blank cards and a question like 'What do you think?'" Too much freedom can be overwhelming. Offering guidance is part of a museum professional's training.[108]

By way of personal example, The Coca-Cola Museum in Atlanta, Georgia, offers a successful structured participatory experience. As part of an exhibit about Coke and popular culture, the museum invites visitors to share their own "Coke Story." Participants sit down at an electronic screen (or use paper that is provided) and type their story. This is then posted electronically on a wall as well as printed on paper for others to read. These memories are then archived; they become a part of the museum's collections. The visitor has contributed to the museum's mission, which is to document the heritage of The Coca-Cola Company and to create a space to share happiness.[109] The goal is to foster engagement through meaningful projects.

Posing different types of participatory experiences also helps museums address questions about accessibility. Since the passage of the Americans with Disabilities Act of 1990, cultural institutions are required by law to provide all citizens full and equal access to all public goods and services. Sometimes this means integrating materials into a mainstream tour for people with physical impairments. Sometimes this means creating special programs. Digital technologies have come to play a new role in creating access. For instance, a number of museums have taken to using 3D printing to create artifakes for sight-impaired persons to experience material culture. (More information about the use of digital methods is discussed in Chapter 7.)

The trend toward participation has also led to a new type of institution: the pop-up museum. As explained by the Santa Cruz Museum of Art & History, "a Pop Up Museum is a temporary exhibit created by the people who show up to participate."[110] The goal is to create a temporary space for people to develop community by sharing stories about objects. Amateurs can become authorities. Public historians can modify the idea of a pop-up museum in a variety of ways. At Florida State University (FSU), graduate students have been creating "On This Spot" pop-up exhibits for a few years. These temporary exhibits printed on yard signs allowed the students to share their research about a historic site with the FSU community at large for about a week.

The idea of participation is also critical in the challenge institutions face in collecting, preserving, and interpreting history with and for marginalized audiences. Lonnie Bunch's experience as the National Museum of African American

Figure 2.8

Figures 2.7, 2.8 and 2.9 My Coke Story is a scaffolded participatory experience. *Source:* Jennifer Koslow.

Figure 2.9

Figure 2.10 Pop-up exhibits foster engagement. *Source:* Jennifer Koslow.

History and Culture's (NMAAHC) first director is indicative of these difficulties.[111] Based on his previous experience working at the National Museum of American History, Bunch knew that the Smithsonian's collections lacked substantial numbers of material artifacts that spoke to the African American experience. In order to build the new museum in the first decade of the twenty-first century he needed to adopt an unorthodox method of collection. Inspired partly by the television program *Antiques Roadshow*, Bunch developed the "Save Our African American Treasures" initiative. In it, citizens were asked to "bring out [their] stuff" and discuss their meaning with the museum's curators.[112] In exchange, museum professionals explained how best to take care of the objects and provided historical context about the material. Bunch needed African Americans to see NMAAHC, a Smithsonian Institution, as their own, which was not a given. The "Treasures" program succeeded in building trust and in building a collection of materials others had long claimed did not exist. In just a few years, NMAAHC acquired almost 35,000 objects through these types of programs and personal networking by Bunch. While Bunch's and his staff's efforts worked they were tremendously time consuming. Building a relationship with traditionally marginalized groups to be granted the privilege of safekeeping a family's heirlooms in perpetuity is an important but difficult ambition for many institutions to achieve.

Interpretation is related to engagement. Interpretation in history-centered institutions is based foremost on best practices for doing history, which was discussed in depth in Chapter 1. Fundamentally, you cannot interpret the history of an object if you do not research the historical context within which the object was created and used. In public spaces, however, interpretation is something more. As explained by Freeman Tilden, who wrote the original guide for National Park Service employees on the subject, interpretation is "an educational activity which aims to reveal meanings and relationships through the use of original objects, by firsthand experience, and by illustrative media, rather than simply to communicate factual information."[113] The ultimate purpose of interpretation, Tilden argued, was to instill a sense of social connection and responsibility for the nation's historic resources: "through interpretation, understanding; through understanding, appreciation; through appreciation, protection."[114]

In addition to the skills that all historians need to possess, public historians need to think about how they will interpret complex ideas in short 100-word labels and brief tours. Several different works can help with interpretation: Freeman Tilden's *Interpreting our Heritage*, Beverly Serrell's *Exhibit Labels: An Interpretive Approach*, and a myriad of handbooks for public speaking. Public Historians should take advantage of these resources to keep on their shelves and review when working in the field.

Public Historians need to know how to be effective communicators of interpretation in both written and oral form. There are a few foundational skills for both types of elucidation. Organization is a crucial component for each. Before you can even begin to write a label for an object or compose your thoughts for a tour, you must think about your audience. Whether you are writing and communicating to adults or fourth graders will shape how you interpret information. Some institutions allow for two different labels or different tours. Either way, unless giving a tour to a group of specialists in the field, it is safe to assume that jargon should be omitted.

In writing a label or giving a speech, you need to determine what is its purpose. Are you informing, persuading, or marking a special occasion, or are you trying to combine more than one of these goals? Most often Public Historians work to educate their audiences about a particular topic. The first line of a speech or a label should contain the main point of your interpretation. It is your thesis statement. It is your argument about why this object is historically significant. This statement should be made clearly and concisely.

Figure 2.11 This example from the National Museum of the American Indian demonstrates how to convey the main point of an exhibit succinctly. *Source:* Jennifer Koslow.

Once you make your main point you need to support it. Develop your main points using an outline as you compose your thoughts. Create an introduction, body, and conclusion. Each sentence in your label or as you speak should build on the previous. If you take too many twists and turns you will lose your audience. If you focus on too many micro details you will lose your audience. Your conclusion should reconnect to your thesis and leave your audience something to think about later. Ultimately, as Tilden explained, you want to talk "with" your visitor, and not "at."[115]

Last, if you are giving a tour, you need to practice. While delivering a memorized speech is a bad idea you do want to develop ideas about how you will communicate and create engagement before meeting with a group of people. You want to practice so you have a sense of timing. You want to know your material to the point where you can be flexible in your delivery. As for labels editing is a long process. Figure out what is a necessary and what is an unnecessary embellishment. Every time you think you have said your thoughts see if you can tell them with one or two fewer words. In sum, public historians need to learn effective written, vocal, and physical delivery and be able to adapt that delivery depending upon their particular audience. In doing so, they will be interpreters who provoke public engagement with and for general audiences.

Practice

1) Visit a museum of history and write about one artifact that made a powerful impression and why.
2) Interview a museum professional about their job.
3) Visit a museum for an hour and find two different spots to sit in each for 15 minutes. Take notes about what people are doing in relation to the various exhibits you were sitting within and then write a brief essay about those observations.
4) Visit an exhibit and analyze the argument (either implicit or explicit) it is making about a historical event or person.
5) Find an object in your home, treat it as a historical artifact, and write an interpretive label for it.
6) Find an object in your home, treat it as a historical artifact, and explain in 3 minutes to the class how it represents something about your family's history.

Further Resources

- American Alliance of Museums: www.aam-us.org.
- Anderson, Gail. *Reinventing the Museum: The Evolving Conversation on the Paradigm Shift.* 2nd. ed. Lanham, MD: Altamira Press, 2012.
- Barrett, Katy. "A Sense of Wonder." *Apollo* 179, no. 617 (February 2014), 54–58.
- Betts, John Rickards. "P.T. Barnum and the Popularization of Natural History." *Journal of the History of Ideas* 20, no. 3 (June–Sept 1959): 353–368.
- Caygill, Marjorie. *The Story of the British Museum.* 2nd ed. The British Museum Press, 1992.
- Cook, James. *The Arts of Deception.* Cambridge, MA: Harvard University Press, 2001.
- Cooks, Bridget R. "Black Artists and Activism: Harlem on My Mind (1969)." *American Studies* 48, no. 1 (Spring 2007): 5–39.
- Dennett, Andrea. *Weird and Wonderful: The Dime Museum in America.* New York, NY: New York University Press, 1997.
- Dubin, Steven. *Displays of Power: Controversy in the American Museum from the Enola Gay to Sensation.* New York, NY: New York University Press, 1999.

- Ewing, Heather. *The Lost World of James Smithson: Science, Revolution, and the Birth of the Smithsonian.* Bloomsbury Press, 2007.
- Giamo, Benedict. "The Smithsonian Enola Gay Exhibit: Public History and the Display of National Identity." *Nanzan Review of American Studies* 19, no. 2 (Fall 1997): 133–144.
- Handler, Richard, and Eric Gable. *The New History in an Old Museum: Creating the Past at Colonial Williamsburg.* Durham, NC: Duke University Press, 1997.
- Harwit, Martin. *An Exhibit Denied: Lobbying The History of Enola Gay.* New York, NY: Springer-Verlag, 1996.
- Hoffer, Peter Charles. *Past Imperfect: Facts, Fictions, Fraud—American History from Bancroft and Parkman to Ambrose, Bellesiles, Ellis, and Goodwin.* Public Affairs, 2007.
- Horton, James Oliver, and Lois E. Horton. *Slavery and Public History: The Tough Stuff of American Memory.* Chapel Hill, NC: University of North Carolina Press, 2006.
- Hoving, Thomas. *Making the Mummies Dance: Inside the Metropolitan Museum of Art.* New York, NY: Simon & Schuster, 1993.
- International Council of Museums: http://icom.museum.
- Karp, Ivan, and Steven Lavine, eds. *Exhibiting Cultures: The Poetics and Politics of Museum Display.* Washington, DC: Smithsonian Institution Press, 1991.
- Kohlstedt, Sally Gregory. "History in a Natural History Museum: George Brown Goode and the Smithsonian Institution." *The Public Historian* 10, no. 2 (Spring, 1988): 7–26.
- Kohlstedt, Sally Gregory. "'Thoughts in Things:' Modernity, History, and North American Museums." *Isis* 96, no. 4 (December 2005): 586–601.
- Leon, Warren, and Roy Rosenzweig. *History Museums in the United States: A Critical Assessment.* Urbana, IL: University of Illinois Press, 1989.
- Levey, Martin. "The First American Museum of Natural History." *Isis* 42, no. 1 (April 1951): 10–12.
- Linenthal, Edward, and Tom Englehardt. *History Wars: The Enola Gay and Other Battles for the American Past.* New York, NY: Henry Holt and Company, 1996.
- Magelssen, Scott. "Performance Practices of [Living] Open-Air Museums (And a New Look at 'Skansen' in American Living Museum Discourse." *Theatre History Studies* 24 (June 2004): 125–149.
- McClellan, Andrew. "P.T. Barnum, Jumbo the Elephant, and the Barnum Museum of Natural History at Tufts University." *Journal of the History of Collections* 24, no. 1 (2012): 45–62.
- Nash, Gary. *First City: Philadelphia and the Forging of Historical Memory.* Philadelphia, PA: University of Pennsylvania Press, 2002.
- Nash, Gary, Charlotte Crabtree, and Ross Dunn. *History on Trial: Culture Wars and the Teaching of the Past.* New York, NY: Vintage Books, 1997.
- Portolano, Marlana. "John Quincy Adams's Rhetorical Crusade for Astronomy." *Isis* 91, no. 3 (September 2000): 480–503.

- Post, Robert C. "A Narrative for our Time: The Enola Gay 'and after that, period.'" *Technology and Culture* 45, no. 2 (April 2004): 373–395.
- Qureshi, Sadiah. *Peoples on Parade: Exhibitions, Empire, and Anthropology in Nineteenth-Century Britain*. Chicago, The University of Chicago Press, 2011.
- Rosenzweig, Roy, and David Thelen. *The Presence of the Past: Popular Uses of History in American Life*. New York, NY: Columbia University Press, 1998.
- Saxon, A.H. "P.T. Barnum and the American Museum." *Wilson Quarterly* (Autumn 1989): 131.
- Sellers, Charles Coleman. *Mr. Peale's Museum: Charles Willson Peale and the First Popular Museum of Natural Science and Art*. New York, NY: W.W. Norton, 1980.
- Serrell, Beverly. *Exhibit Labels: An Interpretive Approach,* 2nd ed. Rowman & Littlefield: 2015.
- Tilden, Freeman. *Interpreting Our Heritage*, 4th ed. Charlotte, NC: The University of North Carolina Press, 2008.

References

1 "ICOM: Museum Definition," International Council of Museums, https://icom. museum/en/resources/standards-guidelines/museum-definition.

2 Roy Rosenzweig and David Thelen, *The Presence of the Past: Popular Uses of History in American Life* (New York, NY: Columbia University Press, 1998), 3.

3 Ibid., 114.

4 Ibid., 105 and 108.

5 Edward P. Alexander, Mary Alexander, and Julilee Decker, *Museums in Motion: An Introduction to the Functions of Museums*, 3rd ed. (1979; Rowman & Littlefield, 2017), 111–113.

6 Katy Barrett, "A Sense of Wonder," *Apollo* 179, no. 617 (February 2014): 55–57.

7 Marjorie Caygill, *The Story of the British Museum*, 2nd ed. (1981; The British Museum Press, 1992), 6.

8 Ibid., 6.

9 Ibid., 12.

10 Ibid., 13.

11 Martin Levey, "The First American Museum of Natural History," *Isis* 42, no. 1 (April 1951): 10–12.

12 Charles Coleman Sellers, *Mr. Peale's Museum: Charles Willson Peale and the First Popular Museum of Natural Science and Art* (New York, NY: W.W. Norton, 1980), 12.

13 Ibid., 18.

14 Gary Nash, *First City: Philadelphia and the Forging of Historical Memory* (Philadelphia, PA: University of Pennsylvania Press, 2002), 134–135.

15 Sellers, *Mr. Peale's Museum*, 9–11.

16 Ibid., 18 and 23.

17 Ibid., 150, 171, and 187.

18 Ibid., 45, and 76–77.

19 Ibid., 127–147 and 143.

20 Ibid., 196, 222, and 228–229.

21 Ibid., 332.

22 A.H. Saxon, "P.T. Barnum and the American Museum," *Wilson Quarterly* (Autumn 1989): 131.

23 James Cook, *The Arts of Deception: Playing with Fraud in the Age of Barnum* (Cambridge, MA: Harvard University Press, 2001), 4.

24 Sadiah Qureshi, *Peoples on Parade: Exhibitions, Empire, and Anthropology in Nineteenth-Century Britain* (Chicago, IL: The University of Chicago Press, 2011).

25 Cook, *The Arts of Deception*, 8–9.

26 Ibid., 8–9.

27 Ibid., 11–12.

28 Andrea Dennett, *Weird and Wonderful: The Dime Museum in America* (New York, NY: New York University Press, 1997), chap. 4.

29 Saxon, "P.T. Barnum and the American Museum," 138.

30 Ibid., 153.

31 John Rickards Betts, "P.T. Barnum and the Popularization of Natural History," *Journal of the History of Ideas* 20, no. 3 (June–Sept 1959): 353–368; Andrew McClellan, "P.T. Barnum, Jumbo the Elephant, and the Barnum Museum of Natural History at Tufts University," *Journal of the History of Collections* 24, no. 1 (2012): 45–62.

32 Heather Ewing, *The Lost World of James Smithson: Science, Revolution, and the Birth of the Smithsonian* (New York, NY: Bloomsbury Press, 2007), 206.

33 Ibid., 112, 139, and 208–209.

34 Ibid., 1–8, 308, and 347–349.

35 Ibid., 319–325.

36 "Measuring Worth," www.measuringworth.com.

37 Marlana Portolano, "John Quincy Adams's Rhetorical Crusade for Astronomy," *Isis* 9, no. 3 (2000): 480–503; Ewing, *The Lost World of James Smithson*, 325.

38 *An Act to establish the "Smithsonian Institution," for the Increase and Diffusion of Knowledge Among Men*, US Statutes at Large 9 Stat. 102, Chapter 178 (August 10, 1849).

39 "About the Smithsonian," www.si.edu/about.

40 Ivan Karp and Steven Lavine, eds., *Exhibiting Cultures: The Poetics and Politics of Museum Display* (Washington, DC: Smithsonian Institution Press, 1991), chaps. 18 and 20.

41 "Dr. George Brown Goode," *Wheeling Register* (Wheeling, West Virginia), September 7, 1896.

42 Gary Kulik, "Designing the Past: History-Museum Education from Peale to the Present," in *History Museum in the United States: A Critical Assessment*, ed. Warren Leon and Roy Rosenzweig, (Urbana, IL: University of Illinois Press, 1989), 7–12.

43 Goode quoted in Sally Gregory Kohlstedt, "'Thoughts in Things:' Modernity, History, and North American Museums," *Isis* 96 (2005): 588.

44 Kulik, "Designing the Past," 8.

45 George Brown Goode "On the Classification of Museums," *Science* 3, no. 57 (1896): 154.

46 Michael Wallace, *Mickey Mouse History and Other Essays on American Memory* (Philadelphia, PA: Temple University Press, 1996), 9.

47 Ibid., 10.

48 Scott Magelssen, "Performance Practices of [Living] Open-Air Museums (And a New Look at 'Skansen' in American Living Museum Discourse)," *Theatre History Studies* 24 (June 2004): 128.

49 Richard Handler and Eric Gable, *The New History in an Old Museum: Creating the Past at Colonial Williamsburg* (Durham, NC: Duke University Press, 1997), 73–74.

50 James Oliver Horton, "Slavery in American History: An Uncomfortable National Dialogue," in *Slavery and Public History: The Tough Stuff of American Memory*, eds. James Oliver Horton and Lois E. Horton (Chapel Hill, NC: University of North Carolina Press, 2006), 49–53.

51 "Report of the National Advisory Commission on Civil Disorders," National Criminal Justice Reference Service, www.ncjrs.gov/pdffiles1/Digitization/8073NCJRS.pdf.

52 Ralph Blumenthal, "Remembering Hoving's Service as Parks Commissioner," *City Room: Blogging from the Five Boroughs*, December 11, 2009, https://cityroom.blogs.nytimes.com/2009/12/11/remembering-hovings-service-as-parks-commissioner.

53 Thomas Hoving, *Making the Mummies Dance: Inside the Metropolitan Museum of Art* (New York, NY: Simon & Schuster, 1993), 64.

54 Steven Dubin, *Displays of Power: Controversy in the American Museum from the Enola Gay to Sensation* (New York, NY: New York University Press, 1999): 22 and 25–27.

55 Allon Schoener, "Harlem on My Mind: A Retrospective Walk through 'The Harlem on My Mind' Exhibition at the Metropolitan Museum of Art, 1969," http://harlemonmymind.org/retrospective.html.

56 Ibid.

57 Clarke quoted in Bridget R. Cooks, "Black Artists and Activism: *Harlem on My Mind (1969)*," *American Studies* 48, no. 1 (Spring 2007): 18.

58 Cooks, "Black Artists and Activism: *Harlem on My Mind (1969)*," *American Studies* 48, no. 1 (Spring 2007): 31–33.

59 Dubin, *Displays of Power*, 31–35.

60 Cooks, "Black Artists and Activism," 19–20; Hoving, *Dancing with Mummies*, 176–177; and Dubin, *Displays of Power*, 23–35.

61 Cooks, "Black Artists and Activism," 26.

62 Charles Peter Hoffer, Past Imperfect: *Facts, Fictions, Fraud – American History from Bancroft and Parkman to Ambrose, Bellesiles, Ellis, and Goodwin* (New York, NY: Public Affairs, 2007), 83.

63 Andrew Gulliford, "The West as America: Reinterpreting Images of the Frontier, 1820–1920," *Journal of American History* 89, no. 1 (June 1992): 200.

64 *New York Times,* May 5, 1991: XX38.

65 "Pilgrims and Other Imperialists," *The Wall Street Journal*, May 17, 1991, A14.

66 Dubin, *Displays of Power,* 160.

67 Michael Kimmelman, "Old West, A New Twist at the Smithsonian," *New York Times*, May 26, 1991, H1.

68 Kim Masters, "Senators Blast Smithsonian for 'Political Agenda,'" *Washington Post,* May 16, 1991, D01.

69 Dubin, *Displays of Power*, 160.

70 Vox Populi, New York Times, July 7, 1991, H25.

71 Dubin, *Displays of Power*, 167.

72 Ibid., 167.

73 Ibid., 171–172.

74 Ibid., 180.

75 *Smithsonian Institution General Background: Policies, Purposes, and Goals from 1846 to Present*, Volume I. Jul. 16, 21, 23, 28, 1970. Subcommittee on Library and Memorials, Committee on House Administration. House; Committee on House Administration. House, 172.

76 *Smithsonian Institution General Background: Policies, Purposes, and Goals from 1846 to Present*, Volume I. Jul. 16, 21, 23, 28, 1970. Subcommittee on Library and Memorials, Committee on House Administration. House; Committee on House Administration. House, 172.

77 *Smithsonian Institution General Background: Policies, Purposes, and Goals from 1846 to Present*, Volume I. Jul. 16, 21, 23, 28, 1970. Subcommittee on Library and Memorials, Committee on House Administration. House; Committee on House Administration. House, 185.

78 Hoffer, *Past Imperfect,* 115.

79 Ibid., 115.

80 Gary Nash, Charlotte Crabtree, and Ross Dunn, *History on Trial: Culture Wars and the Teaching of the Past* (New York, NY: Vintage Books, 1997).

81 Gary B. Nash, "A History of All the People Isn't PC," *The Wall Street Journal*, November 21, 1994, A17.

82 Lynne Cheney, "The End of History," *Wall Street Journal*, October 20, 1994, A22.

83 Nash, "A History of All the People Isn't PC."

84 "The Republican 'Contract with America,'" (1994) http://wps.prenhall.com/wps/media/objects/434/445252/DocumentsLibrary/docs/contract.htm

85 "Martin Otto Harwit," The Bruce Medalists, http://www.phys-astro.sonoma.edu/brucemedalists/Harwit/index.html.

86 Benedict Giamo, "The Smithsonian Enola Gay Exhibit: Public History and the Display of National Identity," *Nanzan Review of American Studies* 19, no. 2 (Fall 1997): 133–144.

87 Martin Harwit, *An Exhibit Denied: Lobbying The History of Enola Gay* (New York, NY: Springer-Verlag, 1996), 103.

88 Giamo, "The Smithsonian Enola Gay Exhibit," 135.

89 "Air Force Association, About Us," Air Force Association, https://www.afa.org/about-us.

90 "Smithsonian National Air and Space Museum, About," https://airandspace.si.edu/about.

91 Harwit, *An Exhibit Denied*, 215–216.

92 Ibid., 215–216.

93 Dubin, *Displays of Power*, 198.

94 John T. Correll, "'The Last Act' at Air and Space," *Air Force Magazine*, September 1994, http://www.airforcemag.com/MagazineArchive/Pages/1994/September%201994/0994lastact.aspx.

95 Harwit, *An Exhibit Denied*, 257, 259, and 345–349.

96 "Boeing B-29 Superfortress 'Enola Gay,'" Smithsonian National Air and Space Museum, https://airandspace.si.edu/collection-objects/boeing-b-29-superfortress-enola-gay.

97 Robert C. Post, "A Narrative for our Time: The Enola Gay 'and after that, period,'" *Technology and Culture* 45, no. 2 (April 2004): 389–390.

98 Stephen E. Weil, "From Being *About* Something to Being *For* Somebody: The Ongoing Transformation of the American Museum," reprinted in *Reinventing the Museum: The Evolving Conversation on the Paradigm Shift*, 2nd edition, ed. Gail Anderson (Lanham, MD: Altamira Press, 2012), 170–190.

99 Weil, "From Being About Something to Being For Somebody," 182.

100 Duncan Cameron, "The Museum, a Temple or the Forum," reprinted in *Reinventing the Museum: The Evolving Conversation on the Paradigm Shift*, 2nd edition, ed. Gail Anderson, (Lanham, MD: Altamira Press, 2012), 51.

101 Ibid., 53.

102 Ibid., 55.

103 Ibid., 59.

104 George E. Hein, "The Constructivist Museum," reprinted in *Reinventing the Museum: The Evolving Conversation on the Paradigm Shift*, 2nd edition, ed. Gail Anderson, (Lanham, MD: Altamira Press, 2012), 123.

105 Hein, "The Constructivist Museum," 126.

106 Ibid.

107 Nina Simon, "Principles of Participation," reprinted in *Reinventing the Museum: The Evolving Conversation on the Paradigm Shift*, 2nd edition, ed. Gail Anderson (Lanham, MD: Altamira Press, 2012), 331–334.

108 Simon, "Principles of Participation," 334–335 and 338.

109 "World of Coca-Cola, Our Story," www.worldofcoca-cola.com/our-story.

110 "A Pop Up Museum," http://popupmuseum.org.

111 Lonnie Bunch, *A Fool's Errand: Creating the National Museum of African American History and Culture in the Age of Bush, Obama, and Trump* (Washington, DC: Smithsonian Books, 2019), chap. 5.

112 Ibid., 92–96.

113 Freeman Tilden, *Interpreting Our Heritage*, 4th ed. (Charlotte, NC: The University of North Carolina Press, 2008), 33.

114 Ibid., 65.

115 Ibid., 37.

3

Preserving Historic Sites and Spaces

The built environment tells us about our history. Historic preservation ensures that historic sites and structures are not lost. It safeguards a sense of place. In some cases, historic preservation is used to resurrect a sense of place where historic sites and structures have been removed from the landscape. Historic preservation is also about maintaining the integrity of a structure's historic character. This means minimizing alterations, damage, or loss of those elements that characterize a historic structure. Preserving structures does not mean never touching them. You can make a structure safe for twenty-first-century living and still maintain the characteristics that make it historically significant. The history section in this chapter will discuss the history of the historic preservation movement from the nineteenth century in the United States to the present. The theory section will discuss the development of cultural heritage practices in the United States.

History

Preserving historic sites and structures in the United States has taken on many different forms. However, one continuous thread is that people, not the government, typically dictate what to save. This makes the United States different than our peers. For instance, in France, King Louis Philippe created a position for an inspector of historic monuments in 1830. The government then inventoried historic structures throughout France and asserted the right to block any modifications to these edifices.[1] Americans did not adopt this top-down approach to historic preservation. Instead, distrust for centralized government coupled with a belief in the rights associated with private property made historic preservation a grassroots affair. There were a few moments in the nation's early history where citizens organized to save a specific structure from destruction (Independence Hall for one).

Public History: An Introduction from Theory to Application, First Edition. Jennifer Lisa Koslow.
© 2021 by John Wiley & Sons, Inc. Published 2021 by John Wiley & Sons, Inc.

However, as an organized movement the origin of historic preservation lay in the actions of a nineteenth-century Virginian woman, Ann Pamela Cunningham. She strove to save Mount Vernon, George Washington's home and death place.

John Washington, George Washington's great-grandfather, purchased the land that became known as Mount Vernon in the 1660s. Lawrence Washington, George's older brother, stipulated in his will that when he died the estate would pass to his only child Sarah. Lawrence's will specified that if Sarah were to die without any offspring the estate would pass to Lawrence's widow, Anne Fairfax. Upon her death, Lawrence willed the estate to George. Lawrence died in 1752, and four-year-old Sarah died two years later. Anne remarried, moved, and leased Mount Vernon to George. Upon her death in 1761, the property became his.

Mount Vernon was the place George Washington built his family (he married Martha Parke Custis in 1759. She was a widow with means and had two children from her previous marriage: four-year-old John and three-year-old Martha). It was where he returned to after serving as the commanding general of the Continental

Figures 3.1 This nineteenth-century print idealizes Marquis de Lafayette's visit to Mount Vernon in 1784. In addition to Lafayette, George Washington, his wife Martha, presumably daughter-in-law Eleanor, and grandchildren Eleanor and George are pictured. *Source:* Library of Congress, Prints & Photographs Division, Reproduction number LC-DIG-pga-01995 (digital file from original print)LC-USZ62-16025 (b&w film copy neg.).

Army and then as the first president of the United States of America. It was the place of his death in 1799, the site of Martha Washington's death three years later, and the location of their tombs.

In the early nineteenth century, Mount Vernon became a site of tourism. Bushrod Washington, George's Washington's nephew and a justice of the US Supreme Court, became Mount Vernon's owner after Martha Washington's death. In 1822, he became so irritated with the number of steamboat passengers disembarking for uninvited day visits that he posted a warning sign. Mount Vernon, he announced, was private property and closed to picnic parties.[2] After Bushrod Washington's death (he and his wife did not have any children), the estate passed to Bushrod's nephew, John Augustine Washington II. He willed the estate to his widow, Jane Charlotte Washington. Their son, John Augustine III, managed the property for her and upon her death in 1855 it became his.

Much as his uncle before him, John Washington found himself confronting numerous visitors making pilgrimages to Mount Vernon. However, given the financial decline of the plantation's profitability (both a result of poor management and bad luck), John Washington attempted to turn tourism into a revenue source. He contracted with one of the steamboat companies to give them exclusive rights to dock, and he invested in the creation of a road to make access to the estate by land easier. Also, he began having the enslaved African American workers of Mount Vernon create materials to sell to tourists as they wandered the estate.[3] Selling the property in its entirety seemed like an increasingly promising way to go.

In the mid to late 1840s, citizens petitioned Congress to consider purchasing Mount Vernon. Calling themselves "memorialists," a group which included the vice president of the United States, president of the US Senate, speaker of the US House of Representatives, a few other US senators and representatives, four cabinet members, the mayor of Washington, and five private citizens, asked Congress to engage in an unprecedented act.[4] They urged Congress to purchase the land, buildings, and tomb for $100,000, the price set by Jane Washington. The memorialists argued that this purchase would do two things. It would allow citizens "the right and privilege of visiting, unrestrictedly, the venerated grounds, mansion, and sepulcher of Washington." An estimated 10,000 people visited the "holy grounds" each year. It would also protect Mount Vernon from "the uncertainties and transfers of individual fortune." The petitioners conceded that Washington's asking amount "may appear to be an exorbitant price." They argued, however, that the money was irrelevant in the face of the "infinite number of purely patriotic reminiscences that must forever be associated with those premises, doubly rendered priceless by containing the remains of [Washington]." Despite these compelling requests, Congress did not take any action. There was no precedent for the government to give that amount of money (almost two and a half million dollars today in relative worth) to a private citizen.[5]

In 1851, the US Army approached John Washington about purchasing the property for a veteran's hospital. Washington decided to ask for $200,000: a price he did not deviate from in later negotiations. In doubling the amount, Washington argued that it accorded with what he believed he could get for it on "the Public Market."[6] The Army Board determined this was beyond its means.

In response to rumors that a group of investors was looking to create a hotel on the site, the state of Virginia began to debate whether it should purchase the property. Governor Joseph Johnson appealed to Virginia's legislators in 1855 to take action. While he admitted that the price should give people pause, he believed some things were more valuable than money. He ended his speech with a powerful implore: "Dollars become as dust when compared with the inestimable patriotism inspired by a visit to the tomb." Despite the plea, the state of Virginia, much like the federal government did not take action. Transferring so much money from the public purse to a private citizen was unprecedented.

At this point, a new figure emerged in leading the fight to save Mount Vernon: Ann Pamela Cunningham. Born into a wealthy Virginian planter family, she suffered a significant back injury falling from a horse as a young woman. Consequently, she found herself visiting Philadelphia quite often to seek the advice of medical professionals (Philadelphia was the American capital of professional medical knowledge at the time.) What this meant for the Cunningham family was frequent trips up and down the Potomac River to reach Washington DC to then travel on to Philadelphia.

After one of these trips, Cunningham's mother, Louisa Cunningham, composed a letter to her daughter about the condition of Mount Vernon and expressed thoughts as to how to change its fortunes. She wrote:

It was a lovely moonlight night that we went down the Potomac. I was on deck as the bell tolled and we passed Mount Vernon. I was painfully depressed at the ruin and desolation of the home of Washington, and the thought passed through my mind: Why was it that the women of this country did not try to keep it in repair, if the men could not do it? It does seem such a blot on our country.[7]

Her 37-year-old daughter responded by penning a letter under the pseudonym "Southern Matron" that was printed by the *Charleston Mercury* in December of 1853. In it, Ann Pamela Cunningham appealed to the "Ladies of the South" to take up this cause. She asked, "can you be still with closed souls and purses, while the world cries 'Shame upon America,' and suffer Mount Vernon, with all its sacred associations, to become, as is spoken of and probable, the seat of manufacturers and manufactories?. . .Never! Forbid it, shades of the dead. . .!"[8]

Figure 3.2   Ann Pamela Cunningham spearheaded the successful movement to save Mount Vernon. Ann Pamela Cunningham, c. 1859. Photographed by Broadbent & Company, Philadelphia. Courtesy of Mount Vernon Ladies' Association.

Cunningham found power in gendered expectations. In the nineteenth century, women in the United States were not expected to engage in partisan politics. For instance, voting regularly occurred in saloons. However, women found power in their alleged moral authority that stood outside of traditional party politics.

Throughout the nineteenth century, women worked to change the laws that governed their lives. They wanted to have custody of their children in divorces. They wanted to control the wages they earned. By the time Cunningham made her plea, women were also engaged in anti-slavery and abolitionist campaigns. They also were involved in numerous organized charity efforts. Hence, while Cunningham's movement to save Mount Vernon moved women into new territory, the idea of feminine activism was not unique to the period within which she lived.[9] Women throughout the nation used the idea of womanhood to advance causes that were important to them. Women's use of their perceived moral authority as a wedge into actions of historic preservation has been described as "personalism."[10]

Cunningham set about saving Mount Vernon through two different strategies: public and personal persuasion. She wrote a letter to Eleanor Washington, John Washington's wife. She wanted Eleanor to ask John if he would be willing to sell the property to an organization of southern women, who would then transfer the title to Virginia.[11] This path did not lead to any positive results. Undeterred, in 1853 Cunningham organized women into a formal society: the Mount Vernon Ladies' Association. She sought help from women from all states in the nation (there were 29 in 1853). In a period of heightened sectional tension (which would break into civil war in 1861), Cunningham characterized the movement to save Mount Vernon as a unifying cause. Thus, the Mount Vernon Ladies' Association became the first mass movement for historic preservation in the United States.

Cunningham structured the group in a hierarchal fashion. As the head of the organization, she was the "Regent." She appointed "Vice-Regents" in states throughout the nation. The "Vice-Regents" appointed "Lady Managers" to work in local communities within each state. The goal was to raise money to purchase Mount Vernon. In addition to direct face-to-face collections through a "circle of friends," women raised funds through events such as balls.[12]

The most high profile mechanism the Mount Vernon Ladies' Association used for raising funds was the enlistment of Edward Everett to the cause. Everett had been president of Harvard University in the 1840s. A former senator from Massachusetts, he was famous for being a gifted orator. One biographer has argued that Everett also viewed saving Mount Vernon as a mechanism for fostering national solidarity in tumultuous times. In support of the Mount Vernon Ladies' Association's quest to raise funds to purchase the site, Everett gave a speech, over a hundred times, on the character of George Washington. He averaged approximately $500 per each performance of his lecture. In the end, his public lectures brought in almost $70,000 to the movement.[13]

By 1856, the Mount Vernon Ladies' Association had raised John Washington's $200,000 asking price. However, he did not want to sell the property to the organization. What finally changed his mind? In June 1856, Cunningham visited Washington to discuss the matter. She missed the steamboat to return to Washington DC and had to spend the night. The next morning, as Washington was waiting with her for her carriage, she tried one more time to convince him of the organization's sincerity. She "assured him that I believed all the ladies concerned felt as I did—while we wished to succeed in our beautiful tribute we were grieved that his feelings were hurt, insulted so repeatedly because of it." All of a sudden, Cunningham recalled, she had an epiphany. She found that with her words "unawares I had at last touched the 'sore spot,' the obstacle no money could have removed." The impediment was of impressions.

Cunningham realized "that [Washington] believed the whole thing had been arranged between the Association and Virginia to put an indignity on him!!"

There had never been a women's association of this type and why was it their charge and not the state of Virginia's to buy the property? Cunningham responded by assuring, "he must let the Association pay the money and not feel that his State or himself were lowered by the act!" In her final act, she held out her hand, and "he put his in mine."[14] Washington sold the property to the association, which has remained in its trust ever since.

Cunningham's organization inspired other women's groups to form to save additional historic sites, typically associated with political figures. By this method, women protected the Hermitage (Andrew Jackson's home), Mary Washington's house (mother of George Washington), and Cedar Hill (Frederick Douglass's home) among others. Throughout the late nineteenth and twentieth centuries, the Daughters of the American Revolution and the Daughters of the Confederacy made historic preservation one of their main activities.[15]

Women's organizations were the most frequent actors in preserving historic sites and structures at the end of the nineteenth century. Still, the federal government did not sit completely idle. The reason was the rise of tourism at Civil War battlefields. As the nation began to create national parks for recreational activities, (Yellowstone, for instance), veterans began to worry about the use of former military sites for leisure.[16] Instead of an outside group lobbying Congress, the lobbyists were internal. Veterans and Congressmen were the same. They did not wish hallowed ground to become the place of picnics.

Henry Boynton, a decorated US Army veteran, was tasked with creating two parks to commemorate the battles of Chickamauga and Chattanooga. His methods became the model. He created a sense of historical space. He mapped and marked troop positions, including those of the Confederates. He attempted to return the landscape to its state at the time of the battles. Afterward, Congress authorized four other military parks: Antietam, Shiloh, Gettysburg, and Vicksburg. Each site was a critical battlefield that helped determine the course of the Civil War. Although Congress pursued slightly different strategies for acquiring land in urban areas from rural ones (in cities it purchased specific properties to tell the story) the main point remained the same. The federal government had an interest in preserving the past. However, battlefield preservation did not lead to a more significant movement by the federal government for historic preservation. First, it was not economically feasible. Second, ideologically, there was still the sense that the government should not be in the business of redistributing public monies to private entities. Hence, the majority of historic preservation work in the early twentieth century was located in the private sector.

While women's organizations continued to save historic properties, the early twentieth century saw a reconfiguration of the meaning and approaches to preservation work. William Sumner Appleton Jr. played a central role in transforming a movement motivated by personalism to one guided by professionalism.[17] In doing so, men came to dominate leadership positions in historic preservation.

Born in 1874, William Sumner Appleton Jr. was descended from one of the first British families to migrate to New England. Family wealth freed Appleton from having to work for a living. He became interested in questions of architecture and archaeology. He became the secretary of the Paul Revere Memorial Association and guided the movement to restore Paul Revere's House in 1907. The house dated from between 1676 and 1681, which made it one of the oldest surviving structures in Boston. Revere lived on the third floor with his family during the American Revolution. By 1900, the house had undergone numerous renovations and had been adapted to many different purposes, including housing a bank, storefront, and tenement for Italian migrants. The question for Appleton was how to figure out what it looked like when Revere resided in it. Here was a hidden history that needed to be revealed. He determined that he needed to consult with architectural and archaeological experts to do so.[18]

After Appleton's success in restoring Revere's house, he chartered the Society for the Preservation of New England Antiquities (SPNEA, now known as Historic New England) in 1910. The cover of the society's first bulletin featured a photograph of the John Hancock house with the caption "Built in 1737 by Thomas Hancock. Destroyed 1863." While the demolition occurred in the infancy of historic preservation, Appleton used it as an example of the dangers of apathy. The Hancock house had stood on a valuable piece of land adjacent to Boston's State House. The family tried to sell the property to the state of Massachusetts for $100,000, which was $25,000 less than it was worth, in 1859. At first, it seemed as if the Boston state legislature would approve the appropriation. Even so, four years later, it took no action. Besides some issues with the title to the property, some legislators objected to the idea of transferring public funds to a private citizen. Appleton did not blame the government for failing to take action. Instead, he believed it was up to private citizens to take responsibility for preserving sites and structures of the past.[19]

Appleton created SPNEA as a vehicle for citizen activism. The goal was to secure buildings – both grand and vernacular – through "gift, purchase, or otherwise, and then to restore them and finally to let them to tenants under wise restrictions." While his first foray into historic preservation resulted in the creation of a historic house museum dedicated to Revere's memory, he advocated something different in this new endeavor. He argued that preservationists could and should modify buildings to fit new uses. The idea of adaptive reuse altered the trajectory of historic preservation in the twentieth century. Appleton changed the justification for saving structures and the results. Patriotism was no longer the sole reason for keeping a building. Also, he emphasized the importance of figuring out through scientific means what a structure looked like in the past. One result of these

BULLETIN OF
THE SOCIETY FOR THE PRESERVATION OF
NEW ENGLAND ANTIQUITIES

VOLUME I   BOSTON, MAY, 1910   NUMBER 1

THE HOME OF JOHN HANCOCK, BEACON STREET, BOSTON
Built 1737 by Thomas Hancock. Destroyed 1863. The fate of this house
has become a classic in the annals of vandalism. Governor Hancock is
said to have intended to bequeath his home to the Commonwealth, but
he died without giving effect to this intention by will. In 1859 a strong
effort was made to have the Commonwealth purchase the house at a low
valuation. This effort failed, and later the heirs offered the house with
some of its contents to the city as a free gift, the house to be moved to
another site. This plan also failed, and in 1863 the house was destroyed.

Figure 3.3 William Sumner Appleton Jr. used the demolition of John Hancock's house as a rallying cry for historic preservation. *Source:* Historic New England institutional records/ Historic New England.

transformations was the diminished role of women to secure leadership roles. As historic preservation became a degreed profession in the twentieth century, universities shut women out of accessing those programs.

In the same period that Appleton was beginning to transform private mechanisms and goals of historic preservation, the federal government also changed its relationship to the movement. In the early twentieth century, it passed the American Antiquities Act of 1906 and ten years later created the National

Park Service (NPS). While neither adopted a top-down approach to identifying historic sites and spaces to save, these laws affirmed that the federal government should support the preservation of historic resources.

The American Antiquities Act of 1906 was not a spontaneous deed. Instead, it was the culmination of years of lobbying for the preservation of America's archaeological sites.[20] After the Civil War, transcontinental railroads used the Southwest as a lure for their businesses. Patrons were promised stops at which they took artifacts as souvenirs. Also, entrepreneurs and scientists both made claims to these ancient sites: the former taking materials to sell and the latter taking materials to study and then put into museums. However, archaeology itself was a nascent field, so it took years of convincing. During the presidency of Theodore Roosevelt, the idea finally found favor.

Roosevelt was not the first person in the United States to propose a more significant role for the federal government in shaping the everyday lives of Americans. At the local and state level, individuals and groups had been agitating for years to regulate the excesses of capitalism and create laws to protect the general welfare. At the federal level, the American Antiquities Act of 1906 was just one of three pieces of legislation passed that year that expanded the social capacity of the federal government, the other two being the Meat Packing Act and the Pure Food and Drug Act. Moreover, many Americans had become familiar with the archaeological history of the United States when they attended World's Fairs and Exhibitions where antiquities were put on display. Through artifacts, people learned about the history of the United States that predated written European records.

According to Francis P. McManamon, former chief archaeologist of the NPS, the American Antiquities Act of 1906 was critical for three reasons. First, "it established basic public policies concerning archeological resources in the United States." Second, "it provided the President with the means of setting aside particularly important places of special preservation, commemoration, and interpretation." Third, the Act "established the requirement of professionalism and a scientific approach for any excavation, removal, and other investigations of archeological resources on public lands."[21] The discipline of archaeology greatly benefited from this federal requirement. By signing the Antiquities Act of 1906 into law, the United States recognized that material culture from the past was a public resource that informs the present.

The creation of the NPS in 1916 was a second federal action toward expanding the role of the federal government in historic preservation. There was a need to manage the various national parks and national monuments that had been created since the 1870s. In 1916, that number stood at 35. The legislation defined NPS's purpose as "conserve[ing] the scenery and the natural and historic objects and the wildlife therein and to provide for the enjoyment of the same in such manner and by such means as will leave them unimpaired for the enjoyment of future generations."[22] In the twentieth century, NPS became the principal federal agency through which the preservation of public resources occurred. It also guided policy and procedures to other federal agencies.

Another meaningful change in the history of historic preservation in the early twentieth century was the reconceptualization of zoning laws. Zoning allows municipal bodies to regulate the use of a property. Cities use it for a variety of purposes from determining where individuals can keep livestock to where they can run a business. However, until the US Supreme Court decision in *Village of Euclid* v *Ambler Realty Company* (1926) it was unclear whether cities could enact this type of regulatory power.[23] Writing for the majority, Supreme Court Justice George Sutherland argued that cities could enact zoning laws as an aspect of its police powers to secure the public welfare. While this particular case was about the sizes and heights of structures that could be erected on specific parcels of land, the ruling was meant to be a general one. Sutherland wrote that the particularities of zoning laws needed to be determined by each community in response to a particular nuisance to be resolved. Although historic preservation was never mentioned in the case, it had significant implications for the movement.

On October 13, 1931, the city council of Charleston, South Carolina became the first city in the nation to adopt a historic-district zoning ordinance. The ordinance created a Board of Architectural Review whose job it was to preserve and protect "old historic or architecturally worthy structures and quaint neighborhoods which impart a distinct aspect to the city and which serve as visible reminders of the historical and cultural heritage of the city, the state, and the nation."[24] Initially, the board focused on regulating the properties south of Broad Street. This area was where the oldest existing structures in the city stood. It was also the heart of the town's formal religious, legal, and financial life. While it could not prevent demolition, it had the power to review requests. In doing so, it could negotiate with property owners and developers on plans. Most importantly, Charleston's zoning law set a precedent that preservation was a civic value.[25]

The idea of thinking about districts rather than individual buildings was also at the heart of another venture in historic preservation making in the early twentieth century: the creation of Colonial Williamsburg. William Archer Rutherfoord Goodwin first moved to Williamsburg as the rector of the Bruton parish church in 1902. The parish had its origins in the 1630s but the contemporary building dated to 1715.[26] Goodwin began making efforts to restore the structure to its original shape, a project that he completed in 1907. Afterward, he left to take a position in Rochester, New York. In February 1923, Goodwin returned to Williamsburg to become a faculty member of the Department of Bible and Literature and Religious Education at the College of William and Mary. Upon his return, he set into motion a plan that used nineteenth-century ideas about the importance of place for evoking patriotism in combination with embracing twentieth-century scientific approaches to historic preservation.

Goodwin viewed Williamsburg as the "Cradle of the Republic" and "birthplace of her liberty."[27] It was the capital of Virginia during the British colonial period. Many of the city's historic structures still stood, albeit not always in the best condition. Goodwin became determined to restore outside appearances back to their eighteenth-century appearance and to recreate buildings that had been demolished. Goodwin used 1770 as the cut-off date for determining the scope of the project.[28] In doing so, he constructed an interpretation about what was significant and what was not. Goodwin knew that to accomplish such an unprecedented feat he would need to secure significant philanthropic financial support.

Goodwin initially appealed to Edsel Ford, son of Henry Ford. He wrote a letter arguing that the Fords were responsible for the physical decay of Williamsburg. Ford's ability to make cars affordable for the average American led to changes in the landscape. Goodwin argued that the resultant "paved roads, filling stations, lunch stands, tourist cabins, billboards, and traffic signals were all intrusions that tended to obliterate the historic atmosphere." He did not receive a positive response. Undeterred, Goodwin kept trying to lobby the Ford Motor Company and its officials.[29]

In the meantime, he secured the help of the local chapter of the Colonial Dames of America. In the spring of 1926, the chapter gave $15,000 toward the purchase of the George Wythe House. (George Wythe was one of the signers of the Declaration of Independence.) Goodwin then set about restoring it. It became important in his more substantial fundraising efforts because it provided him with something to show to potential donors.

A more promising situation arose out of a chance encounter with John D. Rockefeller Jr. In February 1924, Goodwin attended a dinner for the academic honors society Phi Beta Kappa in New York City on behalf of the college.[30] It was there that Goodwin met Rockefeller and did two things. First, Goodwin asked for Rockefeller's financial help in the college's effort to create a Phi Beta Kappa Hall. In two years, the organization would celebrate its 150th anniversary, which was particularly important to the College of William and Mary because it was the site of the first chapter. Rockefeller agreed to lend support. Second, Goodwin also invited Rockefeller to visit Williamsburg.

In 1926, Rockefeller was in Virginia to tour Hampton College, and he stopped to visit the College of William and Mary. Goodwin took him on a tour of Williamsburg. However, he did not bring up his broader idea. In this way, Goodwin laid the groundwork for support by building a relationship. In between this and Rockefeller's next visit, Goodwin met with one of Rockefeller's assistants, Arthur Woods, and presented him with his idea of creating Colonial Williamsburg.[31]

In November 1927, Rockefeller visited the college to attend the dedication of the Phi Beta Kappa Memorial Hall. Before the ceremony, Goodwin met with

Figure 3.4 The Wythe House. The first step in creating Colonial Williamsburg. *Source:* Library of Congress, Prints & Photographs Division, Reproduction number LC-DIG-csas-05821 (digital file from original negative).

Rockefeller and showed him the work he had done to restore the Wythe House. After the service, Rockefeller went on a walk by himself of the town. In the evening, he met with Goodwin and expressed approval of the concept, calling it "irresistible."[32] Although, he was also hesitant about its feasibility. Consequently, at first Rockefeller only earmarked enough money for the production of architectural drawings.

Goodwin moved forward in two directions. His secretary, Elizabeth Hayes, researched the colonial town using archival sources. In particular, she figured out where structures were using newspapers and maps. Goodwin also needed to generate a map of contemporary property lines. For that task he hired William G. Perry, the senior partner of a prestigious architectural firm in Boston. Neither Goodwin nor Perry wanted residents to know what he was doing, so he worked at night with a 50-foot tape measure to avoid attracting attention.

Armed with proof of concept, Rockefeller committed funds to purchase properties. There was a hitch though. Goodwin and Rockefeller feared that costs would escalate if the public found out who was the source of the funds. As a result,

Goodwin and Rockefeller kept Rockefeller's participation a secret. Instead, Goodwin told people that the money came from the college and that he had limited funds. In this sneaky way, Goodwin was able to secure a significant amount of acreage. However, Goodwin desired several properties that no one wished to sell. These were properties owned by descendants of the original titleholders. Goodwin approached them with a proposition they could not refuse. If they sold their property, they could retain a "life interest in their homes" and, thus, remain in them.[33]

After having secured the land and structures, Goodwin then supervised the translation of the architectural drawings into reality. While Hayes's research informed the project, it was still very much the product of the 1920s and 1930s beliefs about the look and feel of British colonial life. One example of this was the choices made about the reconstruction of the colonial capitol building. The old capitol building burned down in 1832. Hence, Goodwin needed to create a new one. He had two options to pick from for a model. One possibility was to create the structure that had been built in 1753, which was how it would have looked during the Revolutionary period. Taking this action would have matched the sense of place being created in the rest of Williamsburg. However, the architects of the project found better documentation for a 1747 version of the capitol and, thus, chose to use it to build a new old capitol.[34]

By 1931, Colonial Williamsburg was taking shape. Over 300 buildings built after 1770 had been demolished. Thirty-four buildings that had existed before 1770 but had since been destroyed were rebuilt.[35] On February 24, 1934, John D. Rockefeller Jr. announced that the majority of the work was complete and Colonial Williamsburg could move on to its next mission, which was education.[36] Since then, Colonial Williamsburg has continued to work to create a sense of place for visitors to experience the past. This has included rethinking the role of slavery in Colonial Williamsburg as well as the history of gender roles. By changing its interpretation, the contemporary site attempts to make visible aspects of historical reality that it originally hid from public view.

While private activities related to historic preservation continued to evolve, the dire economic situation of the 1930s known as the Great Depression prompted unprecedented federal action. Known collectively as the New Deal, President Franklin D. Roosevelt and his appointees created programs and advocated for legislation they hoped would resurrect the nation's economic and social health. Supporting historic preservation was included into these plans in a variety of ways.

For instance, developed in 1933, the Historic American Buildings Survey (HABS) functioned as a major mechanism by which the federal government became an active participant in historic preservation. As part of the New Deal program, HABS was designed to put unemployed architects back to work and preserve history. It

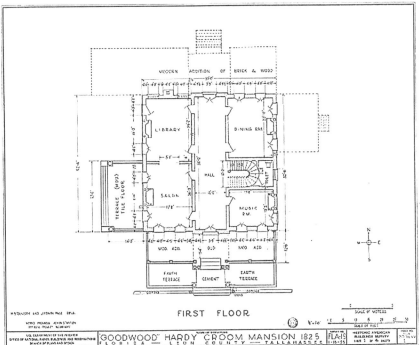

Figures 3.5 and 3.6 In Tallahassee, HABS documented the Goodwood house in two ways: exterior photographs and interior architectural drawings. *Source:* Library of Congress, Prints & Photographs Division, Reproduction number.

was the brainchild of Charles Peterson, who ran the NPS's Branch of Plans and Design and who was an architect. Although the 1930s was a time of economic devastation, there was a sense that economic prosperity could be rekindled through construction projects. Hence, as Peterson explained, historic structures were under threat not only from "natural elements" but also by "real estate 'improvements'" that together "form[ed] an inexorable tide of destruction destined to wipe out the great majority of the buildings which knew the beginnings and first flourish of the nation."[37] His idea was to hire approximately 1000 architects to conduct a national survey using measured drawings and photographs to document historically significant structures. These materials, he argued, would become America's "architectural archive." He lobbied to have them housed in the Library of Congress (the National Archives had yet to be built).

Peterson's project did not include funds to prevent demolition or promote restoration. Instead, Peterson argued, "if the great number of our antique buildings must disappear through economic cause, they shall not pass into unrecorded oblivion."[38] Within a year, HABS produced more than "five thousand sheets of measured drawings and an even larger number of photographs." Approximately 2000 buildings "worthy of being recorded" were identified by HABS.[39] These structures varied from the grand to the vernacular. When the advent of World War II made the necessity of New Deal employment programs obsolete, HABS was discontinued. Thirty years later, Peterson remarked on the significance of HABS. Peterson noted, "owners and occupants were often surprised to learn that they were using buildings significant enough for the Library of Congress to want its plans."[40] Ultimately, HABS created a shared sense of appreciation for historic preservation.

In the mid-1930s, Congress expanded the purview of the federal government to protect historic resources in another way. It passed the Historic Sites Act of 1935. This law "declared that it is a national policy to preserve for public use historic sites, buildings, and objects of national significance for the inspiration and benefit of the people of the United States." In doing so, it turned the federal government from a reactive to proactive participant in historic preservation. The Act also directed NPS to make a "survey of historic and archaeologic sites, buildings, and objects for the purpose of determining which possess exceptional value as commemorating or illustrating the history of the United States." Last, the Historic Sites Act of 1935 extended the purview of protection beyond federal land. The new law applied to any public or private property if the site was extraordinarily significant for telling the history of the United States.[41]

In the 1950s, in the period after World War II, the United States experienced an economic boom. The federal government provided financial support for infrastructure projects. It supported the growth and improvement of inter and intrastate highways. It also buoyed the idea of urban renewal that guided the redevelopment of cities; older structures gave way to new ones. Consequently, many historic resources became vulnerable to the wrecking ball. It was within that context that individuals began to rethink the role of the federal government in historic preservation.

Three things happened, each building on the previous. First, at the suggestion of Ronald F. Lee, a regional director of the NPS and a member of the board of trustees for the National Trust for Historic Preservation, interested parties held a meeting in Colonial Williamsburg in the summer of 1963 to discuss the state of historic preservation. One of the results of this meeting was a call to create a catalog of the nation's historic properties and the consideration of mechanisms to protect them. Second, a year later, President Lyndon B. Johnson appointed a presidential task force on the Preservation of Natural Beauty.[42] One aspect it addressed was urban development. Influenced by its findings, Johnson delivered a message to Congress on the "Natural Beauty of Our Country," wherein he remarked, "in almost every part of the country citizens are rallying to save landmarks of beauty and history." He called upon the government to "do its share to assist these local efforts which have an important national purpose."[43]

Third, US Representative Albert Rains (Democrat from Alabama) and Senator Edmund Muskie (Democrat from Maine) supported the creation of a Special Committee on Historic Preservation to investigate the status of historic preservation in the United States in 1965. This was an independent committee, who found financial support from the US Conference of Mayors and the Ford Foundation. The committee studied historic preservation in the United States and Europe. Random House published the results of the study in January 1966 under the title *With Heritage So Rich*.[44] The book outlined the issues at stake and offered guidance on legislative solutions. First Lady Claudia Alta "Lady Bird" Johnson wrote the foreword. For her, historic preservation was personal:

> For two years I have had the privilege of living in one of the great historic homes of the United States. Daily the lives of the President and of my whole family have been affected by tangible mementoes of earlier Chief Executives and their families. The experience has driven home to me the truth that the buildings which express our national heritage are not simply interesting. They give a sense of continuity and of heightened reality to our thinking about the whole meaning of the American past.[45]

Johnson's foreword articulated why historic preservation mattered. Structures, *With Heritage So Rich* argued, were "sources of memory." They were the tangible remnants of America's past and created a sense of place.

In its conclusions, the report called for a "new preservation" movement that simultaneously expanded the type of participant and the type of historical resource to save. Instead of focusing on exceptional structures with a national focus, *With Heritage So Rich* advocated including those that were important to local communities. The report promoted the idea that "the new preservation must look beyond the individual building and individual landmark and concern itself with the historic and architecturally valued areas and districts which contain a special meaning for the community." It emphatically stated: "In sum, if we wish to have a future with greater meaning, we must concern ourselves not only with the historic highlights, but we must be concerned with the total heritage of the nation and all that is worth preserving from our past as a living part of the present."[46]

A few months after Muskie presented the report to Congress, he and Republican Representative William B. Widnall of New Jersey (Rains had retired) introduced legislation based the report's recommendations.[47] By the end of the year, President Lyndon B. Johnson had signed the National Historic Preservation Act (NHPA) into law. It recognized the primary role of private individuals in saving historic sites and spaces but formally expanded the responsibilities of the federal government in that process. The opening explanation to the Act stated:

> Although the major burdens of historic preservation have been born and major efforts initiated by private agencies and individuals and both should continue to play a vital role, it is nevertheless necessary and appropriate for the Federal Government to accelerate its historic preservation programs and activities, and to give maximum encouragement to agencies and individuals undertaking preservation by private means, and to assist State and local governments and the National Trust for Historic Preservation in the United States to expand and accelerate their historic preservation programs and activities.[48]

The National Trust for Historic Preservation is a non-profit organization that serves as a clearinghouse for information on best practices. The trust was founded in 1949 through a Congressional Charter, which bestowed it symbolic legitimacy. It is not an agency of the federal government.

Significantly, the NHPA of 1966 did not establish police powers for the federal government over historic preservation. Instead, it created a set of directives and guidelines to offer several strategies of encouragement. First, it authorized the secretary of the interior "to expand and maintain a national register of districts, sites, buildings, structures, and objects significant in American history, architecture, archeology, and culture." The idea for a list was based on the Historic

Sites Survey that began in 1935 out of the Historic Sites Act and the 1960 Registry of National Historic Landmarks.[49] In 1966, this new list was titled the National Register of Historic Places, and it remains the nation's catalog of its historic resources.

The NPS administers the register. While individuals or interested groups are the ones who typically are inspired to begin the process, it is up to states to officially nominate a historic site to the National Register. The state historic preservation officer (or tribal preservation officer if the site is on Native American tribal lands) guides the process. Listing a property is a public declaration of its importance to the community, state, or nation. Thus, sites that matter to local history are considered as important to the history of the United States as national history. Last, properties listed on the National Register are eligible for federal tax benefits.

Second, the Act authorized the secretary of the interior to "grant funds to States for the purpose of preparing comprehensive statewide historic surveys and plans, in accordance with criteria established by the Secretary, for the preservation, acquisition, and development of such properties." The survey allowed states to approach historic preservation systematically, after which they developed comprehensive plans for managing historic resources. The secretary of the interior's Standards for the Treatment of Historic Properties continues to provide individuals and communities with the procedures for best practices.[50] Third, the Act authorized the secretary of the interior to found two programs for matching grants-in-aid, one to the states and one to the National Trust for Historic Preservation. Through these three mechanisms, historic preservation in the late twentieth century became a shared experience between individuals, local, state, and the federal government.

In addition to grant programs, the Act established another mechanism for the federal government to use its power of the purse for historic preservation. Section 106 of the Act provided that if a state desired to use federal funds on a project, it must "take into account the effect of the undertaking on any district, site, building, structure or object that is included in the National Register" prior to the distribution of those funds. In 1976, Congress extended Section 106 to include all properties that were eligible for listing, not just those that were listed. The Historic Preservation Act of 1966 (and its subsequent amendments) remains a critical mechanism through which historic preservation is encouraged in the United States. In providing incentives for identifying historic resources, it helped states and localities to create their grant programs as well as the adoption of local ordinances for protecting historic sites and spaces.

The United States is not the only country to rethink its approach to historic preservation in the twentieth century. In 1945, in the aftermath of World War II (and World War I), 50 nations joined to form the United Nations. The goal was to

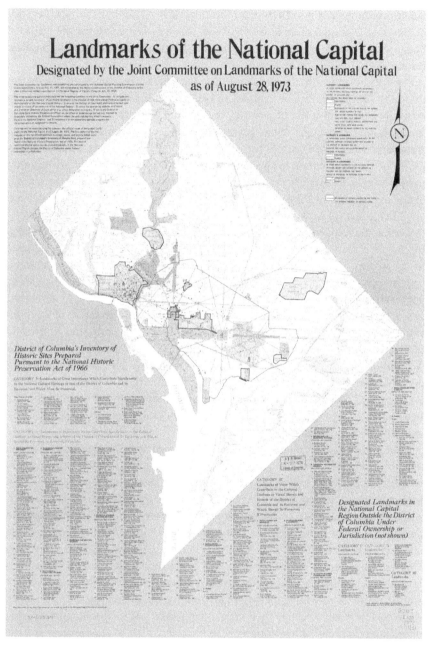

Figure 3.7   After the passage of the National Historic Preservation Act of 1966, states and the District of Columbia created inventories of their historic properties. *Source:* Library of Congress, Geography and Map Division. United States National Capital Planning Commission & United States Joint Committee On Landmarks. (1973) Landmarks of the National Capital. [Washington] [Map] Retrieved from the Library of Congress, https://www. loc.gov/item/75690024/.

"save succeeding generations from the scourge of war" and "to reaffirm faith in fundamental human rights, in the dignity and worth of the human person, in the equal rights of men and women and of nations large and small." The United Nations was also established "to promote social progress and better standards of life in larger freedom."[51] The United Nations Educational, Scientific, and Cultural Organization (UNESCO) was established as a specialized agency within the United Nations to create foundations of peace through mutual knowledge and understanding. UNESCO's constitution declared "that since wars begin in the minds of men, it is in the minds of men that the defences of peace must be constructed."[52] Peace, UNESCO explained, should not be dependent upon treaties.

In the late 1950s, UNESCO came to include historic preservation as one of its activities. The motivation stemmed from the attempt to save the Abu Simbel Temples and archaeological evidence of the Nubia, which would have been destroyed in the process of constructing the Aswan High Dam in Egypt. The movement to save the temples resulted in a compromise. Construction moved forward, the monuments were relocated, and archaeological expeditions were carried out to document and transfer cultural resources to museums.[53]

Since the controversy over the Abu Simbel Temples, UNESCO has continued to formally work to preserve historic sites and spaces upon which there is common agreement that those sites and spaces have value for humanity that crosses political borders. At a convention in 1972, UNESCO coined the term "World Heritage" to identify these types of cultural resources. Additionally, the meeting generated a

Figure 3.8 This photograph from 1904 shows the proximity of the Abu Simbel Temples to the Nile River, an area that would become flooded once the Aswan High Dam was completed in 1970. *Source:* Library of Congress, Prints & Photographs Division, Reproduction number LC-DIG-stereo-1s20768 (digital file from original).

World Heritage List of sites to protect. It also allowed for a group born out of the convention (the World Heritage Committee) to be able to declare sites on the list endangered. This second list was titled "List of World Heritage in Danger." Danger comes in many forms. According to UNESCO, "armed conflict and war, earthquake and other natural disasters, pollution, poaching, uncontrolled urbanization and unchecked tourist development pose major problems to World Heritage sites."[54] As of 2020, there were over 1100 properties on the list, 53 of which were considered in danger. In the United States, 23 sites are on the list, of which one is deemed to have been endangered since 2010: the Everglades National Park.[55]

The history of historic preservation in the United States suggests that creating a sense of place has mattered to its citizens for a long time. Motivations to preserve a historic site and space have differed. For some, it was a personal endeavor. For others, the science of preservation was more important. The role of governments (local, state, and federal) expanded over the twentieth century. While the federal government does not choose what to save, its legislation provides a vehicle to support local endeavors. In the end, historic preservation remains a method for creating community.

Theory

The creation and management of historic resources are most often categorized under the title of cultural heritage. In this theory section, we will discuss the development of heritage practices in the United States. We will look at philosophical questions about how to tell the story of a site. We will also look at the issues related to development. Historic resources are recognized as contributing to a locale's sense of place. But in constructing new roadways, new buildings, and new pathways to navigate the present, how do you meld old and new? In this section, we will discuss how questions of development relate to the preservation or destruction of historic structures.

Should a historic site tell one moment in time or the history of a place through time? Should public historians pursue a strategy of "restoration" or "preservation?" Scholars James L. Nolan Jr. and Ty F. Buckman, explain the methodological difference between the two: "Where the restoration efforts of the [nineteenth century] first two periods sought to return sites to the way they looked at specific historical periods, preservation aims to maintain homes in the conditions in which they were received by curators and preservationists."[56] The decision to pursue one tactic or the other typically depends upon the perspective of the individual or individuals who have taken on the responsibility to save a historic site or space. Their belief about why a place is significant can shape their approach to historic preservation.

The idea of restoring historic sites to focus on a single person has dominated how individuals and associations practiced historic preservation. For example, when Ann Pamela Cunningham began her venture to save the home of George Washington she focused the story of the house on Washington. By comparing and contrasting the historic preservation strategies employed at Monticello (Thomas Jefferson's home) and Montpelier (James Madison's home), we can see the two different approaches in action.[57]

Thomas Jefferson designed Monticello in the 1760s. In many ways, it was a typical plantation: a main house that served as the owner's domicile, outbuildings that served as home and workspace to enslaved African American workers (and in this case some free laborers), and farmland. Construction on the main house began in 1768. It was Jefferson's primary residence until his death in 1826.

In 1833, Uriah Levy, a US naval officer, purchased the house and about 200 of the surrounding acres to save the home of Jefferson from destruction.[58] In his will, Levy left the estate to the US Navy with the understanding that it would be used as a home and school for the orphans of naval officers. Levy died amid the Civil War, and the Confederate States of America confiscated the property and sold it. Jefferson Monroe Levy, Levy's nephew, successfully sued for the deed after the

Figure 3.9 Monticello circa 1900. *Source:* Library of Congress, Prints & Photographs Division, Reproduction number LC-DIG-det-4a17626 (digital file from original).

war. Levy engaged in restoration efforts, including purchasing more of the original land associated with the estate. He also thought about selling the property to the US government, but in keeping with precedent, Congress did not buy Monticello. In the early 1920s Levy sold the property, which included approximately 650 acres, to the Thomas Jefferson Foundation. The organization opened the house to the public in 1924. As the name suggests, the sole focus of interpretation was to be on Thomas Jefferson. The foundation removed any trace of the Levy's existence in the house, which "'did not please the Levy family,' who had held the property for nearly ninety years."[59]

The secretary of the interior's Standards for the Treatment of Historic Properties defines restoration as:

The act or process of accurately depicting the form, features, and character of a property as it appeared at a particular period of time by means of the removal of features from other periods in its history and reconstruction of missing features from the restoration period.[60]

Using Thomas Jefferson's writings and blueprints, the Thomas Jefferson Foundation set about recreating the main house's interior and exterior to resemble its appearance to that of Jefferson's lifetime. For instance, a letter from Jefferson to Mr. Barry, his housepainter, indicated that Jefferson had him paint the house's entry hall floor a grass green. A study of flecks of paint confirmed the action. Although some of the staff were reluctant to change the floor "because it was a beautiful pine floor with a herringbone pattern," the director of restoration William Beiswanger followed the evidence and had it painted.[61]

However, certain aspects of Jefferson's plantation were not immediately restored. At first, there were no attempts to retain evidence of Jefferson's enslaved African American laborers, which numbered over 600 in total during his lifetime. As approaches to history changed in the aftermath of the 1960s, some public historians began to believe that plantation stories ought to include those who built the houses, cooked the food, cleaned the house, took care of children, tended the fields, attended the livestock, and had their bodies rented and sold at the discretion of their owner. Some historic house museums still struggle with incorporating these stories into the fabric of their interpretations.[62]

Historic preservationists began restoring Mulberry Row as a first step toward telling a complete history of Monticello. Several hundred feet south of the main house, Jefferson designed a space for his enslaved and few free laborers to work and live. It has been dubbed Monticello's "Main Street." The number and types of structures varied depending on Jefferson's commercial endeavors. In the early 1990s, the Thomas Jefferson Foundation began to offer tours of Mulberry Row, but it was difficult for visitors to imagine the busy thoroughfare. Consequently, several structures were recreated based on an old insurance policy from 1796, archaeological evidence, and Jefferson's architectural drawings where available. These recreations have helped interpreters focus on the stories of those who lived and worked in these spaces.[63] In addition to the Mulberry tour, docents began interweaving the history of slavery into the principal tour of the main house.

In the summer of 2018, the Thomas Jefferson Foundation unveiled a new exhibit within the main tour: Sally Hemings' room. Within Thomas Jefferson's lifetime, there were rumors that he had fathered several of Sally Hemings children. Hemings was Martha Jefferson's (Thomas Jefferson's wife) half-sister. Martha inherited Sally from her father (also Sally's father) when he died in 1773. Sally Hemings was one of Thomas Jefferson's enslaved workers. Martha Jefferson died in 1782 at the age of 34; Thomas Jefferson was 39; Sally Hemings was 9. Jefferson moved to France to serve as the US envoy in 1784. Three years later, he sent for his youngest daughter, Maria, who was 9. Sally, who was 14, came as her companion. Sally was not the only Hemings to live in Jefferson's French household. Jefferson had brought one of her older brothers, James, who was tasked with learning the art of French cooking.

In 1789, Thomas Jefferson returned with his household to the United States. Shortly after that Sally Hemings began to have children. In total, she had six, of which four survived into adulthood. In 1997, scholar Annette Gordon-Reed published *Thomas Jefferson and Sally Hemings: An American Controversy*. She detailed a reasonable argument making the case that Thomas Jefferson fathered Sally Hemings' children. Gordon-Reed looked at the timing of births. She looked at the fact that the only people Jefferson ever freed from bondage were from the Hemings family. Last, she used the oral histories passed down generation after generation from African Americans who believed they were descendants of Jefferson. The following year, *Nature* published a genetic study that established with 99% accuracy that Thomas Jefferson was the father of Eston Hemings, Sally Hemings youngest son. (The DNA test relied on a unique genetic marker passed on through male descendants in the Jefferson family.)[64]

In 2017, the Thomas Jefferson Foundation restored part of the south wing of the main house. They removed a bathroom that was installed in the mid-twentieth century and revealed a small windowless room with a brick floor, plaster walls, and a hearth.[65] In a nineteenth-century biography Jefferson's grandson, Thomas Jefferson Randolph, claimed that Sally Hemings resided in one of two rooms in the south wing. Although there is no archaeological or textual sources to confirm Randolph's claim, the Thomas Jefferson Foundation has decided to use this space to restore Sally's story to Monticello.[66] They also tried something different. Instead of creating a static image of what the room might have looked like in the early 1800s, the foundation created a "presentation of Sally Hemings as a fully dimensioned human being—a mother, a sister, a daughter, a world traveler." The room is included in the tour of the main structure, thus fully integrating the story of enslaved people into the history of Thomas Jefferson's life and that of Monticello.[67] Although the foundation's techniques for telling history have changed and the story broadened, it is still an example of restoration. Monticello is still the story of Thomas Jefferson and the world within which he lived.

One of the reasons that the Thomas Jefferson Foundation chose restoration is because of the volume of artifacts and related materials they have to document that period. While time-consuming, returning much of the main house to its late eighteenth-, early nineteenth-century appearance was possible. Montpelier, James Madison's home, offers a contrasting methodology.

James Madison's father directed the creation of Montpelier in 1755. Madison remodeled the home (using advice from Thomas Jefferson) in 1809. He died in 1836. In 1899, William du Pont purchased the home. It remained in the du Pont family until 1984, when, upon the death of Marion du Pont Scott, it was bequeathed it to the National Trust for Historic Preservation. Because the house had changed hands a few times before the du Ponts bought it, Madison's furniture was gone. Also, numerous alterations had been made. Instead of trying to restore the house to the period in which Madison resided there, the National Trust took a different approach. It widened theories of preservation to include the idea of process. The National Trust interpreted Montpelier to tell history through time.

Figure 3.10   Montpelier circa 1930s. *Source:* Library of Congress, Prints & Photographs Division, Reproduction number.

The National Trust did this in two ways. First, in addition to the Madisons, the story of the du Ponts was central to the interpretation of the house. For instance, William du Pont Jr. was a significant investor in Thoroughbred horse racing. The trust did not remove the steeplechase course and flat track, which were remnants of that history. Second, the National Trust made changes transparent. For instance, in some rooms, they left open parts of the ceiling to reveal the use of different wood joints. This allowed visitors to see evolving changes in approaches to construction.[68] Today, the museum makes artifacts from the site's long history available to visitors to learn about how the historic landscape of Montpelier was transformed. Its website states: "Explore how Montpelier has changed through time with a wide range of artifacts, including Native American spear points, shoes owned by Dolley Madison, a bayonet from the gun of a Confederate soldier, and bowling pins from the du Pont bowling alley."[69]

Preservationists use both restoration and preservation to guide their work in creating, maintaining, and interpreting historic sites. Decisions on whether to focus on a single person, family, or moment in time are often guided by what materials are left. They are sometimes also governed by gift agreements that might make that requirement specific. However, even in restoration, historic preservationists often look to find ways to bring new interpretive dimensions to the stories they tell.

Another question of cultural heritage practice is the extent to which a surrounding landscape to a structure is essential for maintaining the historical integrity of a site. This is both a practical and a theoretical question. It also raises issues about how a sense of place is developed. Is it derived from the structures themselves or social interactions, or is it some combination of the two?

In investigating the various ways in which New Englanders described what made their towns quintessentially "New England," historian David Glassberg analyzed how community members came to those determinations. Those decisions were often rooted in personal stories. As a result, Glassberg found that there might be multiple interpretations of what made a town distinctive. It also meant that those individual understandings did not always comport with historical documentation.

As Glassberg relates, contemporary representations of New England towns during the British colonial period with a central meeting place for commercial and religious activity was not actually the norm. Most European settlers were dispersed. Main streets developed in the early nineteenth century.[70] Nonetheless, in popular culture, the romanticized version of the hub was an essential feature in depicting a historic New England. Glassberg and a team of scholars and local historic preservationist set out to test the relationship between reality and imagination in 1991.

Glassberg engaged with community members in three different towns in a variety of public meetings. Where he did not see a center in Wilbraham, others did. In the McKnight district of Springfield, gentrification illuminated conflicting perceptions of what were the historical aspects of a neighborhood. To new residents, mostly white, aluminum siding and chain-link fences were aspects to remove while attempting to restore a house to its original Victorian character. To older residents, primarily African American, doing so changed the fabric of a community that put in those features in the 1950s and 1960s when they were able to secure residences in the neighborhood.[71]

The lesson from these different interpretations for public historians engaged in historic preservation, according to Glassberg, is to think differently about the way to assign meaning to a place. He argues that if you ask residents, there is no "single history" for a site. Moreover, sometimes, the source of place making is not corporeal. Instead, a sense of place can be derived from personal memories. Social interaction, he convincingly contends, needs to be taken into consideration. How communities construct a sense of place contributes to how municipalities officially manage cultural resources.[72] Public historians need to pay particular attention to how non-academic audiences determine what is significant about their location and integrate those into interpretations of the past.

Taking into consideration social interactions raises issues about how to determine the value of a site relative to its physicality. If you move a historic structure from its original place, for instance, does it alter a person's ability to interpret its historical significance? In most cases, historic preservationists advocate that landscape matters for establishing historical context. Moving a structure to save it is seen as a last resort.

However, maintaining a structure does not necessarily mean that a site's meaning cannot change. In a series of "provocations" various authors in Max Page and Marla Millers' *Bending the Future: 50 Ideas for the Next 50 Years of Historic Preservation in the United States* suggest that creativity is the key to historic preservation.[73] For instance, Robert Hammond's examination of the High Line in New York City demonstrates the power of allowing historical sites to be rehabilitated and repurposed. Michael R. Allen's piece about Ferguson, Missouri forces historic preservationists to consider the importance of documenting significant sites even after they have been demolished. Remarking on absences in the landscape can be as powerful as marking it.

Another aspect of change is the question of accessibility. The Americans with Disabilities Act of 1990 (ADA) prohibits discrimination based on a person's disability. This made equal treatment a civil right. The ADA classified museums, libraries, galleries, and other places of public display as public accommodations whether publicly or privately funded. The NPS offers guidance to historic properties on how to be ADA compliant. The goal is to create a balance between maintaining the aspects of a structure that are critical to its historical integrity and modifying a structure or site to ensure access. Sometimes these are easy fixes; for instance, installing a ramp, but other times solutions that are more creative are needed.[74] Either way, historic preservationists need to be cognizant of the law and ensure compliance.

So where is a community to turn in attempting to evaluate its historic resources and choosing what course of action to pursue to save them? One way is through the NPS's Certified Local Government (CLG) program. When a community decides to pursue certification, they benefit by opening up opportunities to special funding and technical assistance.[75] The CLG helps communities maintain historic preservation programs. Before being recognized, a community must establish a qualified historic preservation commission. It also must have a mechanism for designating and protecting properties, typically a local ordinance. Hence, many communities have local registers of historic places that often detail requirements for demolition, alteration, and other manipulations of historic properties. To be certified, communities must provide residents with mechanisms for participation in the decision-making process. The CLG helps communities with both the theoretical and practical aspects of historic preservation. They allow for grassroots participation and, ideally, promote inclusivity.

Twenty-first-century ideas about cultural heritage include a desire to maintain a community's sense of place. Different approaches (whether to restore or preserve) depend upon a multitude of factors. Practical as well as theoretical reasons drive these decisions. Public historians engaged in cultural heritage preservation needed to be aware of these differences. They also need to think about the role of social interaction as much as the physical in helping a community determine how and why to save historic sites and structures.

Practice

1) Attend a meeting of your local Architectural Review Board, which reviews proposals to alter, restore, or rehabilitate historic structures in your community. Write up your impressions of the meeting.

2) Visit a site and photograph its main elevation, print it, and label the parts based on the character defining features of styles as discussed in McAlester's *A Field Guide to American Houses*. What does the architecture tell you about the period within which it was constructed?

3) Choose a historic site that is not on the local register of historic places and create the text (between 250 to 500 words) for a sign explaining why the site is historically significant.

4) Choose to visit a site for which you know there is an old photograph, drawing, or painting. Standing in approximately the same location of where you think

the original picture was taken, take (i) a new photograph and (ii) a photograph of the site with the old picture overlaying the current image. Write a brief textual explanation about the site and what you learned comparing the past to the present. Was the past still recognizable? Was the site completely different? How did the landscape change or remain the same?

5) Create a tour (in person or digital) of the National Historic Register sites in your community.

Further Resources

- Glassberg, David. *Sense of History: The Place of the Past in American Life.* Amherst, MA: University of Massachusetts Press, 2001.
- Hallock, Gardiner. "Mulberry Row: Telling the Story of Slavery at Monticello." *Site Lines* 14, no. 2 (Spring 2019): 3–8.
- Handler, Richard, and Eric Gable. *The New History in an Old Museum: Creating the Past at Colonial Williamsburg.* Durham, NC: Duke University Press, 1997.
- Hassan, Fekri A. "The Aswan High Dam and the International Rescue Nubia Campaign." *African Archaeological Review* 24 (2007): 79–90.
- Horton, James Oliver, and Lois E. Horton. *Slavery and Public History: The Tough Stuff of American Memory.* Chapel Hill, NC: The University of North Carolina Press, 2006.
- Hosmer Jr., Charles B. *Presence of the Past: A History of the Preservation Movement in the United States before Williamsburg.* New York, NY: G.P. Putnam's Sons, 1965.
- Hosmer Jr., Charles B. *Preservation Comes of Age: From Williamsburg to the National Trust, 1926–1949.* Charlottesville, VA: University of Virginia Press, 1981.
- Howe, Barbara J. "Historic Preservation: The Legacy of Ann Pamela Cunningham." *The Public Historian* 12, no. 1 (Winter, 1990): 31–61.
- Lindgren, James M. "'A New Departure in Historic, Patriotic Work:' Personalism, Professionalism, and Conflicting Concepts of Material Culture in the Late Nineteenth and Early Twentieth Centuries." *The Public Historian* 28, no. 2 (Spring, 1996): 41–60.
- Mackintosh, Barry. *The National Historic Preservation Act and the National Park Service: A History.* National Park Service, Washington, DC, 1986.
- McAlester, Virginia Savage. *A Field Guide to American Houses: The Definitive Guide to Identifying and Understanding America's Domestic Architecture.* New York, NY: Knopf, 2015.
- McManamon, Francis P. "The Antiquities Act and How Theodore Roosevelt Shaped It." *The George Wright Forum* 32, no 3 (2014): 324–344.

- Nolan Jr., James L., and Ty F. Buckman. "Preserving the Postmodern, Restoring the Past: The Cases of Monticello and Montpelier." *The Sociological Quarterly* 39, no. 2 (Spring 1998): 253–269.
- Page, Max, and Marla Miller. *Bending the Future: 50 Ideas for the Next 50 Years of Historic Preservation in the United States.* Amherst, MA: University of Massachusetts Press, 2016.
- Page, Max, and Randall Mason. *Giving Preservation a History: Histories of Historic Preservation in the United States.* New York, NY: Routledge, 2004.
- Smith, Timothy B. *The Golden Age of Battlefield Preservation: The Decade of the 1890s and the Establishment of America's First Five Military Parks.* Knoxville, TN: The University of Tennessee Press, 2008.
- Watt, Laura A., Leigh Raymond, and Meryl L. Eschen. "On Preserving Ecological and Cultural Landscapes." *Environmental History* 9, no. 4 (October, 2004): 620–647.

References

1 Charles B. Hosmer Jr., *Presence of the Past: A History of the Preservation Movement in the United States before Williamsburg* (New York, NY: G. P. Putnam's Sons, 1965), 23.
2 Ibid., 41.
3 "John Augustine Washington III," George Washington's Mount Vernon, www. mountvernon.org/library/digitalhistory/digital-encyclopedia/article/ john-augustine-washington-iii.
4 "Memorial of Citizens of the United States Praying The Purchase of Mount Vernon by the Government," March 10, 1848. Committee on the District of Columbia. Senate. S. misdoc.82. Serial volume 511: Sessional volume: 1.
5 "Measuring Worth," www.measuringworth.com.
6 Hosmer, *Presence of the Past*, 42.
7 Quoted in Elswyth Thane, *Mount Vernon is Ours: The Story of its Preservation* (New York, NY: Duell, Sloan, and Pearce, 1966), 16.
8 Quoted in Hosmer, *Presence of the Past*, 44.
9 Barbara J. Howe, "Historic Preservation: The Legacy of Ann Pamela Cunningham," *The Public Historian* 12, no. 1 (Winter, 1990): 31–37.
10 James M. Lindgren, "'A New Departure in Historic, Patriotic Work:' Personalism, Professionalism, and Conflicting Concepts of Material Culture in the Late Nineteenth and Early Twentieth Centuries," *The Public Historian* 28, no. 2 (Spring, 1996): 42.
11 Hosmer, *Presence of the Past*, 45.
12 "Mount Vernon Ladies' Associations – Proceedings in California," *San Francisco Bulletin*, May 21, 1859; "Mount Vernon Ladies' Association," *San Francisco Bulletin*, May 26, 1859.

13 Hosmer, *Presence of the Past*, 46–47.
14 Quoted in Hosmer, *Presence of the Past*, 48–9.
15 Howe, "Historic Preservation," 34–37.
16 Timothy B. Smith, *The Golden Age of Battlefield Preservation: The Decade of the 1890s and the Establishment of America's First Five Military Parks* (Knoxville, TN: The University of Tennessee Press, 2008): 34–35.
17 Lindgren, "A New Departure," 51–55.
18 Michael Holleran, "Roots in Boston, Branches in Planning and Parks," in *Giving Preservation a History: Histories of Historic Preservation in the United States*, ed. Max Page and Randall Mason (New York, NY: Routledge, 2004): 96–101.
19 Ibid., 82–83.
20 Francis P. McManamon, "The Antiquities Act and How Theodore Roosevelt Shaped It," *The George Wright Forum* 32, no. 3 (2014): 325–326.
21 "Archeology Program," National Park Service, www.nps.gov/history/archeology/TOOLS/Laws/AntAct.htm.
22 "America's National Park System: The Critical Documents," National Park Service, www.nps.gov/parkhistory/online_books/anps/anps_1i.htm.
23 Village of Euclid v Ambler Realty Co. (No. 31) 272 US 365 (1926), www.law.cornell.edu/supremecourt/text/272/365.
24 "Charleston, South Carolina, Board of Architectural Review," www.charleston-sc.gov/index.aspx?NID=293.
25 Charles Hosmer, *Preservation Comes of Age: From Williamsburg to the National Trust, 1926–1949* (Charlottesville, VA: University Press of Virginia, 1981), 238–240.
26 "Bruton Parish Church—A Brief History," http://images.acswebnetworks.com/1/1318/BPCBriefHistoryJune2011.pdf.
27 Quoted in Hosmer, *Preservation Comes of Age*, 11.
28 Richard Handler and Eric Gable, *The New History in an Old Museum: Creating the Past at Colonial Williamsburg* (Durham, NC: Duke University Press, 1997), 223.
29 Quoted in Hosmer, *Preservation Comes of Age*, 14.
30 Edwards Park, "'My Dreams and My Hope: History of the Restoration," www.history.org/Foundation/general/introhis.cfm.
31 Hosmer, *Preservation Comes of Age*, 12.
32 Ibid., 19.
33 Ibid., 25.
34 Ibid., 38.
35 Ibid., 44.
36 Ibid., 48.
37 Ibid., 549.
38 Ibid., 549.
39 Ibid., 557.

40 Ibid., 558.

41 "Historic Sites Act of 1935," National Park Service, www.nps.gov/history/ local-law/hsact35.htm.

42 Barry Mackintosh, *The National Historic Preservation Act and the National Park Service: A History* (National Park Service, Washington, DC, 1986).

43 Message from the President of the United States, "Special Message to the Congress on Conservation and Restoration of Natural Beauty," 12677–1 H.doc 78, (February 8, 1965).

44 89–2 Cong. Rec. S.2629 (February 9, 1966); Mackintosh, *The National Historic Preservation Act*, preface; Laura A. Watt, Leigh Raymond, and Meryl L. Eschen, "On Preserving Ecological and Cultural Landscapes," *Environmental History* 9, no. 4 (October, 2004): 622–623.

45 "With Heritage So Rich," Preservation 50, http://preservation50.org/about/ with-heritage-so-rich.

46 Ibid.

47 89–2 Cong. Rec. S2629 (February 9, 1966).

48 An Act to Establish a Program for the Preservation of Additional Historic Properties throughout the Nation, and for other Purposes, 80 Stat. 915 (October 15, 1966).

49 Watt, "On Preserving Ecological and Cultural Landscapes," 622.

50 "The Secretary of the Interior's Standards," National Park Service, www.nps.gov/ tps/standards.htm.

51 "United Nations Preamble," United Nations, www.un.org/en/sections/ un-charter/preamble/index.html.

52 "Constitution of the United Nations Educational, Scientific and Cultural Organization," UNESDOC Digital Library, https://unesdoc.unesco.org/ ark:/48223/pf0000261751.page=6.

53 Fekri A. Hassan, "The Aswan High Dam and the International Rescue Nubia Campaign," *African Archaeological Review* 24 (2007): 79–90.

54 "World Heritage in Danger," UNESCO, http://whc.unesco.org/en/158.

55 "World Heritage List: United States of America," UNESCO, http://whc.unesco.org/ en/statesparties/us; "Everglades National Park," http://whc.unesco.org/en/list/76.

56 James L. Nolan Jr. and Ty F. Buckman, "Preserving the Postmodern, Restoring the Past: The Cases of Monticello and Montpelier," *The Sociological Quarterly* 39, no. 2 (Spring 1998): 263.

57 It is not my original idea to compare the two. Instead, I am summarizing the findings of Nolan Buckman. See Nolan, "Preserving the Postmodern, Restoring the Past," 253–369.

58 Malcolm H. Stern, "The Levy Family and Monticello," www.monticello.org/ thomas-jefferson/a-day-in-the-life-of-jefferson/all-my-wishes-end-at-monticello/ the-levy-family-and-monticello.

59 Charles Hosmer quoted in Nolan, "Preserving the Postmodern," 257.

60 "Restoration as a Treatment," www.nps.gov/tps/standards/four-treatments/ treatment-restoration.htm.

61 Beiswanger quoted in quoted in Nolan, "Preserving the Postmodern," 256. Beiswanger served as Monticello's director of restoration from 1969 to 2012. "Director of Restoration Retires After More Than Four Decades at Monticello," https://monticello-www.s3.amazonaws.com/files/old/inline-pdfs/2012w_ DirectorofRestorationRetires.pdf.

62 James Oliver Horton and Lois E. Horton, *Slavery and Public History: The Tough Stuff of American Memory* (Chapel Hill, NC: The University of North Carolina Press, 2006), especially chaps. 2, 6, and 7.

63 Gardiner Hallock, "Mulberry Row: Telling the Story of Slavery at Monticello," *Site Lines* 14, no. 2 (Spring 2019): 3–8.

64 Horton and Horton, *Slavery and Public History*, 137–139. See also www. monticello.org/sallyhemings.

65 "Excavating Monticello's First Kitchen and South Wing," www.monticello.org/ site/blog-and-community/posts/ excavating-monticello%E2%80%99s-first-kitchen-and-south-wing.

66 Jason Daley, "Sally Hemings Gets Her Own Room at Monticello," *The Smithsonian Magazine*, July 5, 2017, https://www.smithsonianmag.com/ smart-news/sally-hemings-gets-her-own-room-monticello-180963944.

67 "Jefferson's Monticello Makes Room for Sally Hemings," June 16, 2018, https:// www.npr.org/2018/06/16/620311433/ jeffersons-monticello-makes-room-for-sally-hemings.

68 Nolan, "Preserving the Postmodern," 258–262.

69 "Mysteries of Montpelier," James Madison's Montpelier, www.montpelier.org/ visit/galleries-and-exhibits.

70 David Glassberg, *Sense of History: The Place of the Past in American Life* (Amherst, MA: University of Massachusetts Press, 2001), 133–137.

71 Ibid., 145–155.

72 Ibid., 157.

73 Max Page and Marla Miller, *Bending the Future: 50 Ideas for the Next 50 Years of Historic Preservation in the United States* (Amherst, MA: University of Massachusetts Press, 2016).

74 "Making Historic Properties Accessible," National Park Service, www.nps.gov/ tps/how-to-preserve/briefs/32-accessibility.htm#planning.

75 "Certified Local Government Program," National Park Service, www.nps.gov/clg.

4

Managing Archives and Historical Records

Archives are cultural agencies that preserve historical memory. The US National Archives defines "archives" as "a place where people can go to gather firsthand facts, data, and evidence from letters, reports, notes, memos, photographs, and other primary sources."[1] The goal is to collect materials that are perceived to have permanent value. Archives also often serve an administrative function for government; government archives are the repositories of official records. The historical profession and archival profession have a long-intertwined history. Archivists manage the raw materials of history. Moreover, Public Historians often work as archivists. For these two reasons, it is appropriate for students of Public History to familiarize themselves with the history and theory of archives.

History

There are many different types of archives. The US National Archives and Records Administration (NARA) likes to remind the public that they are more familiar with archives than they often think. The archivists at NARA point out that most individuals maintain some "personal archives" in their home. This archive "might be in a filing cabinet in your study, a box in the basement, a chest in the attic," but either way NARA argues these materials are records of "important events from your family's history."[2] More formally, there are government archives, independent archives, and community archives. Each plays a different role in preserving the past. For instance, community archives are typically self-conscious spaces for collecting materials for groups who often found themselves either marginalized or omitted from the collecting practices of government institutions.[3] This section focuses on the history of historical associations, state archives, and the US National Archives.

The first organizations to self-consciously create archives in the United States were historical associations. Membership in these early societies was not always

Public History: An Introduction from Theory to Application, First Edition. Jennifer Lisa Koslow.
© 2021 by John Wiley & Sons, Inc. Published 2021 by John Wiley & Sons, Inc.

afforded to all in these early years. Some were based on professional reputation and others on social status. Last, and significantly, these were private organizations rather than state-funded institutions.

In 1791, ten men considered as elites (physicians, reverends, and historians were among the group) joined to form a society in Massachusetts dedicated to preserving the textual history of the United States. Their purpose was

the preservation of books, pamphlets, manuscripts and records, containing historical facts, biographical anecdotes, temporary projects, and beneficial speculations, conduces to mark the genius, delineate the manners, and trace the progress of society in the United States, and must always have a useful tendency to rescue the true history of this country from the ravages of time and the effects of ignorance and neglect.[4]

They incorporated the society three years later as the Massachusetts Historical Society (MHS).

The founders actively sought materials to add to its collections. One of the founders, Jeremy Belknap, explained: "there is nothing like having a *good repository,* and keeping a *good lookout,* not waiting at home for things to fall into the lap, but prowling about like a wolf for the prey."(italics in the original)[5] According to one of MHS's historians, "by 1844 the Society could report 100 volumes of bound manuscripts including. . .the bound manuscript journal of Governor John Winthrop kept from the time of his departure from England in the *Arbella* in 1630 until his death in 1649."[6] The MHS published documentary collections to make these materials accessible beyond the physical archives that were open to scholars.

In the early years of the new republic, several men followed MHS's lead. A society formed in New York in 1804, the American Antiquarian Society at Worcester created in 1812, an organization formed in Philadelphia in 1824, and another in Virginia in 1831.[7] Each was founded with similar principles to MHS. For instance, New York's charter indicated that its mission was "to discover, procure, and preserve whatever may relate to the natural, civil, literary and ecclesiastical history of the United States in general, and of the State in particular."[8] As a result, New York's nineteenth-century newspaper collection grew to be among the largest in the nation. For those doing work before the existence of electronic databases, this proved to be exceedingly crucial for research.[9]

In 1854, Lyman Copeland Draper became the secretary of the State Historical Society of Wisconsin, and he changed the nature of funding for future historical societies. He successfully advocated for permanent state funding. Draper, who had experience collecting historical manuscripts, moved from New York to Wisconsin in 1852 in the hopes of securing a position with the state. He joined the historical society and was elected to its executive committee. Before Draper's arrival, the institution was in a financially precarious situation.[10] One solution would have been to raise the fee to join to $5.00, which would have made it unaffordable to many. (The relative cost today is $122.[11]) Instead, Draper was able to secure an appropriation of $500 from the state legislature. (The relative price today is $15,400.00) This far outweighed the income the society had received from dues and gifts, which was $52.52.[12]

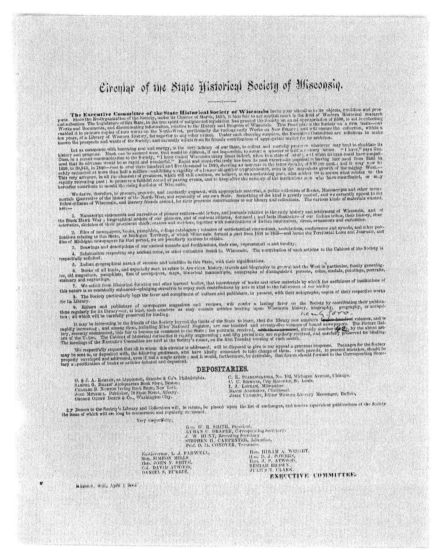

Figure 4.1   The State Historical Society of Wisconsin used a circular to explain its funding source and its collecting goals. *Source:* Library of Congress, Rare Book and Special Collections Division, Printed Ephemera Collection. State Historical Society Of Wisconsin. (1855) Circular of the State Historical society of Wisconsin ... Madison Wis April 1. Madison. [Pdf] Retrieved from the Library of Congress, https://www.loc.gov/item/rbpe.18901600/.

Since that first appropriation, the state of Wisconsin has continued to fund the society. This provided a model for other states. By way of example, Iowa founded a Historical Society in 1857 and received $250 annually from the state's legislature.[13] Similarly, Kansas used Draper's model and its historical society began receiving an annual sum in 1877.[14] The State Historical Society of Wisconsin also developed a variety of programs to disseminate information and provide educational opportunities to residents throughout the state, including a magazine, a "traveling historymobile, and four or five branch museums."[15] Others also adopted these kinds of programs.

In most states, these societies continue to collect, preserve, and interpret the history of the United States. Sometimes the line between research facility and museum is quite blurred. For instance, the Chicago Historical Society (CHS) was founded in 1856 and functioned as the city's only public library for a period. However, the Great Chicago Fire of 1871 reduced the building and its contents to rubble. Rebuilding began in the late 1870s, but CHS's most significant transformation happened in 1920. In that year, CHS agreed to purchase Charles F. Gunther's enormous collection of manuscripts, rare books, art, and other artifacts of Americana material culture. The historical society leased land in Lincoln Park from the city of Chicago in perpetuity to build a new structure to house these materials.[16] The new building was both a museum and research facility. Visitors could walk through a replica of the room in Washington in which Lincoln died (Gunther had collected his deathbed) or the foyer to Independence Hall from Philadelphia.[17] Although it had been functioning as a museum since the mid-twentieth century, it was not until 2006 that CHS was formally renamed the Chicago History Museum. This action did not mean, however, that it eschewed collecting textual material. Instead, it is both an archive and a museum.[18] The Chicago History Museum, like many other state historical societies, continues to operate as an independent archive committed to collecting, preserving, and interpreting local history.

The story of states taking an active role in preserving government records is interlinked with the story of the American Historical Association (AHA). When the AHA was founded in 1884, the organization was home to historically minded scholars, who were themselves splitting off from the American Social Science Association. In addition to "the promotion of historical studies," AHA's self-stated mission included "the collection and preservation of historical manuscripts."[19] Thus, in its early history, the AHA engaged in a series of studies to aid scholars in identifying historical materials among the various states.

In 1899, the AHA appointed a Public Archives Commission to "investigate and report on the character of the historical public archives of the several States and the United States and the means taken for their preservation and publication."[20] In 1900, a preliminary report conveyed the precarious state of public record throughout the nation. A survey of Ohio found its official documents to be in "a very confused state, with many gaps in the files, due in part to the burning of the old statehouse in the early part of the century." The Commission made an example out of Nebraska, arguing that it was an illustration of "a typical case of the loss of important records through ignorance and carelessness." Here the surveyor found that "the janitors at the capitol, in the course of their cleaning, found a box of manuscripts, and concluding that they were of no value, burned them." The result was that "as near as can made out, the entire records of the constitutional convention of 1875 went up in smoke."[21] The impact of the study was significant. According to Whitehill, "within a decade [the Public Archives Commission] had issued forty-one reports on State and municipal archives, and, in response to this stimulus, half of the states passed laws relating to the preservation and custody of their records."[22] This became particularly important in the South where most states did not have active historical societies.

In creating official repositories for public records, states adopted several different strategies. Some created independent commissions. Some created departments within state government. Others placed an archives program into another division. In 1901, Alabama was the first to create a Department of Archives and History. Mississippi followed suit in 1902. Here we see a direct connection to the AHA as Mississippi's first director, Dunbar Rowland, was an active member on the Public Archives Commission.[23] Rowland also provides an example of how contemporary politics shaped the collecting policies of these official repositories. Rowland's belief in white supremacy led him to prioritize collecting materials to preserve the history of the Confederate States of America. He wrote:

> If there is one duty of this Department which should stand before all others it is that sacred duty to preserve the record of the deeds of the Confederate soldiers of Mississippi who gave up everything for country and made forever heroic the time in which they lived.[24]

Rowland did not attempt to collect materials that would have outwardly contested this construction of memory.

As the number of state archives grew in the twentieth century and the US National Archives was established in the 1930s (a story we will get to in a moment), so did the number of self-identified archivists. In 1936, this led to the creation of the Society of American Archivists (SAA). As the process for managing information developed in the twentieth century, so did the elaboration of professional identities. In 1955, a group formed for records managers: the American Records Management Association. While different, there is a substantial overlap between the two professional fields. Hence, in 1974, the National Association of State Archives and Records Administrators formed and ten years later was renamed the National Association of Government Archives and Records Administrators.[25]

The United States did not open a National Archives until 1933. This was relatively late compared to Western European countries. France, whose revolution occurred shortly after the American Revolution, established an archive (Archives Nationales) amid that upheaval (1793). The creation of this archive was literal and figurative: records belonged to the people, not the King.

There is no single reason that the United States did not establish a National Archives until the twentieth century. Most history in the United States occurred locally and, as the section above explained, states and historical societies established archives to preserve that history. Also, there was a general hesitancy to increase the role of the federal government. The story, then, of the National Archives is a winding one, with several starts and stops along the way.

Discussion about the preservation of federal government records occurred after the states ratified the US Constitution and a new national government was formed in 1789. Members of this experiment in governance knew that the records of the Continental Congresses would be valuable materials to save. Without an official archive to receive them, the records were given to the State Department to store.[26]

As the young republic developed, Congressmen began to contemplate the creation of a National Archives. However, before establishing an archive, an account of records and their circumstance needed to be made. In 1810, Massachusetts US Representative Josiah Quincy directed a congressional committee whose job it was to investigate the "condition of the 'ancient public records and archives of the United States.'" The committee discovered that these materials were "in a state of great disorder and exposure; and in a situation neither safe nor convenient nor honorable to the nation." President James Madison responded by signing legislation to provide some protections for federally related government materials. First, records essential for commerce needed security. Hence, the General Post Office and Patent Office were to be given "better accommodation." Also, the legislation provided $20,000 for fireproof rooms within which "all the public papers and records of the United States," specifically those "in the custody of the state, war or navy departments," were to be placed. However, the creation of nonflammable spaces to put documents in was not the same thing as a National Archives.[27]

Unfortunately, early nineteenth-century precautions against fire were inadequate. In 1833 the first treasury building burned to the ground. In 1836, a fire destroyed the General Post Office and the Patent Office: the two buildings were next to each other. The fire started in the basement of the Post Office in the early hours of December 15. While "most of the books and papers of the General Post Office were saved," the same could not be said of the contents of the Patent Office. The fire left skeleton structures.[28]

Interest in establishing a true National Archive emerged at the end of the nineteenth century. As explained in the section on state archives, the AHA played a significant role in prompting states to build archival infrastructures. Members of

Figure 4.2 J. Franklin Jameson was indefatigable in working to establish a National Archives for the United States. *Source:* U.S. National Archives and Records Administration (NARA)

the AHA also discussed the importance of a National Archives. In 1893, for instance, Ellen Hardin Walworth, co-founder of the Daughters of the American Revolution, presented the paper, "The Value of a National Archives to a Nation's Life and Progress" at one of the AHA's panels at the World's Columbian Exposition of 1893 in Chicago, Illinois.[29] More influential was the appointment of J. Franklin Jameson to the position of president of the AHA.

In 1882, Jameson received the first doctorate of history Johns Hopkins University ever awarded. His dissertation was titled "The Origin and Development of the Municipal Government of New York City." He then taught at Johns Hopkins, Brown University, and the University of Chicago.

In 1905, Jameson left his academic position to become the director of the Department of Historical Research at the Carnegie Institution's Bureau of Historical Research in the capital. (Andrew Carnegie donated ten million dollars in 1902 to create a "scientific research foundation in Washington to 'conduct, endow, and assist investigation in any department of science, literature, or art, and to this end to cooperate with governments, universities, colleges, technical schools, learned societies, and individuals.'"[30]) As the director, Jameson created a space to support historical research. Surveys were made of European archives and guides produced as to the materials within. He supervised several documentary publications related to the political and legal history of the United States, including judicial cases relating to slavery and the correspondence of Andrew Jackson.[31] During this time, he also served as the managing editor for the *American Historical Review*, which was the primary journal of the AHA. In 1907, Jameson became the first historian with a PhD to become president of the AHA.

Jameson's affiliation with the AHA gave him "institutional credibility in pursuing his scholarly objectives."[32] It also helped him in his 20-year lobbying effort to convince US presidents and congressmen that the United States should establish a National Archives. Described as "indefatigable," his colleagues at the AHA remembered him as the "prime mover and the most devoted worker in the long campaign to educate officials and legislators and the public to a realization of the importance of adequate provision for the records of the Federal government."[33] He began his campaign in 1908, and it succeeded in 1926.

One of the questions that came up in his education efforts was whether the Library of Congress could serve as a National Archives. He continually had to explain that the Library of Congress collected and cared for "manuscript materials which are primarily historical" while a National Archives should be responsible for the preservation of the "main masses of administrative papers" of the federal government.[34] The librarian of Congress, Herbert Putnam, explained to Theodore Roosevelt the dissimilarity: "There is a clear distinction between such manuscript collections as the Papers of the Continental Congress, of the [*sic*] Washington and other personal collections, and those records which are accumulated from the ordinary operations of the various executive departments."[35]

While Jameson often found that US presidents from Theodore Roosevelt to Calvin Coolidge supported his cause, executive power did not extend to the control over the purse. Congress, while also seemingly supportive, failed to appropriate money for a building. In conversing with Coolidge, Jameson expressed his frustration: "Is it not more strange than creditable, that a thing which all legislators have for a decade agreed ought to be done, has in a decade not been achieved – even though the decade has been marked by war and needed economies?"[36]

While Jameson engaged in a campaign to convince lawmakers to support the creation of a National Archives, a few events helped inform public opinion on his cause. Fire, for one, continued to be an issue. On March 29, 1911, New York's Capitol burned. The library within had served as the home for the state's records dating back to the eighteenth century. On January 10, 1921, a fire broke out in the US Commerce Department Building in Washington DC. It housed the US Census: five were damaged (1860, 1870, 1880, 1900, and 1910.) The 1890 Census was lost in its entirety.

A second informative event was World War I, known as the Great War at the time. The US's official participation lasted a little over a year and a half and approximately four million men registered through the draft. After the war, Congress chartered a veteran's organization, the American Legion. Its goal was to assist veterans. In doing so, it served as a lobbying group. While Jameson had previously joined with the AHA, historical societies, patriotic hereditary societies (for instance, the Daughters of the American Revolution), the voting power of those groups was limited. In contrast, the American Legion afforded Jameson with an ally with significant electoral influence throughout the nation. As Victor Gondos explained, the power of the American Legion meant that congressmen had "to think twice about failing to support the archival demand."[37] With the help of the American Legion, Jameson was successful in lobbying the US Congress to pass the Public Buildings Act of 1926 on May 25 of that year.

Once funds were available, land was purchased halfway between the US Capitol and the White House, between Pennsylvania and Constitution Avenues. It used to be the site of the Center Market. When President Herbert Hoover laid the cornerstone on February 20, 1933, he described its meaning for every citizen of our democracy:

> The building which is rising here will house the name and records of every patriot who bore arms for our country . . . there will be aggregated here the most sacred documents of our history, the originals of the Declaration of Independence and of the Constitution of the United States . . . The romance of our history will have habitation here in the writings of statesmen, soldiers, and all the others, both men and women, who have built the great structure of

Figure 4.3 The US National Archives under construction. *Source:* U.S. National Archives and Records Administration (NARA).

our national life. This temple of our history will . . . be one of the most beautiful buildings in America . . . It will be one of the most durable . . . Devoutly, the Nation will pray that it may endure forever . . . the repository of records of our beloved country.[38]

The National Archives building was completed in 1935. This led to a different issue. Where were the records of the federal government and what condition were they in? In 1934, Congress passed an Act providing for an archivist. On advice and consent of the US Senate, Franklin D. Roosevelt appointed R.D.W. Connor of North Carolina as the first archivist of the United States. (He had been the state archivist for North Carolina and a professor of history at the University of North Carolina at Chapel Hill.) Connor supervised a significant survey that began in May of 1935. It was a massive undertaking. What he found were problems of mold, water, light, dirt, vermin, and other safety hazards including potentially flammable jeopardy. Five years later, when the survey was complete, Connor and his team had identified three million cubic feet of records, thirty-four and a half million feet of film, and millions of photographs and maps to be rehoused at the National Archives.[39]

Figures 4.4 and 4.5 Once completed, the US National Archives moved records out of jeopardy. *Source:* U.S. National Archives and Records Administration (NARA).

Figure 4.5

Until 1943, there was still some question as to what materials should be put into the National Archives. Congress passed an Act to Provide for the Disposal of Certain Records of the United States Government to provide clarification. It defined the records to be collected as

all books, papers, maps, photographs, or other documentary materials regardless of physical form or characteristics, made or received by any agency of the United States Government in pursuance of Federal law or in connection with the transaction of public business and preserved or appropriate for preservation by that agency or its legitimate successor as evidence of the organization, functions, policies, decisions, procedures, operations, or other activities of the Government or because of the informational value of data contained therein.[40]

Although it took until the twentieth century for the United States to establish a National Archives, citizens of the nation worked to collect and preserve archival records in the centuries before this action. Individuals recognized the value of saving documentary evidence about the past and formed historical societies. In the nineteenth century, states also began to maintain their administrative records. The expansion of the federal government provided new impetus in the twentieth century to preserve the records of its governance. In combination, the public has access to a wealth of material that documents the history of the United States at multiple levels.

Theory

There is a long history of how people have approached collecting, preserving, and managing archival records. Dutch archivists Samuel Muller, Johan Feith, and Robert Fruin published the first foundational text, *Manual for Arrangement and Description of Archives*, in 1898.[41] Since that time discussion about what to acquire, how, and why along with issues of how to organize archival materials has remained both an international story and an evolving one. In the United States, along with its European peers, the earliest archives related to the governance of the state. As notions of democracy expanded in popular culture (and politics), so too did ideas about who archives serve and the types of materials they should represent.

In this section on theory, we will look first at how archives compare to other institutions of information (libraries and record centers). After, we will look at the main guiding principles of archival theory. Last, we will briefly look at what happens inside an archive. In sum, this introduction should provide you with familiarity with how archives work in general while understanding that each archive carries its particularities in terms of content and management.

Record centers, libraries, and archives are related institutions. However, it is vital to recognize the distinctions between these entities. Most importantly, each serves a fundamentally different purpose. Whether a Public Historian is working in one of these settings or interfacing with staff who do, they need to be mindful of their different characters.

Record centers maintain records that are no longer needed for everyday use. Managers have retention schedules that help them identify how long to hold documents and when it is ok to destroy them. By way of example, you might have a file at home with your tax returns. Depending on the nature of your return, the Internal Revenue Service recommends retaining the return and related records for three years.[42] Record managers also identify records that have permanent value and are set to be sent to the institution's archives if it has one. Records managers can work in both the private and public sector.

Libraries are incredibly diverse. They can be public or private, small or large, free or fee-based. In general, libraries are places to access information. Libraries tend to obtain material that is published, and that is not unique. They also organize materials by subject, and not by how they were acquired.

In contrast, archives are concerned with preserving the raw materials of history. As defined by the SAA, "archival collections are the natural result of the activities of individuals and organizations and serve as the recorded memory." They explain, "this distinctive relationship between records and the activities that generated them differentiates archives from other documentary resources."[43] Although some of this material might be published, it is typically unique. Think of the difference between the original physical contract between J.K. Rowling and her publisher for *Harry Potter and the Sorcerer's Stone* versus the millions of copies of the book sold in the United States. Most archival materials tend to be unpublished. These records typically do not circulate outside of the structure they are housed. They are organized by provenance, which means that the archivist identifies the materials by the individual, family, or organization that amassed the materials before those materials were archived.

One of the results of these differentiations has been the development of different professional organizations. Archivists initially found a home within the AHA, which was established in 1884. With the growth of so many state archives and, in 1934, the National Archives, archivists formed their association in 1936: the SAA.[44]

Archivists work with records. An archival record can take on many forms. While traditionally it has referred to two-dimensional textual documents, depending on their mission, an archive might collect other kinds of records (oral histories, for example, are a non-textual record). Archival records have often been interpreted as evidence of the past.[45] In the aftermath of postmodern theoretical interrogations about the meaning of texts and truth in the 1990s, this definition came into question. Could a record have a purpose outside of the person interpreting it? Geoffrey Yeo offers a productive way to think about archival records. He encourages archivists to think about a record as a type of representation of past activities. He suggests that we think about records as "persistent representations of activities created by participants or observers of those activities or by their authorized proxies."[46]

In working with archival records, archivists are guided by two main principles: (i) the principle of provenance and (ii) the principle of original order. According to one of the seminal texts on the topic by T.R. Schellenberg, "the principal of provenance stem[med] from the French principle of *respect pour les fonds*," which was implemented in the French Archives Nationales in 1839. The French minister of public instruction, François Guizot, stipulated that "records should be grouped according to the nature of the institution that has accumulated them."[47] In doing so, records of various agencies were to remain distinct once they found their way to the archives. The agency, in the archives, becomes a "record group." As an example, all of the records related to Florida's governors are listed as one "record group" (00100) in the State Archives of Florida's database.

The principle of original order is related to provenance. According to Schellenberg, this principle grew out of work by archivists in the Prussian State Archives in the

1880s. They stated, "official papers are to be maintained in the order and with the designations which they received in the course of the official activity of the agency concerned."[48] The purpose in keeping them in the original order is that it might offer a window into understanding the logic of the original creator of the records, albeit acknowledging that at times it may not. These two principles guide archivists as they work to acquire, appraise, arrange, and describe records with the ultimate goals of preserving them and making them accessible to users.

Obtaining an archival collection is called acquisition. Public historians who are archivists need to be mindful that what is in vogue in the historical profession does not drive their decisions. As F. Gerald Ham warned in 1975, to do so would make archivists "at best nothing more than a weathervane moved by the changing winds of historiography."[49] Current archival theory suggests that collecting policies should be based on knowledge of historical methodology (acquiring a diverse set of records that speak to a range of perspectives) rather than a specific range of historical questions. Public historians working in an archive, public or private, need to know the regulatory and philosophical perspectives that guide acquisitions for the particular institution within which they are working. The mission of an archive guides its collection policy. As Ham advised archivists, that does not mean that they should act as mere custodians. Instead, archivists need to recognize that they play an influential role in determining what is saved for documenting human culture.[50]

Historically, the power of archivists over what to collect inadvertently and sometimes deliberately resulted in the exclusion of voices of marginalized groups. For example, if an archivist was charged with collecting the papers of elected officials, and historically most elected officials are white men, it is easy to see how minorities and women's perspectives on historical events were left out of archival collections. The development of community archives in the latter half of the twentieth century was one way in which amateur archivists addressed the problem of omission.

By way of example, a number of LGBTQ archives began as community archives. For instance, Jim Kepner established the Western Gay Archives out of his own personal collections in 1971. Kepner wrote for *ONE Magazine*, which was the first mass-produced periodical devoted in content and audience to a gay community, from the early 1950s to the early 1960s. Renamed and expanded from the 1960s to the present, the University of Southern California Library incorporated the ONE National Gay & Lesbian Archives into its library system in 2010.[51]

Yet, even this early archive did not always collect materials that spoke to the diversity of the LGBTQI2S (lesbian, gay, bisexual, transgender, queer (or questioning), intersex, and two-spirit) experience. In the late 1980s, Luis Alberto Campos de la Garza recognized the absence of archival material that spoke to experiences of gay Latinos. When the late scholar Horacio N. Roque Ramírez investigated the history of the queer Latino and Latina community of San Francisco, he needed to turn to de la Garza's collection to find textual and photographic evidence of the past. Ramírez also conducted a significant number of oral histories to unearth the hidden history of this community.[52] Just as Lonnie Bunch had to create creative ways to amass a collection for the National Museum of African American History and Culture, those who seek to include marginalized voices in archives often need to include dedicated non-professionals as part of the process.

In acquiring collections, archivists appraise their value. There are different ways to define value. Active records serve the needs of their creators, which is a type of value. Non-active records may serve historic and cultural needs beyond that of what their creator needed. This can be an additional value.[53] As Reto Tschan explains, "appraisal must be based on the needs of the creator in fulfilling their own administrative and legal functions." At the same time, "an archives which preserved only those records created by governmental or organizational bureaucracies would fail to meet our expectations of the role which archives have come to play in providing a sense of national and cultural history."[54]

Some archivists allow the creator to determine what should be transferred to an archive. Others believe that archivists should work with the creator to decide what should be preserved. Others leave it for the archivist on their own to make the decision. Depending on the size and complexity of a collection, any option has benefits and drawbacks. Deciding what records to keep is never a superficial matter.

Once acquired, archivists process a collection. Processing includes arrangement and description. The SAA explains the difference. According to the SAA, "arrangement is the intellectual and/or physical processes of organizing documents in accordance with accepted archival principles, as well as the results of these processes." This differs from description, which "is the creation of an accurate representation of the archival material by the process of capturing, collating, analyzing, and organizing information that serves to identify archival material and to explain the context and records systems that produced it, as well as the results of these processes."[55] Archivists use both arrangement and description to make materials useful for patrons whether they are political aides reviewing past policies to write new laws, genealogists looking to identify family members, or scholars investigating historical questions. Archivists work with non-academic and academic audiences, with amateurs and professionals, and people who identify in between these categories.

Historically, archivists applied a set standard for arranging a collection. They grouped material based on the provenance of the collection and original order. This translated into organizing by the following hierarchical categories: record group, series, file, and item. As part of this process, archivists refoldered material into acid-free folders, weeded out duplicates, and took out metal staples and other fastener devices. The goal was to implement preservation strategies during the processing procedure. The deliverable product at the end of processing was a detailed finding aid, which contained multiple layers of information. However, there was a drawback to these practices. They resulted in a tremendous backlog of collections to process. Traditionally, unprocessed collections were not opened to the public.

In 2005, archivists Mark A. Greene and Dennis Meissner studied the literature on best processing practices. They analyzed grant applications and surveyed archivists to determine the significant issues facing archivists in terms of processing and offered some suggestions for remedies. They found that archival backlog was a global problem. Processing collections down to the item level is exceedingly time-consuming. Greene and Meissner called into question strategies that might not be effective in climate-controlled environments. For instance, metal staples do not rust. They also noted that reorganizing all materials might not be necessary. In the age of electronics, it is sometimes easier to make an intellectual inventory of materials than it is to rebox all of the content.[56] Ultimately, they advocated for more flexibility in processing collections. They argued that most do not need item-level processing. Instead, they suggested, "for the great majority of materials significant arrangement, description, and conservation efforts ought not to take place below [the series] level."[57]

The ultimate goal is to provide access to users. Depending upon the institution, archives might be open to the public or, if private, an institution might ask for references before giving access to its materials. Increasingly, archives have attempted to provide online access to contents. However, there are issues of digital preservation that make this a complicated task. Digital preservation is more than merely putting the material in a cloud storage facility. It is an intellectual question as much as a monetary one. (Digital issues will be discussed at greater length in Chapter 7.)

In the twenty-first century, archivists continue to discuss how to approach the collection, preservation, and interpretation of archival records. Public historians work with archivists. They also might be archivists. Thus, it is exceedingly vital for them to continue to familiarize themselves with the significant issues that arise for discussion and to pay heed to changes in best practices.

Practice

1) Visit an archive in person. Choose a collection to examine. Write up the experience of your visit.
2) Interview an archivist about their job.
3) Visit an archive virtually. Analyze what materials are online as compared to what is not digitized. Offer an analysis as to why some materials have and have not been digitized.
4) Research the history of your school's archives, or city, county, and/or state.
5) Create an archival collection of your family's records. Organize into a record group, series, file group, and items. Write a summary of how you made your acquisitions and how you intellectually appraised the records.

Further Resources

- Alexander, Edward P. "The New York State Historical Association Reaches Sixty." *New York History* 40, no. 4 (October, 1959): 414–425.
- Cook, Terry. "What is Past is Prologue: A History of Archival Ideas Since 1898, and the Future Paradigm Shift." *Archivaria* 43 (Spring 1997): 17–63.
- Cox, Richard J. "Archival History: Its Development, Needs, and Opportunities." *The American Archivist* 46, no. 1 (Winter, 1983): 31–41.
- Flinn, Andrew, Mary Stevens, and Elizabeth Shepherd. "Whose Memories, Whose Archives? Independent Community Archives, Autonomy, and the Mainstream." *Archival Science* 9 (2009): 71–86.
- Galloway, Patricia. "Power and History: Dunbar Rowland and the Beginning of the State Archives of Mississippi." *The American Archivist* 69, no. 1 (Spring–Summer, 2006): 79–116.
- Gondos Jr. Victor. *J. Franklin Jameson and the Birth of the National Archives, 1906–1926*. Philadelphia, PA: University of Pennsylvania Press, 1981.
- Greene, Mark A., and Dennis Meissner. "More Product, Less Process: Revamping Traditional Archival Processing." *The American Archivist* 68, no. 2 (Fall–Winter, 2005): 208–263.
- Ham, F. Gerald. "The Archival Edge." *The American Archivist* 38, no. 1 (January, 1975), 5–13.
- McCoy, Donald R. *The National Archives: America's Ministry of Documents 1934–1968*. Chapel Hill, NC: University of North Carolina Press, 1978.
- Ramírez, Horacio N. Roque. "A Living Archive of Desire: Teresita la Campesina and the Embodiment of Queer Latino Community Histories." In *Archive Stories: Facts, Fictions, and The Writing of History*, edited by Atoinette Burton, 111–135. Durham, NC: Duke University Press, 2005.
- Ramírez, Horacio N. Roque. "Memory and Mourning: Living Oral History with Queer Latinos and Latinas in San Francisco." In *Oral History and Public Memories*, edited by Paula Hamilton and Linda Shopes. Philadelphia, PA: Temple University Press, 2008: 165–186.
- Rothberg, Morey D. "The Brahmin as Bureaucrat: J. Franklin Jameson at the Carnegie Institution of Washington, 1905–1928." *The Public Historian* 8, no. 4 (Autumn, 1986): 46–60.
- Scanlan, Kathryn A. "ARMA v. SAA: The History and Heart of Professional Friction." *The American Archivist* 74 (Fall–Winter 2011): 428–450.
- Schellenberg, T.R. "The Principles of Arrangement." *The American Archivist* 24, no. 1 (January, 1961): 11–24.
- Shelley, Fred, and J. Franklin Jameson. "The Interest of J. Franklin Jameson in the National Archives: 1908–1934." *The American Archivist* 12, no. 2 (April 1949): 99–130.

- Society of American Archivists. *Describing Archives: A Content Standard.* Chicago, IL: Society of American Archivists, 2013.
- Tschan, Reto. "A Comparison of Jenkinson and Schellenberg on Appraisal." *The American Archivist* 65, no. 2 (Fall–Winter, 2002): 176–195.
- Wakimoto, Diana K., Debra L. Hansen, and Christine Bruce. "The Case of LLACE: Challenges, Triumphs, and Lessons of a Community Archives." *The American Archivist* 76, no. 2 (Fall–Winter 2013): 438–457.
- Whitehill, Walter Muir. *Independent Historical Societies.* Boston, Massachusetts: The Boston Anthenœum, 1962.
- Yeo, Geoffrey. "Concepts of Record (1): Evidence, Information, and Persistent Representations." *The American Archivist* 70, no. 2 (Fall–Winter 2007): 315–343.

References

1 "What's An Archives?" National Archives, www.archives.gov/about/info/ whats-an-archives.html.

2 Ibid.

3 Andrew Flinn, Mary Stevens, and Elizabeth Shepherd, "Whose Memories, Whose Archives? Independent Community Archives, Autonomy, and the Mainstream," *Archival Science* 9 (2009): 71–86; Diana K. Wakimoto, Debra L. Hansen, and Christine Bruce, "The Case of LLACE: Challenges, Triumphs, and Lessons of a Community Archives," *The American Archivist* 76, no. 2 (Fall–Winter 2013): 439–440.

4 Walter Muir Whitehill, *Independent Historical Societies* (Boston, MA: The Boston Anthenœum, 1962): 8.

5 Edward P. Alexander, "The New York State Historical Association Reaches Sixty," *New York History* 40, no. 4 (October, 1959): 415.

6 Whitehill, *Independent Historical Societies*, 12.

7 Alexander, "The New York State Historical," 414.

8 Ibid.

9 Whitehill, *Independent Historical Societies*, 59.

10 Ibid., 247–248

11 "Measuring Worth," www.measuringworth.com.

12 Whitehill, *Independent Historical Societies*, 249.

13 Ibid., 275.

14 Ibid., 279.

15 Alexander, "The New York State Historical," 417.

16 Whitehill, *Independent Historical Societies*, 211.

17 Ibid., 212.

18 "Chicago Historical Society Collection Management Policy," https://chm-cdn-1. s3.amazonaws.com/uploads/2016/10/Collections-Management-Policy_-2015-09-18-final-revision.pdf.

19 Annual Report of the American Historical Association for the Year 1897, 55th Congress, 2nd Session, H. Doc 577 (1898).

20 "American Historical Association Annual Report 1899," American Historical Association, www.historians.org/about-aha-and-membership/aha-history-and-archives/annual-reports/annual-reports-1895-1909.

21 American Historical Association, *Annual Report for the Year 1900, Volume II: Report of the Public Archives Commission*. H. Doc., 548 pt. 2, 19.

22 Whitehill, *Independent Historical Societies*, 480.

23 Patricia Galloway, "Power and History: Dunbar Rowland and the Beginning of the State Archives of Mississippi," *The American Archivist* 69, no. 1 (Spring–Summer, 2006): 82.

24 Galloway, "Power and History," 98.

25 Kathryn A. Scanlan, "ARMA v. SAA: The History and Heart of Professional Friction," *The American Archivist* 74 (Fall–Winter 2011): 428–450.

26 Victor Gondos Jr, *J. Franklin Jameson and the Birth of the National Archives, 1906–1926* (Philadelphia, PA: University of Pennsylvania Press, 1981): 3.

27 Gondos, *J. Franklin Jameson and the Birth of the National Archives*, 4.

28 Ibid., 6.

29 Ibid., 11. For more on Walworth's life in history-making see Carolyn Strange, "The Battlefields of Personal and Public Memory: Commemorating the Battle of Saratoga (1777) in the Late Nineteenth Century," *Journal of the Gilded Age and Progressive Era* 14 (2015): 194–221.

30 Morey D. Rothberg, "The Brahmin as Bureaucrat: J. Franklin Jameson at the Carnegie Institution of Washington, 1905–1928," *The Public Historian* 8, no. 4 (Autumn, 1986): 51.

31 "John Franklin Jameson," *The American Historical Review* 43, no. 2 (January 1938): 246.

32 Rothberg, "The Brahmin as Bureaucrat," 55.

33 "John Franklin Jameson," *The American Historical Review* 43, no. 2 (January 1938): 247.

34 J. Franklin Jameson quoted in Fred Shelley and J. Franklin Jameson, "The Interest of J. Franklin Jameson in the National Archives: 1908–1934," *The American Archivist* 12, no. 2 (April 1949): 103.

35 J. Franklin Jameson quoted in Shelley, "The Interest of J. Franklin Jameson," 104–105.

36 Ibid., 121.

37 Gondos, *J. Franklin Jameson and the Birth of the National Archives*, 103.

38 Ibid., 1–2.

39 Donald R. McCoy, *The National Archives: America's Ministry of Documents 1934–1968* (Chapel Hill, NC: University of North Carolina Press, 1978): 61–70.

40 An Act to Provide for the Disposal of Certain Records of the United States Government, Public Law 115, 78th Cong., 1st sess. (July 7, 1943), 380.

41 Terry Cook, "What is Past is Prologue: A History of Archival Ideas Since 1898, and the Future Paradigm Shift," *The American Archivist* 74, no. 2 (Fall–Winter 2011): 20–22.

42 "Tips for Managing Your Tax Records," Internal Revenue Service, www.irs.gov/newsroom/tips-for-managing-your-tax-records.

43 Society of American Archivists, *Describing Archives: A Content Standard* (Chicago, IL: Society of American Archivists, 2013): xv.

44 Richard J. Cox, "Archival History: Its Development, Needs, and Opportunities," *The American Archivist* 46, no. 1 (Winter, 1983): 33.

45 Geoffrey Yeo, "Concepts of Record (1): Evidence, Information, and Persistent Representations," *The American Archivist* 70, no. 2 (Fall–Winter 2007), 320.

46 Ibid., 334.

47 T.R. Schellenberg, "The Principles of Arrangement," *The American Archivist* 24, no. 1 (January, 1961): 13–14.

48 Quoted in Schellenberg, "The Principles of Arrangement," 18.

49 F. Gerald Ham, "The Archival Edge," *The American Archivist* 38, no. 1 (January, 1975): 8.

50 Ibid., 13.

51 "History," ONE Archives at the USC Libraries, https://one.usc.edu/about/history

52 Horacio N. Roque Ramírez, "A Living Archive of Desire: Teresita la Campesina and the Embodiment of Queer Latino Community Histories," in *Archive Stories: Facts, Fictions, and The Writing of History*, ed. Atoinette Burton (Durham, NC: Duke University Press, 2005): 119; Horacio N. Roque Ramírez, "Memory and Mourning: Living Oral History with Queer Latinos and Latinas in San Francisco," in *Oral History and Public Memories*, eds. Paula Hamilton and Linda Shopes (Philadelphia, PA: Temple University Press, 2008): 178.

53 Reto Tschan, "A Comparison of Jenkinson and Schellenberg on Appraisal," *The American Archivist* 65, no. 2 (Fall–Winter, 2002): 181.

54 Ibid., 195.

55 Society of American Archivists, *Describing Archives*, xvi.

56 Mark A. Greene and Dennis Meissner, "More Product, Less Process: Revamping Traditional Archival Processing," *The American Archivist* 68, no. 2 (Fall–Winter, 2005): 208–263.

57 Greene, "More Product, Less Process," 252–253.

5

Marking History

Monuments preserve historical memory in public spaces. Unlike historical scholarship that changes over time depending on questions a historian asks, and the sources they look at, the history expressed on and through monuments typically stays fixed. The history a statue conveys speaks to the perspective of its creators and the historical moment of its creation. People erect monuments to commemorate a past person or event. These authors intend to instill specific values through these memorials. They hope that their monument will become an instrument for everyday civic education.

Monuments are also expressions of power. In studying monuments, it is essential to ask who had the money to pay to design and create a physical marker. It is also critical to inquire about who could sway local, state, or federal government officials to agree to place a monument in a public space. This chapter focuses on commemoration in a US context but it is important to recognize that these issues are not unique to the United States. Nonetheless, the particulars of memorialization differ depending on national dynamics. The history portion of this chapter examines the creation of several different monuments to discuss their power and, at times, their contested nature. This section is organized by statue and space as opposed to being described in a strict chronology. The theory section explains the process of creating markers and monuments.

History

Before we begin to look at the history of specific monuments, there are a few larger contextual questions to ask about commemoration and memorialization. First, if you destroy a monument or relocate it from its original placement, are you erasing history? The American Historical Association (AHA) attempted to offer guidance amid debates about the removal of Confederate statues from public

Public History: An Introduction from Theory to Application, First Edition. Jennifer Lisa Koslow.
© 2021 by John Wiley & Sons, Inc. Published 2021 by John Wiley & Sons, Inc.

spaces in the mid to late 2010s, which answers this question from the perspective of professional historians. The AHA explained that "a monument is not history itself; a monument commemorates an aspect of history, representing a moment in the past when a public or private decision defined who would be honored in a community's public spaces."[1] Monuments are "interpretations" of the past. Just as historians revisit historical interpretations in their professional lives, there is no reason why citizens cannot do the same for honorific structures.

Removing a statue is both a legal question and a moral question.[2] Removal can provoke strong emotions. In May of 2017, the mayor of New Orleans Mitch Landrieu decided to remove Confederate statues from the city's public spaces. He explained: "There is a difference in remembrance of history and reverence of it."[3] Landrieu discussed how these monuments were erected at the same moment and within the same intent as Jim Crow laws, which established a system of white supremacy in political, economic, and social institutions. When the monuments went up, African Americans had no public mechanism to voice resistance. Landrieu also recited from a primary source to remind any doubters that the reduction of African Americans was at the heart of the Civil War. He quoted Alexander Stephens, the vice president of the Confederate States of America, who stated that the Confederacy's

> cornerstone rests upon the great truth, that the negro is not equal to the white man; that slavery – subordination to the superior race – is his natural and normal condition. This, our new government, is the first, in the history of the world, based upon this great physical philosophical, and moral truth.

Landrieu admitted that growing up in New Orleans he had never thought about the meaning of the monuments he passed. As the city contemplated their removal, African American citizens changed his mind. One particularly powerful commenter asked Landrieu to imagine himself as an African American parent explaining to his child "who Robert E. Lee is and why he stands atop of our beautiful city." He asked:

> Can you look into that young girl's eyes and convince her that Robert E. Lee is there to encourage her? Do you think she will feel inspired and hopeful by that story? Do these monuments help her see a future with limitless potential? . . . We all know the answer to these very simple questions. When you look into this child's eyes is the moment when the searing truth comes into focus for us.

Thus, Landrieu concluded that "to literally put the Confederacy on a pedestal in our most prominent places of honor is an inaccurate recitation of our full past."

He argued, "it is an affront to our present, and it is a bad prescription for our future." He would no longer ask anyone to pay reverence to the Confederate cause.

New Orleans placed Lee's statue in a warehouse while it determines what to do with it. The city can draw upon many different examples from around the globe for next steps. Generally, governments adopt one of three possible strategies: do nothing, destroy, or repurpose. Perhaps the most creative example for resolving contested memories exists in Budapest. After the fall of the communist regime in Hungary in the early 1990s, the new government removed the symbols of communism that were scattered throughout Budapest and moved them to an outdoor park on the outskirts of the city. Hungarian architect Ákos Eleőd conceived and designed the experience. Eleőd believed that the "truth of democracy is proved by the historical process." He argued, "this park is not about the statues or the sculptors, but a critique of the ideology that used these statues as symbols of authority." Here was an imaginative solution for people, as Eleőd described, to "get to know [the past], analyse it and think about it!"[4]

While the debates over Confederate monuments in the United States have occupied much of the public's attention in the 2010s, they are by no means the only contested monuments in the history of the United States. In this chapter, we will look at the Haymarket Monument in Chicago as a way in which to analyze controversy. We will also engage with the history of the National Mall, not all of which created controversy.

James W. Loewen, author of *Lies Across America: What Our Historic Sites Get Wrong*, concluded, "America's most toppled Monument is Haymarket Monument in Chicago."[5] What was Haymarket, and how should it be remembered? Investigating this question provides us with a useful example of how memories can be contested. The history of the memorialization of Haymarket also offers us a way to see how different communities can find common ground.

Let us start with the question of "what was Haymarket?" In the late nineteenth century, across the nation, industrial workers asserted that they had certain rights. Without their labor, factories could not produce materials. They argued that at the very least they should be entitled to work an eight-hour day. The idea was eight hours for work, eight hours for recreation, and eight hours for rest. During the first week of May of 1886, thousands of workers paraded in the streets of Chicago, attended meetings, and went on strike to declare support. They found themselves in conflict with police at several different points. One clash on May 3 at the McCormick reaper factory left two strikers dead. A mass demonstration was called for the next day at the Haymarket Square to protest police actions. At least one of the first leaflets distributed called for revenge.

The Haymarket meeting on the evening of May 4, 1886, started peacefully. Mayor Carter H. Harrison was there to observe, as were almost 200 policemen. Although the crowd was dwindling and although Harrison had told the police not to engage, one of the police officers ordered his men to move into the crowd to force it to dis perse. As the police began to move into the group, one of the protestors threw a bomb at the police. It killed Officer Mathias Degan instantly. The police responded by firing into the crowd and chaos ensued. In the end, eight policemen died, sixty were injured, and an undetermined number of protestors were hurt.

For those in the middle-class, the event reinforced their fears that labor organizing was radical. For those in the working-class, the event strengthened their sense of injustice. Harrison took action to suppress citizens' first amendment rights: the right to peaceably assemble, the free exercise of speech, and the freedom of the press. Harrison issued a proclamation prohibiting meetings in public places. The mass demonstrations for an eight-hour day were brought to a halt. After hundreds of arrests, the state of Illinois put eight men, who were known anarchists on trial for murder. Although no individual was ever definitively tied to the bomb that was thrown, the eight men were found guilty of conspiracy to commit murder. The prosecution used the men's thoughts and ideas as conveyed through speeches and writings to convince the jury of their guilt. Seven of the men were initially sentenced to death. On November 11, 1887, two of the rally's organizers, George Engel and Adolph Fischer, along with two speakers, August Spies and Albert Parsons, were hanged in the Cook County jail. (Of the other three, one committed suicide the night before the execution and the other two had their sentences commuted.) Citing the absence of definitive evidence connecting the defendants to the bomb, Governor John Peter Altgeld pardoned the last remaining defendants in 1893.

On the event's third anniversary, in 1889, the city of Chicago erected a monument to its fallen policemen in the Haymarket. The memorial statue consisted of a statue of a captain with one arm raised standing atop a high pedestal. The inscription read: "In the name of the people of Illinois, I command peace." Frank Degan, Mathias Degan's teenage son, unveiled the monument.

The city did not allow those associated with the protestors to erect a marker to their fallen. Instead, in 1893, they built their memorial in Waldheim cemetery, which was located in a suburb of Chicago. Here, at the site of burial for Engel, Fischer, Spies, and Parsons, Albert Weiner created a sculpture of a woman, the symbol of justice. She looks outward while laying laurel leaves (a symbol of victory) atop the head of a dying worker that she stands in front of protecting. The inscription repeated Spies's last words: "The day will come when our silence will be more powerful than the voices you are throttling today."

Over time, Chicago's Haymarket monument faced several difficulties. The intersection sat in the middle of an exceedingly congested Randolph Street. It was also apparently vandalized multiple times. Consequently, the city moved it a mile away to the intersection of Randolph and Ogden in 1900. There it stood until May 4, 1927, when on the 41st anniversary of tumultuous events in Haymarket, a streetcar jumped its tracks, hit the pedestal, and the statue fell to the ground. It

HAYMARKET SQUARE

Figure 5.1   Haymarket Square in 1893. The monument is in the bottom right-hand corner of the picture. *Source:* Library of Congress, Prints & Photographs Division, Reproduction number LC-USZ62-134212 (b&w film copy neg.)LC-USZ62-29792 (b&w film copy neg.).

was then moved into the adjacent Union Park. In the 1950s, however, police advocated for the statue's placement back to its original, or near its original, site. The city complied, and in 1958, it returned it albeit on the north side of Randolph.

Eleven years later, amidst the turmoil of the late 1960s, the Haymarket monument became a new site for radical leftist protest. On October 5, 1969, the Weathermen attempted to destroy the memorial by exploding dynamite between the statue's legs. They did so in the middle of the night. The figure hurtled into the air, and parts of the legs landed on the Kennedy expressway. However, no one was hurt. The statue was fixed at the cost of almost $5,000 and returned to its position. A year later, the Weather Underground (virtually the same group as before) attempted to blast the statue apart again after midnight. Again, no one was hurt. Still, the figure lost one leg. The other leg was found over 200 feet away. Chicago's mayor, Richard J. Daley, decried the bombing as "a senseless and vicious attack on the entire community."[6] It was rebuilt again at the cost of $8,000. Daley ordered the Chicago Police Department (CPD) to place 24-hour security around the statue.

Figure 5.2 The Haymarket Martyrs' Monument in Waldheim Cemetery (now known as Forest Home Cemetery). Library of Congress, Prints & Photographs Division, Reproduction number LC-DIG-stereo-1s12399 (digital file from original) LC-USZ62-61671 (b&w film copy neg. of half stereo).

Also, the city installed a hidden video camera fixed on the figure in a nearby building as an additional security mechanism. The expense for the surveillance systems cost the city almost $70,000 annually.

After a few years, the CPD argued that the city would be better served to have the officers attend to community needs other than protecting the statue. In 1972, the city moved the figure into the lobby of its police headquarters.[7] Four years later, the police moved the statue after realizing that "if terrorists mailed a bomb to police headquarters, they could still blow the statue up and them too!" They put it in an atrium inside the Chicago Police Academy, which was not open to the public. The original pedestal on Randolph Street remained until 1996 when it was demolished as part of a "street improvement plan."[8]

The Haymarket statue remained in the Chicago Police Academy until 2007. In June of that year, the figure was put atop a new pedestal outside of Chicago's Police Headquarters. The great-granddaughter of Officer Mathias Degan, Geraldine Docekal, along with her two sons unveiled the monument. Although the base was redesigned, it still included the original inscription.

Until the early 1990s, there was nothing to mark the event in Haymarket Square. In 1992, the Chicago Landmarks Commission installed a plaque in the sidewalk.

Dedicated by Mayor Richard M. Daley (son of Richard J. Daley), the marker indicated a sea change in the way in which the historical event was understood. The label described its importance as the "site of the Haymarket Tragedy." The text succinctly described the incident without assigning blame to either side. It read:

> A decade of strife between labor and industry culminated here in a confrontation that resulted in the tragic death of both workers and policeman. On May 4, 1886, spectators at a labor rally had gathered around the mouth of Crane's Alley. A contingent of police approaching on DesPlaines Street were met by a bomb thrown from just south of the alley. The resultant trial of eight activists gained worldwide attention for the labor movement and initiated the tradition of "May Day" labor rallies in many cities.[9]

Lying flat into the sidewalk, neither the marker nor its text seems to have incited anyone to vandalize the commemoration.

In 2004, the city of Chicago installed a new memorial sculpture in Haymarket Square on the site where the speakers' wagon was located. The artist, Mary Brogger, created a semi-abstract piece. While it is clear that the figures are giving speeches and that they are symbolically being supported and lifted by the workers below, they remain undefined in their features. The accompanying text fills several side panels. It addresses how this one event has held different meanings for people in memory, from questions of the right to assembly to articulations for anarchy. Among those present at the dedication were members of the CPD. As members of a union, they too recognized that they had benefited from the rise of the labor movement.[10]

Between 1889 and 2004, the city of Chicago allowed different memorials to the events in Haymarket. In doing so, the city picked sides over whose interpretation would be broadcast to the public. At first, the monument reflected elite and middle-class beliefs that portrayed all aspects of the labor movement as subversive to the social order. The policeman commanded order: he did not engage in conversation about why and how the industrial system disproportionately favored employers over employees. As society changed and federal and state governments recognized the rights of labor, so too did people's perception of the meaning of the Haymarket event. Instead of a "riot," it became known as a "tragedy." The tragedy was two-fold. It was a tragedy for the lives lost and a tragedy for the suppression of civil rights. The contemporary monument presents both views. It creates a sense of place by mediating contested memories.

Now that we have analyzed one monument through time, let us turn our attention to our nation's capital. Most Americans are familiar with the National Mall. Images of the Washington Monument, the Lincoln Memorial, the Vietnam Memorial, and other national monuments to political, military, and social leaders

Figure 5.3   The contemporary Haymarket Memorial. *Source:* Jennifer Koslow.

waft across our televisions at least once a year every fourth of July. But when did the National Mall become a civic space and, in particular, a place for working out contested issues? That story begins in the late nineteenth century.

In the early 1900s, Congress turned to Daniel Burnham to propose a plan to redesign the space between the Potomac River, the US Congress, and the White House. Burnham, an architect from Chicago, had been made famous by his work designing the layout of the Columbia World's Exposition in 1893 in Chicago. His had produced urban designs for several different cities including Cleveland and San Francisco. His work was part of the City Beautiful Movement, in which members ascribed to using architecture to create civic order. The movement was particularly influential at the turn of the twentieth century when many felt disoriented by the changes brought by urbanization, industrialization, and massive immigration.

Since US Senator Joseph McMillan headed the commission, the resultant proposal was known as the McMillan Commission Plan of 1902. Burnham's goal was to develop a guide for expansion "keeping pace with national advancement, until [Washington] becomes the visible expression of the power and taste of the people of the United States."[11] At the heart of the new space was the National Mall. Instead of winding paths and trees, it was cleared to create an inward-looking experience. The Center Market and railroad depot were moved out and off to the side. The plan made space for new federal buildings, which were to be designed in a neoclassical style. (There was one exception. The Smithsonian castle of Gothic and Romanesque style was allowed to stay.) Overall, Burnham desired the new symmetry to instill a sense of stability and order.

One existing memorial that Burnham incorporated into his design was the Washington Monument. The first proposals to build monuments to Washington occurred even before his death, which was in 1799. Pierre Charles L'Enfant's plan in 1791 for the capital city included an equestrian statue of Washington (an archetype for political–military figures at the time.) After Washington's death, there was a discussion about moving his tomb from Mount Vernon to the capital. Neither plan was adopted. In 1833, the Washington National Monument Society formed to renew focus and fundraising to create a memorial in the nation's capital. In the 1840s, the organization chose a Doric (inspired by Ancient Greece) obelisk design proposed by architect Richard Mills. Obelisks were recognizable ageless commemorative symbols of honor. The goal was to build the tallest structure in the world. Mills also proposed placing a "circular colonnade" around the bottom of the structure to "be known as the 'National Pantheon.'"[12] The Society laid the cornerstone on July 4, 1848.

In 1855, the Washington National Monument Society ran out of money to build the monument. The monument was only roughly 150 feet high. The organization turned to Congress for funding. However, at approximately the same time, members of the Know-Nothing party (a semi-secret organization that was anti-immigrant and anti-Catholic) secured membership on the organization's board and took over. Members of Congress did not wish to support the Know-Nothings and did not appropriate funds. Construction remained stymied until after the conclusion of the Civil War. In 1876, Congress assumed responsibility for the monument's completion. It provided funds and appointed Lieutenant Colonel Thomas Lincoln Casey of the US Army Corps of Engineers to supervise the construction. Casey did two things. He stripped the obelisk of any proposed ornamentation. Casey also added an elevator. He used it in building the monument. Afterward, it was a novel way to travel to the top. (There were also stairs.) When completed in 1884, the memorial rose over 500 feet in the air. The monument conveyed power in two ways. First, if you stood at its base and looked up, you felt its enormity. Second, if you looked out from the observation level, you experienced your authority over the world below.[13]

The McMillan plan guided the development of the National Mall in the early twentieth century. Memorials were created in dialogue with the Capitol and the Washington Monument. The Lincoln Memorial is a good example. Congress approved funding for a memorial in 1910. Two major New York architects competed: Henry Bacon and John Russell Pope. Each suggested building a pantheon to house a seated figure. Bacon's proposal also included the text of two speeches: the Gettysburg Address and the Second Inaugural Address. He argued that words mattered: "I believe these two great speeches made by Lincoln will always have a far

Figures 5.4 The Washington Monument under construction. *Source:* U.S. National Archives and Records Administration (NARA).

greater meaning to the citizens of the United States and visitors from other countries than a portrayal of periods of events by means of decoration."[14]

Bacon's design was chosen. His temple housed an almost twenty-foot tall seated figure of Lincoln. The 36 exterior columns represented the 36 reunited states. Daniel Chester French created the sculpture based on his study of photographs. French's Lincoln conveyed the weight of events. He sits in quiet repose with one hand relaxed, the other clenched. It was a stark contrast to other contemporary depictions. For instance, Augustus Saint-Gaudens's 1887 sculpture in Chicago rendered Lincoln standing, as if about to give a speech. [15] Saint-Gaudens humanized Lincoln. French set him apart.

In creating the Lincoln Memorial, the federal Commission of Fine Arts considered the relationship between its memorials. It desired the Lincoln Memorial to be in a conversation, not in competition, with the Washington Monument and the

Figure 5.5   The Washington Monument today? *Source:* Jennifer Koslow.

Capitol's dome. Bacon argued that its placement on the Potomac completed a story about the nation:

> On the great axis, planned over a century ago, we have at one end the Capitol, which is the monument of the Government, and to the west, over a mile distant from the Capitol, is the monument to Washington, one of the founders of the Government. If the Lincoln Memorial is built on this same axis still farther to the west, by the shore of the Potomac, we will there have the monument of the man who saved the Government, thus completed an unparalleled composition which can not fail to impart to each of its monuments a value in addition to that which each standing alone would possess.[16]

Sentiments about the importance of creating a coherent sense of space continued to drive developments of the National Mall throughout the twentieth century.

Figure 5.6 Daniel Chester French's Lincoln conveys the weight of events. *Source:* Jennifer Koslow.

The majority of memorials created on the National Mall in the twentieth century celebrated either political or military figures in US history. The development of the Vietnam Veterans Memorial in the late 1970s and early 1980s was a significant change. It was designed to be both a cathartic and therapeutic experience.[17] Jan Scruggs, a Vietnam War veteran, became determined to create a memorial in the nation's capital in 1979. He helped found the Vietnam Veterans Memorial Fund, who then lobbied Congress to allow the group to carry out the project. Congress authorized the organization to do so on July 1, 1980, which President Jimmy Carter then signed into law. Congress stipulated a few conditions. It determined the general location of the monument. Congress required that the secretary of the interior, the Commission of Fine Arts, and the National Capital Planning Commission give their approval to the plans. Last, Congress dictated that no public funds be used.[18]

The Vietnam Veterans Memorial Fund ran a competition for a design proposal. It was open to any US citizen 18 years of age or older. The rules stipulated that the design "be reflective and contemplative in nature, harmonize with its surroundings, be entirely apolitical, and include all of the names of the almost 58,000 dead

Figure 5.7 Maya Lin's winning submission. Library of Congress, Prints & Photographs Division, Reproduction number LC-DIG-ppmsca-09504 (digital file from original drawing) LC-USZC4-4915 (color film copy transparency)LC-USZC4-1353 (color film copy transparency)LC-USZC4-1027 (color film copy transparency of top left)LC-USZC4-1028 (color film copy transparency of bottom right)LC-USZ62-90338 (b&w film copy neg.) LC-USZ62-90337 (b&w film copy neg. bottom left)LC-USZ62-90340 (b&w film copy neg. bottom right)LC-USZC2-1501 (color film copy slide).

and missing."[19] Anonymous entry 1026 won. The architect was Maya Lin, a 21-year-old student at Yale University.

Maya Lin was born in Athens, Ohio, in 1959. Hers was an artistic family. Her father was a ceramist and her mother was a poet and scholar of Chinese literature. They had migrated from China in the late 1940s and found faculty employment at Ohio University. In Lin's final year at Yale, she was enrolled in a class that focused on funereal architecture. They examined different ideas about "how people, through the built form, express their attitudes toward death."[20] The students chose to use the Vietnam Veterans Memorial Fund competition as inspiration for their final class project. Lin's experiences on campus shaped her ideas.

In conducting research, Lin consciously decided to omit any information specifically about the Vietnam War. Instead, she chose to focus on other soldier memorials. Sir Edwin Lutyens's memorial particularly moved Lin. The monument was to those who died at the Battle of the Somme in Thiepval, France, during World War I. At the time, the French army did not use dog tags to identify bodies. Lutyens decided to include the 100,000 names of those listed as missing. Professor Vincent Scully described the monument's structure as a process; the enormity of the loss you were confronted with by the list of names carved onto a gigantic archway. Scully described this feature as "a gaping scream." Individuals had to walk through the arch to reach the cemetery, where the bodies of 70,000 men were interred.[21] At Yale, Lin felt the power of names every time she walked through Woolsey Hall, which was where the school engraved the names of alumni who died while serving in the United States military.

Before Lin and her peers could design their memorials, they needed to see the site. Consequently, Lin, along with some of her classmates, traveled to Washington DC. Lin described the region as a quiet oasis on the mall. It proved inspirational. Lin described her instinctive process:

> I imagined a knife and cutting into the earth, opening it up, an initial violence and pain that in time would heal. The grass would grow back, but the initial cut would remain a pure flat surface in the earth with a polished, mirrored surface, much like the surface of a geode when you cut it and polish the edge.[22]

On that polished surface, the names would be carved. Lin proposed putting them in chronological order beginning and ending at the apex of the memorial. She did this for two reasons. The first reason was logistical. She knew no one wanted to search through a list of John Smiths. Second, and, more importantly, this design made the memorial come full circle. In this way, the monument paid played tribute to the individual as well as seeing death as a collective. Also, Lin thought about the relationship between the new memorial with the old. She pointed one wall to the Washington Monument and the other to the Lincoln Memorial to "bring the Vietnam Memorial into historical context."[23]

Lin believed that when people were confronted with the enormity of lost lives, it was "up to each individual to resolve or come to terms with this loss." In explaining her design, she stated, "for death is in the end a personal and private matter, and the area contained within this memorial is a quiet place meant for

personal reflection and private reckoning." The reflectiveness of the black granite, she felt, created "an interface between the world of the living and the world
of the dead."[24]

When Lin submitted her proposal, she did so "never expecting to hear about it
again."[25] She was surprised to learn that she had beat out more than 1400 entries.
Upon graduation, she moved to Washington DC. Working with the architectural
firm Cooper-Lecky, Lin worked to help realize the design. However, controversy
ensued. The memorial's color (black versus the traditional white), the absence of
additional adornment, the listing of names, were all atypical aspects compared to
most of the other monuments on the mall. Some critics did not realize that the
listing of names was a requirement by the Vietnam Veterans Memorial Fund.
Some brought their prejudices to the idea of a black memorial. Some people's
opinions about gender and race shaped the discourse against Maya Lin's design.
For a period, it looked like the entire project might come to a halt.

Out of these various controversies, the US Commission of Fine Arts came up
with two compromises. It added an American flag and a sculpture of three soldiers
to the site. However, they were not placed atop the apex as some desired. Instead,
they were placed at the entranceway to the site. Later, a statue of female nurses
was added to this section.[26]

On November 13, 1982, the Vietnam Veterans Memorial was dedicated. The
National Park Service estimated that over twenty million people visited the memorial within its first 10 years of existence. It has inspired the creation of a three-
quarter size replica of the memorial that continues to be installed temporarily
around the nation. The Vietnam Veterans Memorial Fund also has created a virtual experience for those who cannot come to Washington DC.[27] The memorial
has done for many people what Scruggs and Lin hoped it would do. It has offered
veterans, their families, and the public space to reflect, reconcile, and heal. Despite
(or perhaps because of) its abstract nature, the monument created a sense of place.

The latest memorial statue to be added to the National Mall is dedicated to the
memory of Martin Luther King Jr. In 1983, a few alumni of the Alpha Phi Alpha
fraternity discussed the idea of creating a piece in Washington DC dedicated to the
memory of King. They secured the official support of the fraternity and then
lobbied Congress. On November 12, 1996, Congress authorized Alpha Phi Alpha
to supervise the construction of a memorial, which President Bill Clinton then
signed into law. Two years later, President Clinton signed into law legislation that
allowed the monument to be constructed in "Area 1" on the National Mall. Area
1 is reserved for markers of "deep symbolic significance to the nation."[28] The
memorial was unique for several reasons. First, it did not honor a US president or
commemorate a war. Second, it was the first memorial in Area 1 that honored an
African American. (In 1974, a monument to Mary McLeod Bethune was installed
in Lincoln Park, about a mile east of the Capitol.) Last, in stark contrast to the

Figure 5.8 The Vietnam Veterans Memorial continues to draw visitors of all ages. *Source:* Jennifer Koslow.

debates over establishing a federal holiday in honor of King in the early 1980s, the King memorial enjoyed overwhelmingly bipartisan support.

Once authorized, Alpha Phi Alpha created the Martin Luther King Jr. National Memorial Project through which to develop the monument. The organization needed over $100 million which it raised through private donations: many of which came through corporate funding. It also chose the Roma Design Group, which was based in San Francisco, to supervise the design. The firm, which was composed of architects, landscape architects, and urban designers, created a "Council of Historians" to advise the project. Dr. Clayborne Carson of Stanford University drew the design group's attention to a line from King's speech at the March on Washington in 1963, wherein he said: "With this faith we will be able to hew out of the mountain of despair a stone of hope." Roma Design Group then used this as a touchstone to create the memorial.

The Roma Design Group also asked the Council of Historians to select additional quotes to use around the monument based on four themes: justice, democracy, love, and hope. The designers instructed the historians to limit their selections to no more than 30 words in length, which is the same length as this sentence, which is not very long.[29] The monument left out the radical nature of King's politics.

Amid the 1960s, King's use of nonviolent action to force confrontations made him a very unpopular figure to many. A Gallup poll from August of 1966 determined that 63% of Americans polled had an unfavorable view of King.[30] That statistical figure stands in stark contrast to a Gallup poll taken in August 2011, the year of the monument's unveiling, in which 94% of those polled viewed King favorably. What changed between King's death in 1968 and the erection of the memorial in 2011 was the public's memory of King's politics.[31]

Part of the change stemmed from the way King's story came to be told in primary and secondary schools. To help children identify with the material, they are often taught the quote: "I have a dream that my four little children will one day live in a nation where they will not be judged by the color of their skin but by the content of their character." In the same speech, however, King discussed the cruel contemporary realities African Americans were forced to endure. King was specific about the economic, social, and political injustice African Americans faced. He refuted the calls for gradual change stating, "there will be neither rest nor tranquility in America until the Negro is granted his citizenship rights." He warned his fellow citizens that "the whirlwinds of revolt will continue to shake the foundations of our nation until the bright day of justice emerges." King called attention to the damage wrought by the "manacles of segregation," "the unspeakable horrors of police brutality," and "vicious racists" who held political authority in the South.[32] Instead of a dream, these observations reflect a nightmare.

Roma wanted the textual messages on the monument to foster a sense of Martin Luther King Jr.'s importance to global movements against injustice. They chose to include optimistic words toward achieving those goals.[33] From the 12 various addresses, the most repeated words were: we, our, must, peace, justice, and love. In contrast, words like equality, injustice, race, and struggle only appear once. While the quotes capture King's sentiments, they do very little to help a person place King into mid-twentieth century racial politics. As evidence of this, one quote was truncated in such a way that it made King appear to be boasting of his accomplishments, which was the opposite point of the original speech. The quote came under severe criticism and ended up being erased (not an easy task) from the monument.

The King quotes were only one way that Roma Design Group constructed an interpretation of the past. The 30-foot high statue of King carved out of granite was another. The group selected a photograph from which they asked Lei Yixin, a Chinese sculptor, to make the figure. His selection and the depiction caused two different controversies.

Lei Yixin has an international reputation for making enormous figures out of granite. (Working for the Chinese government as a master sculptor he has been called upon to make massive renditions of Mao Zedong.) Upon announcing the choice, the California chapter of the National Association for the Advancement of Colored People publicly objected. Gwen Moore, the chapter's president, argued, "it's an insult. This is America and, believe me, there's enough talent in this country that we do not need to go out of the country to bring in someone to do the work."[34] Although the Memorial Foundation disagreed, they brought in Ed Dwight, an African American sculptor, to consult on the project. (Dwight's primary medium was bronze, which was why he was not chosen to carve the final monument.)[35]

A second issue related to the sculpture was King's stance and facial gesture. The US Commission of Fine Arts argued that the "stiffly frontal image, static in pose, confrontational in character" image was unsettling. The commission explained that it reminded them of the monuments erected to dictators. The proposed model was shown to two of King's children, Martin Luther King III and Bernice King. His son remarked, "well, if my father was not confrontational, given what he was facing at the time, what else could he be?"[36]

Figure 5.9 The Martin Luther King Jr. Memorial inspires contemplation. *Source:* Jennifer Koslow.

In the end, the disjuncture between the quotes and the sculpture present the viewer with an interesting mystery. Who was King and how should he be remembered by society? Robert Harris believes that the memorial will preserve a sense of King's significance even if it obscures "the movement for which he lost his life."[37] Kevin Bruyneel's appraisal after studying the monument and speaking with visitors on the site's second day of being open was that the memorial conveyed "a consensual narrative . . . that advocates the idea that the contemporary US is a post-racial polity." However, Bruyneel also found that visitors always make their own meaning, which in some cases offered a counter-narrative.

Monuments suggest a history that is typically set in stone. However, how people interpret the past changes as new evidence is found or old evidence is reinterpreted with a fresh eye. Consequently, how monuments are interpreted does not remain static. They are pieces of material culture that tell us about a particular time and place. Typically expensive to create, they tell us about who and why a person or organization invested in commemorating an event or person. Those monuments that sit on public lands tell us about how that monument spoke to those who were in power. Disputes over the construction of monuments and contemporary controversies remind us that their creation and placement is not always a neutral expression.

Theory

There is no single path for putting up a memorial. An individual, organization, and an institution can spearhead the movement to construct one. In the United States, municipal, state, and the federal government typically do not instigate their creation. Most monuments memorialize local affairs and are paid for by local organizations. However, the placement of monuments on public lands, and in some cases the appropriation of public funds, means that monuments are never a private matter.

Historically, professional historians were not typically consulted in the construction of monuments. This is not to say that groups have not been historically-minded when they decide to engage in the process of monument making. For instance, the United Daughters of the Confederacy believed that their work marking history in the built environment through designating historic sites and creating monuments rested on sound historical research.[38] They did not consider the racial biases embedded in the history that they were reading and creating. Today, groups looking to develop memorials can fall into the same trap if they only engage with the historical literature that confirms their preconceptions. So, in a world where no set of agreed-upon best practices exist for the creation of monuments, what can Public Historians offer for those who wish to engage in marking history?

Historians research and evaluate evidence to reach reasonable conclusions about the past. Since the early 2000s, college administrators, faculty, and students across the United States have begun considering whether their institutions played a role in perpetuating a system of slavery in the United States. Historians have been asked to sit on committees to research those histories and offer recommendations on how institutions can remember that past.[39] Amid controversies over whether to remove Confederate memorials from public spaces, the AHA "urge[d] communities faced with decisions about monuments to draw on the expertise of historians both for understanding the facts and chronology underlying such monuments and for deriving interpretive conclusions based on evidence." For those who might not know how and where to find a historian to consult, the AHA facilitates referrals: "Indeed, any governmental unit, at any level, may request from the AHA a historian to provide consultation. [The AHA] expect[s] to be able to fill any such request."[40]

Sometimes it is not the historian themself but their work that informs commemorative acts. Ruth Sergel's projects commemorating the Triangle Shirtwaist Factory Fire, which claimed 146 lives in New York City in 1911, provide an excellent example. As a young teen in the 1970s and 1980s, Sergel, a multimedia artist, was captivated by the tragedy after reading Leon Stein's *The Triangle Fire*. The majority of the victims were young immigrant women. While the building was itself fireproof, the safety measures in the workplace were inadequate. When a fire broke out the women were trapped. The event led New York to adopt regulatory measures to address worker safety. Sergel's interest in the event continued into her adulthood.

Sergel has created several temporal memorials to commemorate those who died in the fire. One of those projects is "Chalk." Sergel had an idea after reading journalist David Von Drehle's book, published in 2004, about the fire, within which she found a list of the dead with the addresses of their homes. Enlisting her friends to help, she passed out the list of names and asked people to chalk in front of the deceased's home. The project has continued ever since. It has also grown. Sergel notes, "I've never met most of the chalkers" yet, many participate every year. For Sergel chalking marks not just death but life. She explains, "this was her home; she was part of a family, a community, a neighborhood."[41]

In developing Chalk and other commemorative projects, Sergel's sense of the immigrant women was informed by Annelise Orleck's work, *Common Sense and a Little Fire: Women and Working-Class Politics in the United States, 1900–1965* published by the University of North Carolina Press in 1995. Sergel read history to help her develop collaborative commemorative projects that included a diverse group of labor activists, cultural workers, artists, writers, and educators, among others. By doing so, she not only understood the specifics of the fire better but the world within which these women lived. In doing so, in understanding these

Figure 5.10 Every March 25, "Chalk" inspires the public to remember the 146 workers, mostly young immigrant women, who died in the Triangle Shirtwaist Factory Fire. *Source:* Photo Courtesy of Joanne Borts. Chalk Project Street Art by Joanne Borts (Union Activist, Broadway Actor, Community Organizer) and Tine Kindermann, (Berlin-born, NY-based Artist with a focus on Social Justice).

women as workers, Sergel hoped to prompt society to confront contemporary questions of social justice.

In sum, Public Historians can offer a historical perspective to those who wish to understand the history of existing monuments and proposals for adding new ones to the landscape. However, no mechanism forces institutions, groups, and individuals to include historians as part of the process. In this way, monument making is different than that of exhibiting history in museums, preserving historic sites, and managing historical records. Amateur historians may or may not consult with professional public historians and academic histories. Nevertheless, when asked, Public Historians can be of public service in helping to generate civil conversations about the complexity of monument making.

Practice

1) Pick a monument and analyze it in the following ways: (i) What is the point of the monument? (ii) Read the text on the plaque and determine who is telling the story (look for sentences that are in the passive voice, i.e. "the sandwich

was eaten by a student." The active voice would be "a student ate the sandwich." You know who is doing the action in the active voice. It is obscured in the passive voice.) (iii) Do the words and artwork provoke any emotional response? (iv) Do you have any questions about the text or artwork? Do you think there might be another story to tell? If so, whose?

2) Sit for 15 minutes near a monument and observe, i.e. people watch. Does anyone stop and look at the memorial? If so, what do they do?

3) Research the history of past events on campus. (Use yearbooks and old student newspapers.) Take a piece of chalk and make a temporary marker on campus – i.e. mark a spot in history.

4) Create an inventory of the different historical markers on your campus. Analyze the results.

5) Create a map of the different historical markers on your campus. Create a tour (virtual or face-to-face) based on the map.

Further Resources

- Bruyneel, Kevin. "The King's Body: The Martin Luther King Jr. Memorial and the Politics of Collective Memory." *History & Memory* 26, no. 1 (Spring–Summer 2014): 75–108.
- Clarke, Max, and Gary Alan Fine. "'A' for Apology: Slavery and the Discourse of Remonstrance in Two American Universities." *History & Memory* 22, no. 1 (Spring–Summer 2010): 81–112.
- Cox, Karen L. *Dixie's Daughters: The United Daughters of Confederacy and the Preservation of Confederate Culture.* Gainesville, FL: University of Florida, 2003.
- Harris Jr., Robert L. "Reflections on the Building of the Martin Luther King National Memorial in Washington, D.C." *The Journal of African American History* 103, no. 3 (Summer 2018): 402–417.
- Levinson, Stanford. *Written in Stone: Public Monuments in Changing Societies.* Durham, NC: Duke University Press, 1998.
- Loewen, James W. *Lies Across America: What Our Historic Sites Get Wrong.* New York, NY: The New Press, 1999.
- Peroco, James A. *Summers with Lincoln: Looking for the Man in the Monument.* New York, NY: Fordham University Press, 2008.
- Piehler, Kurt. *Remembering War the American Way.* Washington, DC: Smithsonian Institution Press, 1995.
- Savage, Kirk. *Monument Wars: Washington D.C., the National Mall, and the Transformation of Memorial Landscape.* Berkeley, CA: University of California Press, 2005.

- Sergel, Ruth. *See You in the Streets: Art, Action, and Remembering the Triangle Shirtwaist Factory Fire.* Iowa City, IA: University of Iowa, 2016.
- Theriault, Kim Servart. "Re-membering Vietnam: War, Trauma, and 'Scarring Over' After 'The Wall.'" *The Journal of American Culture* 26, no. 4 (December 2003): 421–431.
- Walters, Lindsey K. "Slavery and the American University: Discourses of Retrospective Justice at Harvard and Brown." *Slavery & Abolition* 38, no. 4 (2017), 719–744.

References

1 American Historical Association, "Statement on Confederate Monuments," August 28, 2017, www.historians.org/news-and-advocacy/aha-advocacy/aha-statement-on-confederate-monuments.

2 Sanford Levinson, *Written in Stone: Public Monuments in Changing Societies* (Durham, NC: Duke University Press, 1998), 75–129.

3 Katherine Sayre, "Read Mayor Mitch Landrieu's Speech on Removing New Orleans' Confederate Monuments," *The Times-Picayune*, May 23, 2017, https://youtu.be/csMbjG0-6Ak.

4 "The Biggest Statues of the Cold War," www.mementopark.hu/pages/conception.

5 James W. Loewen, *Lies Across America: What Our Historic Sites Get Wrong* (New York, NY: The New Press, 1999), 152–155.

6 "Haymarket Statue Bombed," *Chicago Tribune*, October 7, 1969; "Daley Decries Haymarket Bombing; Vows to Rebuild," *Chicago Tribune*, October 6, 1970.

7 "Haymarket Riot Statue Move Sought," *Chicago Tribune* July 18, 1971; "Moving Day Nears for Haymarket Statue," *Chicago Tribune*, January 13, 1972.

8 Loewen, *Lies Across America*, 152–155.

9 "Site of the Haymarket Tragedy," City of Chicago, Chicago Landmarks, http://webapps1.chicago.gov/landmarksweb/web/landmarkdetails.htm?lanId=1322.

10 Stephen Kinzer, "In Chicago, an Ambiguous Memorial to the Haymarket Attack," *New York Times, September* 15, 2004.

11 Senate Committee on the District of Columbia and the Park Commission, The Improvement of the Park System of the District of Columbia, McMillan Commission Plan for Washington, DC, S. Rep. No. 166 (1902), www.nps.gov/parkhistory/online_books/mcmillan/index.htm.

12 Kirk Savage, *Monument Wars: Washington D.C., the National Mall, and the Transformation of Memorial Landscape* (Berkeley, CA: University of California Press, 2005), chap. 3; Washington National Monument Society, *A Brief History of the Washington National Monument Society* (Washington, 1953), 11.

13 Savage, *Monument Wars*, 131–133.

14 The United States Commission of Fine Arts, et al., *Lincoln Memorial Commission Report* (Washington, DC: GPO, 1913): 13.

15 Peroco, James A., *Summers with Lincoln: Looking for the Man in the Monument* (New York, NY: Fordham University Press, 2008), chap. 4.

16 The United States Commission of Fine Arts, et al., *Lincoln Memorial Commission Report* (Washington, DC: GPO, 1913): 13.

17 Savage, *Monument Wars*, 265–270.

18 Joint Resolution to Authorize the Vietnam Veterans Memorial Fund, Inc., to establish a memorial, Public Law 96–297, 96th Cong. (July 1, 1980).

19 Kim Servart Theriault," Re-membering Vietnam: War, Trauma, and 'Scarring Over' After 'The Wall,'" *The Journal of American Culture* 26, no. 4 (December 2003): 423.

20 Maya Lin, "Making the Memorial," *The New York Review of Books*, November 2, 2000.

21 Ibid.

22 Ibid.

23 Maya Lin, [Vietnam Veterans Memorial. Competition Drawing.] Photograph. Washington DC, 1980 or 1981. From Library of Congress. www.loc.gov/item/97505164.

24 Lin, [Vietnam Veterans Memorial. Competition Drawing]; Lin, "Making the Memorial."

25 Lin, "Making the Memorial."

26 Savage, *Monument Wars*, 277.

27 Vietnam Veterans Memorial Fund, www.vvmf.org.

28 *Overhaul Plans for National Mall, Hearings on H.R. 581–40, Before the Subcommittee on National Parks, Forests and Public Lands of the House Natural Resources Committee*, 112th Cong. (2012) (statement of Stephen E. Whitesell, Regional Director, National Capital Region, National Park Service, Department of the Interior).

29 Robert L. Harris Jr., "Reflections on the Building of the Martin Luther King National Memorial in Washington, D.C.," *The Journal of African American History* 103, no. 3 (Summer 2018): 413.

30 Kevin Bruyneel, "The King's Body: The Martin Luther King, Jr. Memorial and the Politics of Collective Memory," *History and Memory* 26, no. 1 (Spring–Summer 2014): 77.

31 Ibid., 77.

32 "I Have a Dream: Full Text March on Washington Speech," National Association for the Advancement of Colored People, www.naacp.org/i-have-a-dream-speech-full-march-on-washington.

33 "Quotations, Martin Luther King, Jr. Memorial," National Park Service, www.nps.gov/mlkm/learn/quotations.htm.

34 Quoted in Bruyneel, "The King's Body," 86.

35 Harris, "Reflections," 411–412.

36 Quoted in Bruyneel, "The King's Body," 87.

37 Harris, "Reflections," 417.

38 Karen L. Cox, *Dixie's Daughters: The United Daughters of Confederacy and the Preservation of Confederate Culture* (Gainesville, FL: University of Florida, 2003).

39 Lindsey K. Walters, "Slavery and the American University: Discourses of Retrospective Justice at Harvard and Brown," *Slavery & Abolition* 38, no. 4 (2017), 719–744; Max Clarke and Gary Alan Fine, "'A' for Apology: Slavery and the Discourse of Remonstrance in Two American Universities," *History & Memory* 22, no. 1 (Spring–Summer 2010): 81–112.

40 American Historical Association, "Statement on Confederate Monuments."

41 Ruth Sergel, *See You in the Streets: Art, Action, and Remembering the Triangle Shirtwaist Factory Fire* (Iowa City, IA: University of Iowa, 2016), 22–23; http://streetpictures.org/chalk.

6

Recording Memory as History

In the early 1990s, two historians, Roy Rosenzweig and David Thelen, were able to quantify what many already knew to be true: people trust personal accounts for learning about the past. In a survey about Americans' perceptions of history and methods of connections to it, Rosenzweig and Thelen asked respondents to rank "trustworthiness of sources on a 10-point scale." The majority of Americans trusted stories from relatives and eyewitnesses more than anything else except museums.[1] Recording spoken history preserves memories for future historical research and contemporary community identity.

This chapter looks at the historical development of recording spoken history in the United States from the 1930s. Part of this history is about changes in technology: from using paper and ink to the invention of audio recording devices. While technological transformations were significant, imagination also played a critical role. Who and what would be recorded, and how, often depended upon the perceptions of the interviewer. However, interviewees have always influenced the content and form of the transformation of the spoken word into alternate enduring forms. Since the late 1940s, recording personal stories has become known as "oral history." This chapter explains the development of oral history as a methodology within the historical profession.

History

There are many places you could begin a history of the recording of personal accounts for the preservation and interpretation of history. For instance, the ancient Greek historian Thucydides interviewed eyewitnesses to the Peloponnesian War. In the late nineteenth century, Hubert Howe Bancroft used stenography to document the memoirs of political leaders of the American West; he called the product "dictations."[2] In the 1930s, Myles Horton founded the Highlander Folk

Public History: An Introduction from Theory to Application, First Edition. Jennifer Lisa Koslow.
© 2021 by John Wiley & Sons, Inc. Published 2021 by John Wiley & Sons, Inc.

School in Tennessee. He wanted to create a space where people learned to "value their own experience, to analyze their own experience, and to know how to make decisions."[3] An essential element of the educational process was listening to each other and discussing each other's stories.

This history of oral history begins with two folklorists, John and Alan Lomax, as they transitioned from textual to audio methods for recording memory. Their story is indicative of the varied genealogical and interdisciplinary nature of oral history. They are also familiar figures to many outside of the oral history classroom.

John Lomax and his son, Alan Lomax, never used the term oral history. Nevertheless, in hindsight, much of their work recording the voices and music of Americans in the early to mid-twentieth century speaks to the spirit of con-temporary uses and goals of oral history. John Lomax was born in Mississippi in 1867 and grew up in Texas in a family of modest means. His parents were deter-mined to secure their 10 children access to formal education, including at least one year of college. After a year at Granbury College and a summer at Eastman Business College, John Lomax became a teacher. When he was 28 he returned to study, and enrolled at the University of Texas and completed a bachelor of arts in two years. When he finished his degree, he became the school's registrar. However, his desire for an academic life did not dim. In 1903, he became an instructor in English at Texas A&M University and, two years later, secured a sabbatical to pursue graduate studies at Harvard. There he desired to combine his interest in folk songs (especially cowboy ballads) and English literature. He began searching and collecting cowboy songs for his research, which eventually morphed into a life-long pursuit of obtaining a variety of different types of folklore.[4]

By the 1930s Lomax was a renowned folklorist and he worked as an unpaid consultant to the Library of Congress's Archive of American Folk Song, which had been established in 1928. (He desired this relationship because he did not have an academic appointment. Lomax had lost his job to Texan politics, become a banker, and then administrator for an alumni organization. Hence, this affiliation provided him with the status he needed when requesting money from philanthropic and scholarly sources for his collecting expeditions.) Lomax, along with his son Alan, worked on adding to the archive and toward producing an anthology of American folklore to be published by Macmillan.

Amid the Great Depression, the federal government created programs to put people back to work. One of these programs, the Federal Writers' Project (FWP) of the Works Progress Administration (WPA), was tasked with collecting the personal histories of former enslaved men and women. While Lomax did not work for the WPA for very long, his impact on the Slave Narrative project was profound.[5] Under his supervision, WPA workers collected more than 2300 interviews between 1936 and 1939. Recorded by hand and then transcribed, and in some cases edited, the federal government archived the memories (and occasionally a photographic portrait) of these men and women about life before the Civil War.[6]

The idea of collecting the history of freedmen and women originated independently 10 years prior at three different historically African American colleges: Southern, Prairie View, and Fisk University. Historian John B. Cade, who moved from Southern to Prairie View in the early 1930s, began gathering firsthand accounts from formerly enslaved people as a way to counter the dominant academic narrative that asserted that African Americans benefited from slavery. World War I and the Great Migration of African Americans from the South to the North in search of economic opportunities undergirded interest in the cultural study of African American lives.

The federal government became involved in the collection of slave narratives by accident. The original focus of the FWP was to employ individuals to create guides to American cities and states that included information about the history and geography of these sites. Over time, the FWP expanded its efforts and accumulated knowledge about folklife. John Lomax directed these endeavors.

When the FWP began collecting life histories of ordinary Americans, there was no directive to focus on formerly enslaved people. However, Carita Doggett Corse, who directed the Florida Writers' Project, understood the importance of collecting the stories of freedmen and women. A historian with a master of arts degree from Columbia University, Corse used interviews for her publications on the history of Florida.[7] She instructed members of Florida's FWP, which included Zora Neale Hurston, to seek out these individuals for inclusion in the project. Corse then sent a number of these life histories of freedmen and women to the central office in Washington, bringing them to Lomax's attention. He later systematized and expanded these efforts by instructing every state with a Writers' Project that existed in April of 1937 to seek out former slaves and capture their memories. Lomax advised workers to abstain from inserting personal opinions about the narratives they collected. Instead, he reminded them "the Federal Writers' Project is not interested in taking sides on any question. The workers should not censor materials collected regardless of its nature."[8]

It is important to note that in many ways, Lomax's procedures differed from contemporary best practices for oral history. First, although Lomax's instructions were for the interviewee to remain neutral toward the history they were recording, Lomax did not take into consideration other factors that shaped the interviews. For instance, Jim Crow laws in the South mandated African American subservience to white people in public spaces. Lomax did not consider the impact this might have on the stories formerly enslaved people might tell to an interviewer depending upon the interviewer's racial identity. Looking at the narratives from Georgia indicated that African Americans were more willing to speak of the hardships they experienced to another African American. However, Lomax's own positive experiences collecting folklore among African Americans coupled with the fact that there were few African Americans hired by the FWP helps explain why he did not make using African American interviewers a priority.[9]

The project closed in 1939, and soon World War II shifted federal work programs in a very different direction. The Library of Congress retained the narratives and related documents. Benjamin Botkin, who succeeded Lomax, had the interviews bound into a series of volumes and placed into the Rare Book Room. Until the 1970s, the collection was unpublished, was not indexed, and it did not circulate. Historians, who were trained to value written documents created close to an event, were skeptical about the utility of personal reminiscences for decoding the past. Most of the interviewees were of advanced age remembering back on their childhoods, which made historians wonder about the subjective nature of these life histories as sources. Historians began to adopt new methodologies in the 1960s, 1970s, and 1980s, which led them to interrogate the purpose and nature of all sources. As a result, many historians found that these recordings were exceedingly important for uncovering perceptions about slavery from those who had been its subjects.

Recording interviews on audio in the 1930s was possible but difficult, which helps explain why the FWP collected the narratives of formerly enslaved people by pen and paper. In collecting folklore, Alan Lomax, John Lomax's son, initially borrowed a hand-wound cylinder recorder from Mina Edison, Thomas A. Edison's widow. However, it was not very practical for recording in the outdoors.[10] In the summer of 1933, Alan Lomax procured a new Ediphone, which was lighter and was designed to record voices better but was not ideal for capturing music.[11] A few months later, the Lomaxes acquired a new and better recording device, but it weighed 315 pounds. They transformed their car into a portable recording studio, driving it to the singers whenever possible and lugging it "across fields and creeks, onto front porches and into houses."[12] Lomax recalled the transition from paper to audio:

In the beginning, when recording instruments were unsatisfactory, this work of preservation was carried on in largely manuscript form, but in recent years with the development of fine portable recording machines, the Library [of Congress] has been steadily enlarging its collection of records of folk-songs made in the homes of the people who know them."[13]

Alan Lomax was John and Bess Lomax's third child and second son. Born in 1915 in Austin, Texas, Alan worked with his father on folklore collecting projects at first and then on his own. When the Library of Congress acquired his lifetime project, Lomax's library contained "5,000 hours of sound recordings, 400,000 feet of motion picture film, 2,450 videotapes, 2,000 scholarly books and journals, hundreds of photographic prints and negatives, and over 120 linear feet of manuscripts."[14]

Figure 6.1 John Lomax recorded Harriett McClintock outside at a crossroads near Sumterville, Alabama, in 1940 as Ms. McClintock's great-grandchildren and Ruby Pickens Tartt watched. *Source:* Library of Congress, Prints & Photographs Division, Reproduction number LC-DIG-ppmsca-38814 (digital file from original negative).

Alan Lomax began collecting life histories as part of his work collecting folk songs. The idea for including oral biographies came from his father, who discussed the work he had supervised as part of the FWP, in particular, the collection of slave narratives. Alan Lomax realized the power of recording oral history in audio in a moment of serendipity in 1938 with jazz musician "Jelly Roll" Morton. Originally intending to document a few songs, Alan Lomax impulsively "decided to do a full-scale interview." According to Lomax,

[he] sat down on the floor, looked up, and said "Jelly Roll, where did you come from and how did it all begin?" [Jelly Roll] then began to play the piano and talk. It came out of nowhere, the fact that he decided to do that. We hadn't agreed on it at all. Sort of half closing his eyes, he gave that immortal definition of his family, and New Orleans.

Lomax titled these sessions the "Autobiography of Jelly Roll Morton" and it was the first of several recorded life histories he undertook.[15]

In the early 1940s, Lomax developed different educational radio programs related to folk music and American culture. One was "America in the Summer of 1941," which Lomax described as a way to let "the people explain themselves and their lives to the entire nation." In addition to folk music, the program "recorded people's opinions on the war in Europe, asking whether they thought the United States should become involved in it, and documented the Tennessee Valley Authority's work in Union County, Georgia."[16] Another was titled "This is History." Lomax recorded "people of various localities discussing their problems, telling stories, singing songs, etc." Lomax's goal was "to tell the story of some community or some community activity in the words of the people of that community." He believed the final product had a "very permanent quality and live[d] up to its title, This is History."[17] He labeled these projects "Documentary Recording."[18] One aspect that was unique to Lomax's work was his commitment to "giv[e] voice to marginalized American communities" through his radio shows.[19]

The Lomaxes experiences offer contemporary public historians a sense of how capturing people's stories on paper and audio can be an essential means for preserving the history of the American experience in all its diversity. The Lomaxes transition from manuscript to audio also demonstrates how technology offered new possibilities. Listening to aural sources stimulated the senses in different ways than written descriptions. However, these efforts did not shape the ways historians working in universities practiced their craft in the mid-twentieth century. Instead, we must turn to the history of Allan Nevins to see where the inspiration for the term "oral history" and its methodology lie.

The term "oral history" is tied to Allan Nevins. While Nevins might have been aware of the FWP to collect slave narratives and the Lomaxes numerous efforts to collect folklore, he did not leave any personal or public papers indicating that either were a source of inspiration for his efforts to systematically capture via audio technology the stories of people's pasts. Unlike the FWP and the Lomaxes, however, Nevins's work directly influenced the creation of "oral history" as a distinct field in the historical profession. Although he rejected the term, he is often described as oral history's "founding father."[20]

Allan Nevins was born in 1890 in a small rural town in Illinois to a family of farmers. The town, Camp Point, invested in its citizens' education and Nevins obtained a high school diploma before heading to the University of Illinois at the age of 18. It was here that Nevins became interested in newspaper work as a way to combine his academic interests with a sense of civic duty. Five years later, in 1913, Nevins graduated with a master's degree in English. He then headed to New York City to work at the *Evening Post*. For the next 15 years, Nevins worked as a journalist. He also began writing books on historical figures in public policy, which won him attention from academic historians.[21] In 1927, Nevins accepted a one-year position at Cornell University. The following year, Columbia University offered him an adjunct position, which it transformed into a permanent position three years later. Nevins's path to an academic job was unusual but not unheard of in the early twentieth century when the historical profession was still in the process of professionalizing.

Nevins's move from professional journalist to professional historian did not disrupt his belief in making history accessible to those outside of universities. In the 1930s, his books on US President Grover Cleveland and Hamilton Fish (Ulysses S. Grant's secretary of state) earned him Pulitzer Prizes. Scholar Ian Tyrell has argued that Nevins served as an essential bridge between the worlds of academic and amateur historians.[22] Nevins's nonconventional path into the historical profession shaped his perspective on historical sources: he desired the collection of contemporary sources for future historical research.[23] He first expressed this idea in *The Gateway to History* published in 1938. While the vast majority of the book focused on explaining historical methods and theories to amateurs, Nevins also made a general plea to professional historians to develop "some organization" to make "a systematic attempt to obtain, from the lips and papers of living Americans who have led significant lives, a fuller record of their participation in the political, economic, and cultural life of the last sixty years." Nevins believed that this "period in which America has been built into the richest and most powerful nation the world has ever seen, and socially and economically has not only been transformed but re-transformed."[24]

Within *The Gateway to History*, Nevins discussed the use of personal accounts for writing history. While he wanted them included, he believed they needed to be interrogated. He viewed them as biased by nature in contrast to what he felt were more objective testimonies: "a government is largely impersonal and a newspaper often tries to be; but when we come to records made by individuals in their private capacity, new difficulties appear." Nevins advised students to "evaluate [testimony] as first-hand or hearsay, fresh or stale, prejudiced or unprejudiced, corroborated or uncorroborated, vague or definite." After evaluating eyewitness testaments, Nevins instructed writers of history to "hunt in every nook and cranny for corroboration – or, what is equally valuable, contradiction." Last, he advised students to lay "documents side by side" to construct a reasonable interpretation about the past.[25]

Establishing the Columbia Oral History Research Office in 1948 was in step with his vision of increasing the source base upon which history could be written. Technology influenced his decision to pursue this direction. As a subsequent director, Louis Starr, explained, "the automobile, the airliner, and the telephone between them [were] steadily obliterating history's most treasured resource, the confidential letter. . . . we no longer confide[d] to one another in writing, as earlier generations did. . . we talk[ed]."[26] Nevins decided to turn technology from a limit to a benefit. Using a portable tape recorder was key to this new endeavor. It allowed Nevins to do something that, as far as he knew had not been done in earlier uses of interviews by historians. He could record verbatim individual historical memory. Nevins believed these conversations would be more frank than written autobiographies where the author had time to rethink what they wanted to say. While Nevins did not reference the work of the FWP, he was aware of the efforts by the US Armed Services to conduct combat interviews during World War II. These interviews, however, had not been tape-recorded.[27] Even if he had known about the FWP, its goals were very different than those of Nevins. The FWP collected material for non-academics while Nevins wanted to secure resources for future scholarship.[28] Nevertheless, Nevins believed that Columbia would not fund his experiment in what appeared to be a new historical methodology. Instead, he needed to find grant money to support the initial endeavor.[29]

In 1945, Frederic Bancroft, a renowned historian, died, and the trustees of Columbia University set up a prize for the best book in either American history or diplomacy. Allan Nevins's *The Ordeal of the Union* won the initial award in 1948. The Bancroft Prize came with a $4000 grant. Nevins used the money to establish the Oral History Research Office (OHRO). Although Columbia University did not provide monetary support, it afforded Nevins space in two rooms in the basement of Butler Library. The research associates transcribed their interviews from "old Tandbergs" which "were so large they couldn't be taken home."[30] Nevins continued to secure grant money to fund various interview projects, often convincing a leading business to support projects which related to their industries. For instance, he persuaded McDonnell Douglas to help fund a project to document the history of aviation.[31]

When Nevins began collecting oral histories in the late 1940s, he focused on securing the thoughts and recollections of people who his colleagues would have recognized as significant. In this way, although his method appeared to be new, it also fit within the norms of traditional history.[32] In May of 1948, Nevins set out to conduct his first official interview. His student, Dean Albertson accompanied him. Nevins interviewed George McAneny, who "had been instrumental in the whole planning and design of the New York subway system."[33] They took the subway, lugging a 40-pound tape recorder with them.[34]

The name "oral history" seems to be one that Nevins used from the beginning to describe this endeavor. In recollecting on the precise question of the name, Dean Albertson recalled that Nevins had used the "name 'oral history'. . . on the day that [he] first discussed the matter with him in his Fayerweather Hall office at Columbia in February or March 1948." According to Albertson, the term itself was "inconsequential." Instead, the critical aspect was the ideas behind the process: research, interview, transcription with the interviewee, and depositing the materials in an archive for future access. So, how and why Nevins came up with the term is still a bit of a mystery.[35] (At the first National Colloquium on Oral History in 1966, historians shared humorous stories about how the name confused those within and without academia. Was it about dentistry? Were offices of oral history where students took their oral qualifying exams?)

Nevins's attitudes toward what constituted oral history played a role in shaping the direction of the field. For Nevins, oral history was a product developed together by the interviewee and interviewer. The transcript of the interview was sent to the interviewee for corrections. The copy returned was then put into the permanent file. As Elizabeth Mason, OHRO's associate director explained: "In the first place, it was far more authentic, (which is true) for instance, he believed that the final version of the transcript should contain the editorial notes of the interviewee."[36] His successor, Louis Starr, "insisted on . . . complete approval of the transcripts by the interviewees."[37] However, not everyone wholly followed this method. Nevins's student and original assistant director, Dean Albertson, "wouldn't allow a page that had a strikeover on it" to go into the files. He, instead, "always retyped" his transcripts into a final version.[38] The University of California, which established a program a few years after Nevins, retyped, edited, and included photographs in

Figure 6.2   Dean Albertson (left) and James P. Warburg (right) create an oral history. Warburg served as an important advisor to President Franklin D. Roosevelt on economic issues during the Great Depression. *Source:* Columbia University Libraries.

their oral histories. The bound version, however, cost much more than Nevins's approach and it also took longer to produce. Columbia's OHRO produced at least twenty oral histories a year in comparison to the one or two the University of California created.[39]

Allan Nevins served as the office's director until 1958, when he was forced to retire because of an age limit.[40] He moved to the Huntington Library in California, where he continued to research and write. He remained involved with the Columbia OHRO by serving as the chair of its advisory board. The office itself became a consultant to many others, including students of journalism, social work, and education and continues to do so today.

The Columbia OHRO was the first of its kind. However, within a few years, the University of California at Los Angeles (UCLA) and the University of California both created centers for oral history. One of the reasons for the growth of oral history was technological. Tape recorders became affordable, available, and easier to operate.[41]

The various programs differed in procedures. For instance, in contrast to Nevins exposing the process of editing, the California programs were "very meticulous on editing and the form of the final product."[42] The University of California also printed all of the original questions in the transcript, which was something Columbia sometimes left out.[43]

In the 1960s, a variety of people engaged in some form of interviewing process desired the creation of a national organization to provide a forum for discussing methodologies, theories, and practicalities for doing oral history. Jim Mink of UCLA is typically credited with establishing the Oral History Association (OHA). He organized the first meeting in 1966 at Lake Arrowhead, which is near Los Angeles. A year later, a second meeting was held at Arden House in New York, which was Columbia University's conference center. The 145 people attending adopted a constitution.[44] Louis Starr was elected as the organization's first president.

Samuel Hand, a historian from the University of Vermont who became the founding editor of *The Oral History Review*, remembered that the conference at Arden House was unlike the meetings he attended for other historical organizations, such as the Organization of American Historians and the American Historical Society. Instead of being dominated by historians, this conference was populated by a more interdisciplinary group including physicians and archivists.[45] The OHA remains an interdisciplinary organization today. It continues to hold an annual meeting, award prizes, support the publication of a major journal (*The Oral History Review*), and provide guidelines on best practices, ethics, and related issues for those wishing to do oral history either at the community or academic level.

There are different reasons that oral history became popular among historians and the public in the late twentieth century. Elizabeth Mason believed that the Bicentennial had a remarkable effect, almost "like a forest fire." She said "every town and village in the country thought, 'Ah! That's what we'll do for the bicentennial. We'll interview the older residents.'" People contacted Columbia, and Mason referred them to the OHA.[46]

In thinking back on the trajectory of oral history, Samuel Hand believed that Alex Haley's work was a turning point. Hand credited Haley with popularizing oral history and the "idea of family history."[47] Haley discussed his work collecting his family's history at the Seventh Annual Colloquium on Oral History held in Austin, Texas on November 10, 1972. This was four years before the book *Roots: The Saga of an American Family* was published and five years before the television miniseries broke Nielsen records.

Speaking to the OHA in 1972, Haley described how he used his skills as a journalist to investigate his family's history. While looking at the Rosetta Stone at the British Museum, he became inspired to investigate the stories he had heard sitting on his grandmother's porch in Henning, Tennessee. By that time, Haley was in his late thirties. He was retired from the Navy, where he had given twenty years of service, and working as a journalist, most recently completing an autobiography with Malcolm X. The story of the deciphering of the hieroglyphics on the stone reminded Haley of the African sounds embedded in his family's history whose meaning he did not know. It was "a long narrative history of the family which had been passed down literally across generations."[48]

In remembering his time with his grandmother, Cynthia Palmer, Haley explained that she "pumped that story into me as if it were plasma."[49] He realized looking back that "it was by all odds the most precious thing in her life – the story which had come down across the generations about the family going back to that original African."[50] His research took him to Senegal, Africa, where he sat for hours listing to the *griot* Kebba Kanga Fofana, who spoke of the "ancestral history of the Kinte Klan."[51] In the fifth hour of Fofana's narrative, he uttered the following: "About the time the king's soldiers came, the eldest of these four sons, Kunta, went away from this village to chop wood and was seen never again." While Fofana "went on with his story," Haley realized that the oral history of his grandmother and Fofana had converged.[52]

Much like Nevins had called for students to corroborate (or contradict) personal testimonies with as many other sources as they could find, Haley set about tracking down as many documents as he could to connect the two stories. He scoured maritime records in the archives of Lloyd's of London and the Library of Congress, among others. In doing so, Haley was able to figure out when his ancestor Kunta Kinte was kidnapped in Africa, the name of the ship (the *Lord Ligonier*) he was transported on to the Americas, the date the *Lord Ligonier* docked in Annapolis, the record of the ship's holdings when it arrived (98 Africans out of 140 had survived the almost three-month long journey of

5000 miles from the Gambia River to Maryland), and found the deed of Kunta Kinte's sale into slavery.[53]

Haley's account of his research was gripping. His story also spoke to a different way to think about who or what constituted oral history. In Africa, he described *griots* as "living archives of oral history." He explained that "they are the old men who, from the time they had been in their teen-ages, have been part of a line of men who tell the stories as they have been told since the time of their forefathers, literally down across centuries." While there wasn't a tape recorder to capture a person's words exactly, which was becoming the norm of "oral history" in the United States, Haley asserted that preservation of memory by the griots captured the same essence.[54] He argued that any suspicions about whether these recollections could be counted on for historical fact should be set aside: "The reason it astounds us is because in our culture we have become so conditioned to the crush of print that most people in our culture have almost forgotten what the human memory is capable of if it is trained to keep things in it."[55] Haley's story, especially about how family history was passed down in many African American families orally, offered those doing an oral history with a sense of legitimacy about trusting memories as a mechanism for documenting the past.

The question of how to evaluate oral sources in comparison to written ones continued to be debated within the history profession. As Samuel Hand explained, when he went to graduate school in history in the 1950s, his professors (and himself) believed that "oral history was inferior to a written source, because a written source was generally created closer to the event so that made it superior." In retrospect, he explained the fallacy of his thinking: "But then when you think about it and you give it some deliberate thought, it doesn't quite work out that way."[56] The question of the reliability of written versus oral sources gave way in the debates about sources in general during the 1990s, when theories of Postmodernism ignited all sorts of questions about how to read and evaluate different documents about the past.

Studs Terkel was another influential figure in popularizing oral history in the late twentieth century. Born in New York City, Terkel moved to Chicago, Illinois, as a child. His parents ran a boarding house from 1926 to 1936. Although he graduated from the University of Chicago with a law degree in 1934, Terkel did not go on to practice law. Instead, he found employment with the FWP. In 1952, Terkel went on air on 98.7 WFMT in Chicago with the *Studs Terkel Program*. Starting in the late 1960s, he began taking his interviewing projects and turning them into best-selling books. In 1985, his book *The Good War: An Oral History of World War II* won a Pulitzer. In 1997, President Clinton awarded Terkel the National Humanities Medal for "deep[ening] the nation's understanding of the humanities and broadened our citizens' engagement with history, literature, languages, philosophy, and other humanities subjects."[57]

Some historians have argued that Terkel's work was not oral history. Terkel's interviews, while engaging, often did not appear to engage with methodological questions that interested scholars in the field. Moreover, his editing process was extensive.[58] This increased the emotional aspects of the interviews and, presumably, the reader's engagement. However, it also meant that the interviews were not printed verbatim. While he removed his questions from the printed text, Terkel's voice was interwoven throughout because of his editorial choices. At the heart of his work was a sense of activism. People's stories were important because they helped people connect the past with their present.[59]

As Michael Frisch has argued, Terkel's approach has much to offer to oral historians.[60] In many respects, Terkel was conventional. He researched his interviewees and the subjects they were to discuss. He also drew multiple perspectives into his work. For instance, in the preface to *Hard Times*, he advised readers that for those persons whose tales were related inside its pages, "their rememberings are their truths." Terkel's work helped explain to general audiences how historical interpretation functioned, which differed from the conventional approach of memorization used in most high school history classes. Terkel argued "the precise fact or the precise date is of small consequence" because *Hard Times* was "not a lawyer's brief nor annotated sociological treatise." Instead, Terkel maintained that the book was "simply an attempt to get the story of the holocaust known as The Great Depression from an improvised battalion of survivors."[61] In reviewing Terkel's lifetime of work, Frisch concluded that despite whatever reservations oral historians might have had about Terkel,

[his] enduring works of history preserve many voices and present his own, all in a rich, productive, transparent, engaged conversation that readers will continue to find it easy and meaningful to join. Which is exactly what characterized the best historians and the histories they leave us.[62]

In the twenty-first century, StoryCorps has become a significant popularizer of oral history. David Isay, who produced different programs for radio, came up with the idea for StoryCorps out of his own experience with recording his grandparents as a child. Although the tape appears to be lost, he wishes that he could find it for two reasons. First, for the joy it would give his family to hear their voices again. Second, for what he feels they could learn from the stories on the tape. He believes that ordinary people's perspectives are essential for understanding the past.[63] Since 2003, StoryCorps has provided a mechanism for recording stories. First through a recording booth in Grand Central Station in New York City, for which Studs Terkel cut the ribbon to mark the opening, and then through mobile-booths, which have been taken around the country. Sometimes the goal is to record something specific, such as people who identify as LGBTQI2S (lesbian, gay, bisexual, transgender, queer, intersex, and two-spirit) and the voices of those incarcerated. StoryCorps' mission is to "preserve and share humanity's stories in order to build connections between people and create a more just and compassionate world."[64] Isay envisioned the project as "the spiritual heir to the documentary work created under the W.P.A."[65] The interviews are played over National Public Radio and archived in the American Folklife Center at the Library of Congress.

The recordings of StoryCorps are compelling because they are self-consciously emotive. However, critics argue that it is not oral history in the traditional sense because of an inherent bias. Alexander Freund characterizes it as such: StoryCorps believes that "telling and listening to stories is positive, healing, and empowering, and can lead to personal transformation and social change."[66] But is this necessarily so? In focusing on the individual, does StoryCorps undercut the underlying purpose of social history and oral history: the study of how history is shaped by economic, political, religious, and cultural institutions.[67] In addition, the stories are mediated in their retelling. Initial interviews generally run 40 minutes but are edited down to 10–15 minutes for the radio, along with music and a voice-over added for continuity at moments. Aspects of the interview are moved around to create a narrative.[68] In this way, the works are curated much like a museum exhibit.

Although telling individual stories is not the same engaging in the totality of the historian's craft, it is a step in that direction. Oral history provides narrators with the ability to shape the collection, preservation, and interpretation of history. Individual stories are not history, but Public Historians can use them to help make sense of the intersection between memory and history.

Theory

Since scholars began using "oral history" as a specific term in the 1950s, there has been variation as to what the term constitutes. In this way, oral history is similar to any other type of historical approach: methods, definitions, and practices do not remain static. This section presents the main theoretical issues that have concerned oral historians since the mid-twentieth century.

Authorship is a major theoretical problem in oral history. Who is the author of an oral history: the interviewer or the interviewee? Saul Benison, one of Columbia University's OHRO's first research associates, described oral histories as a "mutual creation" between the "historian-interviewer who has determined the historical problems and relationships to be examined" and the "participant in past events."[69] Michael Frisch argued that the interviewer and interviewee shared authority over the oral history.[70] According to Frisch, an oral history by its very nature was a process in which the interviewer and interviewee interpreted the past together.[71] Today, many oral historians prefer to use the term "narrator" to describe the interviewee as a way to connote the power dynamic that exists between the two individuals in conversation. It is important to remember that in an experience of shared authority, the narrator can choose to remain silent on a subject, and the interviewer-historian must respect the narrator's right to privacy.[72]

Oral histories serve multiple purposes, both personal and public depending on the authors' intentions. They can be used by a researcher in collaboration with other historical materials to construct an interpretation about the past in a conversation with other historians. A community can use oral histories to promote civic engagement. A person might want to create a verbal account to pass down their memories to their family. Thus, oral history can be of use to both amateur and academic historians. None of these purposes are necessarily exclusionary to any other.

A second compelling question for oral historians is about the purpose and nature of transcription. At its heart, the issue is about accessibility. For those working in the early oral history programs in the 1960s there was no question that transcription was an essential aspect of oral history. Although transcription is a time-consuming activity, the product provides a textual record of the conversation. Indexing these transcripts added an informative layer for retrieving information about key concepts, terms, and events.

However, there was no singular agreement on what the finished product should contain. As Saul Benison explained, in the beginning, the outcome of oral history was a "new kind of historical document." He believed that the "mutual creation" of the oral history "contribute[d] to both [its] strengths and weakness" as a primary source.[73] He desired transparency. Consequently, he felt that in addition to a transcript of the interview itself, the finished product should include the questions of the "historian-interviewer" along with their "bibliographies of the primary and secondary material used by the interviewer" to construct those questions.[74] Benison's point about research still holds today. Oral histories are much more engaging if the interviewer has conducted background research into the person and topic for which they are interviewing them about.

In the early years of oral history programs, transcriptions also offered a mechanism for sustainability. Purchasing audiotape and preserving it was expensive. Instead, oral history programs typically saved only a sample for posterity and then reused the tapes. As Saul Benison explained, this was done despite knowing that the vocal inflections on the recordings "contribute a truth to the oral history account that the typed page can never convey."[75]

In the twenty-first century, however, there are new technologies and new ideas about the purpose of transcription. Digital software tools have expanded the range of possible ways to develop accessibility. These tools allow editors to annotate interviews (audio and video) and make them searchable without a verbatim transcription. However, digital tools do not necessarily lead to greater access. For instance, keyword searches do not always capture concepts that narrators and historian-interviewers generated in the mediated process of transcription.

Another theoretical issue for oral historians is the issue of questions. Scholars agree that open-ended questions, ones without a yes or no answer, offer the narrator the highest chance for self-reflection. There is less agreement on whether to allow the narrator access to the questions before the interview. The utility is that it might jog someone's memory more productively for the interview. A downside is that the narrator might feel that they need to rehearse or that they can only stick to the questions being asked. Some scholars do not provide questions but do give a general sense of the types of questions they might ask. Another option is to ask the narrator what they would be most comfortable with in preparing for the oral history.

Last, oral historians are concerned with oral histories as both primary source documents and as texts to be decoded. Theoretical approaches to cultural studies prompt historians to think about how the conversations being recorded relate to constructions of race, class, gender, and the dynamics of power.[76] In this respect, investigating oral communications is not that different than written ones. Theory can help in the meaning-making process, but it does not replace the action of document collection.

Practice

1) Listen to an interview by Studs Terkel and describe how Terkel listened to the person he was interviewing. Explain how Terkel documented a memory that contributes to our historical knowledge about a topic. https://studsterkel.wfmt.com/

2) Using one or two of the slave narratives of the FWP of the 1930s, read through the narrative and answer the following questions: (i) If there are no questions transcribed, come up with the list you think the interviewer asked the interviewee. (ii) If there is no information about the interviewer listed, what would you say is their gender and racial identity? Explain how you reached your conclusion. (iii) If the interviewer is listed, do they have a Wikipedia page? If so, does it discuss their participation in the FWP? If not, try adding that information to the page. (iv) What does the document tell you about life in the 1930s? www.loc.gov/collections/slave-narratives-from-the-federal-writers-project-1936-to-1938

3) The Oral History Archives at Columbia University has placed some of its oral histories online. Watch a video of one of the oral histories from the Carnegie Corporation Oral History Project. As you watch think about how this oral

history resembles the strategies Nevins suggested when he began the program and how it differs. www.columbia.edu/cu/lweb/digital/collections/oral_hist/carnegie/video-interviews

4) Listen to one of the interviews at StoryCorps at least two times, and as you listen, take notes on how the editing aided in making it compelling. www.storycorps.org

5) Students can conduct an oral history. In order to do so, they will need to research a person, the events surrounding that person's life (create a bibliography of the sources used in this investigation), come up with open-ended questions, record the interview (either just audio or audio and video), construct a transcript (either full transcript or shortened version to provide a sense of topics and at what point they were discussed), and allow the narrator to review and edit the transcript. The OHA is a tremendous resource for learning about best practices, technology, and providing links to various forums of discussion on the hows and whys of doing oral history: www.oralhistory.org. The Library of Congress has information on its website to give some guidance: www.loc.gov/folklife/familyfolklife/oralhistory.html as does the Oral History Center at the Bancroft Library, University of California http://www.lib.berkeley.edu/libraries/bancroft-library/oral-history-center/oral-history-tips. Two popular guidebooks to doing oral history are Valerie Raleigh Yow, *Recording Oral History: A Guide for the Humanities and Social Sciences* (Rowman & Littlefield, 2014) and Donald A. Ritchie, *Doing Oral History* (Oxford University Press, 2014).

Further Resources

- Benison, Saul. "Reflections on Oral History." *The American Archivist* 28, no. 1 (January 1965): 71–77.
- "Born in Slavery: Slave Narratives from the Federal Writers' Project, 1936 to 1938," Library of Congress, www.loc.gov/collections/slave-narratives-from-the-federal-writers-project-1936-to-1938.
- Fetner, Gerald L. *Immersed in Great Affairs: Allan Nevins and the Heroic Age of American History*. Albany, NY: State University of New York Press, 2004.
- Filene, Benjamin. "Listening Intently: Can StoryCorps Teach Museums How to Win the Hearts of New Audiences," in *Letting Go?: Sharing Historical Authority in a User-Generated World*, edited by Bill Adair. Philadelphia, PA: The Pew Center for Arts & Heritage, 2011.
- Freund, Alexander. "Under Storytelling's Spell? Oral History in a Neoliberal Age." *Oral History Review* 42, no. 1 (2015): 96–132.
- Frisch, Michael. *A Shared Authority: Essays on the Craft and Meaning of Oral and Public History*. Albany, NY: State University of New York Press, 1990.

- Frisch, Michael. "From a Shared Authority to the Digital Kitchen, and Back," in *Letting Go?: Sharing Historical Authority in a User-Generated World,* edited by Bill Adair. Philadelphia, PA: The Pew Center for Arts & Heritage, 2011.
- Gustavson, Andrea. "From 'Observer to Activist:' Documentary Memory, Oral History, and Studs Terkel's 'Essence' Narratives." *Journal of American Studies* 46 (2012), 110–116.
- Haley, Alex. "Black History, Oral History, and Genealogy." *Oral History Review* 1 (1973): 1–25.
- Hamilton, Paula, and Linda Shopes. *Oral History and Public Memories.* Philadelphia, PA: Temple University Press, 2008.
- The Oral History Association: www.oralhistory.org.
- Shopes, Linda. "'Insights and Oversights:' Reflections on the Documentary Tradition and the Theoretical Turn in Oral History." *Oral History Review* 41, no. 2 (2014): 257–268.
- Szwed, John. *Alan Lomax: The Man Who Recorded the World.* New York, NY: Viking, 2010.

References

1 Roy Rosenzweig and David Thelen, *The Presence of The Past: Popular Uses of History in American Life* (New York, NY: Columbia University Press, 1998), 21. The ranking was as follows from most to least trustworthy: (i) museums, (ii) personal accounts from grandparents or other relatives, (iii) conversation with someone who was there (witness), (iv) college history professors, (v) high school teachers, (vi) nonfiction books, and (vii) movies and television programs.

2 Willa Klug Baum, "Oral History: A Revived Tradition at the Bancroft Library," *The Pacific Northwest Quarterly* 58, no. 2 (April 1957): 57.

3 Daniel R. Kerr, "Allan Nevins is Not My Grandfather: The Roots of Radical Oral History Practice in the United States," *Oral History Review* 43, no. 2 (2016): 373.

4 John Szwed, *Alan Lomax: The Man Who Recorded the World* (New York, NY: Viking, 2010): 5–11.

5 Norman R. Yetman, "'Born in Slavery:' An Introduction to the WPA Slave Narratives," *Library of Congress Information Bulletin* 60, no. 4 (April 2001): 91.

6 Yetman, "Born in Slavery," 86–95.

7 "Carita Doggett Corse," Florida Commission on the Status of Women, http://fcsw.net/dt_team/carita-doggett-corse; Yetman, "Born in Slavery," 92.

8 John Lomax quoted in Yetman, "Born in Slavery," 93.

9 Yetman, "Born in Slavery," 93.

10 Szwed, *Alan Lomax*, 35.

11 Ibid., 35–36.

12 Ibid., 43.

13 Ronald D. Cohen, ed., *Alan Lomax Assistant in Charge: The Library of Congress Letters, 1935–1945* (Jackson, MS: University of Mississippi, 2011): 70.

14 William R. Ferris, "Alan Lomax: The Long Journey," *Southern Cultures* 13, no. 3 (Fall 2007): 133.

15 Szwed, *Alan Lomax*, 123–125.

16 Ibid., 179.

17 Cohen, *Alan Lomax*, 284.

18 Ibid., 306.

19 Rachel Donaldson, "Broadcasting Diversity: Alan Lomax and Multiculturalism," *The Journal of Popular Culture* 46, no. 1 (2013): 60.

20 Oral History Association, "Definitions of Oral History" (audio recording), September 26, 1966, transcript and audio recording, https://texashistory.unt.edu/ark:/67531/metadc953771/m1. In his talk to the Oral History Association on September 26, 1966, Nevins told his colleagues that he wanted to dispel the myth that he created oral history. He said oral history "founded itself," and it would have "sprung into life" without him.

21 Gerald L. Fetner, *Immersed in Great Affairs: Allan Nevins and the Heroic Age of American History* (Albany, NY: State University of New York Press, 2004): chap. 1.

22 Ian Tyrell, *Historians in Public: The Practice of American History, 1890–1970* (Chicago, IL: University of Chicago Press, 2005): 62.

23 Gerald L. Fetner, *Immersed in Great Affairs*, 140.

24 Allan Nevins, *The Gateway to History* (New York, NY: D. Appleton-Century Company, 1938): iv.

25 Nevins, *The Gateway to History*, 188 and 204.

26 Louis Starr quoted in Saul Benison, "Reflections on Oral History," *The American Archivist*, 28, no. 1 (January 1965): 72.

27 Forrest Pogue, "Louis Starr: A Remembrance," *Oral History Review* 8 (1980): 94. On Pogue's participation in conducting combat interviews during World War II see Forrest C. Pogue and Holly C. Shulman, "Forrest C. Pogue and the Birth of Public History in the Army," *The Public Historian* 15, no. 1 (Winter, 1993): 31–34 and 45–46.

28 Jerold Hirsch, "Before Columbia: The FWP and the American Oral History Research," *Oral History Review* 34, no. 2 (2007): 10.

29 Richard Polsky, "An Interview with Elizabeth Mason," *Oral History Review* 27, no. 2 (Summer–Fall 2000): 161.

30 Ibid., 160.

31 Ibid., 163.

32 Hirsch, "Before Columbia," 10.

33 Polsky, "An Interview with Elizabeth Mason," 162.

34 Ibid., 162.

35 Charles T. Morrissey, "Why Call It 'Oral History?' Searching for Early Usage of a Generic Term," *Oral History Review* 8 (1980): 23 and 38.

36 Polsky, "An Interview with Elizabeth Mason," 163–164.

37 Forrest Pogue, "Louis Starr: A Remembrance," *Oral History Review* 8 (1980): 95.

38 Polsky, "An Interview with Elizabeth Mason," 164.

39 Ibid., 172.

40 Polsky, "An Interview with Elizabeth Mason," 159.

41 Baum, "Oral History," 58.

42 Polsky, "An Interview with Elizabeth Mason," 171.

43 Baum, "Oral History," 59.

44 Polsky, "An Interview with Elizabeth Mason," 171. Charles W. Crawford, "Oral History: The State of The Profession," *Oral History Review* 2 (1974): 1.

45 Tracy E. K'Meyer, "An Interview with Samuel Hand: 'Reel Life: The Early Years of the OHA/OHR'" *Oral History Review* 26, no. 2 (Summer–Fall 1999): 112.

46 Polsky, "An Interview with Elizabeth Mason," 172.

47 Hand quoted in K'Meyer, "An Interview with Samuel Hand," 124.

48 Alex Haley, "Black History, Oral History, and Genealogy," *Oral History Review* 1 (1973): 1.

49 Haley, "Black History," 5.

50 Ibid., 5.

51 Ibid., 15.

52 Ibid., 16.

53 Ibid., 24.

54 Ibid., 12.

55 Ibid., 12.

56 K'Meyer, "An Interview with Samuel Hand," 113.

57 "National Humanities Medal," National Endowment for the Humanities, www.neh.gov/our-work/awards-honors.

58 Andrea Gustavson, "From "Observer to Activist:' Documentary Memory, Oral History, and Studs Terkel's 'Essence' Narratives," *Journal of American Studies* 46 (2012), 110–116.

59 Gustavson, "From 'Observer to Activist'" 104–105.

60 Michael Frisch, "Studs Terkel, Historian," *Oral History Review* 41, no. 2 (2014): 269–278.

61 Studs Terkel, *Hard Times* (New York, NY: Avon Books, 1970): 17.

62 Frisch, "Studs Terkel," 278.

63 "An Introduction to StoryCorps," StoryCorps, https://storycorps.org/about.

64 "An Introduction to StoryCorps," https://storycorps.org/about.

65 Benjamin Filene, "Listening Intently: Can StoryCorps Teach Museums How to Win the Hearts of New Audiences," in *Letting Go? Sharing Historical Authority in a User-Generated World*, ed. Bill Adair, (Philadelphia, PA: The Pew Center for Arts & Heritage, 2011): 178.

66 Alexander Freund, "Under Storytelling's Spell? Oral History in a Neoliberal Age," *Oral History Review* 42, no. 1 (2015): 105.

67 Ibid., 108.

68 Filene, "Listening Intently," 187–188.

69 Saul Benison quoted in Linda Shopes, "'Insights and Oversights:' Reflections on the Documentary Tradition and the Theoretical Turn in Oral History," *Oral History Review* 41, no. 2 (2014): 258–259.

70 Michael Frisch, *A Shared Authority: Essays on the Craft and Meaning of Oral and Public History* (Albany, NY: State University of New York Press, 1990): xx.

71 Michael Frisch, "From a Shared Authority to the Digital Kitchen, and Back," in *Letting Go?: Sharing Historical Authority in a User-Generated World*, ed. Bill Adair (Philadelphia, PA: The Pew Center for Arts & Heritage, 2011): 127.

72 Selma Thomas, "Private Memory in Public Space: Oral History and Museums," in *Oral History and Public Memories*, ed. Paula Hamilton and Linda Shopes (Philadelphia, PA: Temple University Press, 2008): 98–100.

73 Benison, "Reflections on Oral History," 73.

74 Ibid., 73.

75 Ibid., 76.

76 Linda Shopes, "'Insights and Oversights:' Reflections on the Documentary Tradition and the Theoretical Turn in Oral History," *Oral History Review* 41, no. 2 (2014): 262–268.

7

Digitizing History

This chapter examines the theory and practice of how history is collected, preserved, and interpreted using digital mediums. In the history section of this chapter, you will learn about the history of computers, the history of the World Wide Web, and the history of scholars using computers for historical analysis. The theory section explores the critical debates surrounding the opportunities and limitations in using digital media in historical practice. The question for Public Historians is not whether to embrace or reject the digital but rather how and when to use it effectively.

History

The desire for developing computers was articulated long before people began to be able to realize that aspiration. For instance, in 1936, British mathematician Alan M. Turing published a paper proposing the idea of using algorithms – essentially step-by-step instructions –to program an instrument to do a set of calculations. The idea became known as the Turing machine. However, when first theorized, it was just that: an abstract theory. In the late 1930s, the desire became realized into something tangible. Bell Telephone Laboratories, for example, created the Complex Number Calculator in 1939.

The price tag for developing computers was very costly. World War II facilitated the process for many countries, including the United States and Great Britain. Governments invested in the emergent technology for the war effort. Great Britain constructed Colossus to break Nazi codes.[1] The United States built the electronic numerical integrator and computer (ENIAC).

Using money from the US Army, John Mauchly and J. Presper of the University of Pennsylvania's Moore School of Electrical Engineering designed and supervised the building of ENIAC between 1943 and 1945. According to historian David Alan Grier,

Public History: An Introduction from Theory to Application, First Edition. Jennifer Lisa Koslow.
© 2021 by John Wiley & Sons, Inc. Published 2021 by John Wiley & Sons, Inc.

Figure 7.1 The enormous ENIAC. *Source:* Library of Congress, Prints & Photographs Division, Reproduction number LC-USZ62-110437 (b&w film copy neg.).

the ENIAC can best be understood "as a collection of electronic adding machines and other arithmetic units, which were originally controlled by a web of large electric cables."[2] The goal was to create a machine that could "calculate trajectory ballistics thousands of times faster than other calculating machines."[3] The war ended before ENIAC could be used. Nonetheless, the US Army's $400 000 investment was not for naught.[4] On February 15, 1946, ENIAC was presented to the public. *The New York Times* described the invention as "an amazing machine which applies electronic speeds for the first time to mathematical tasks hitherto too difficult and cumbersome for solution."[5] While swift in making calculations, the machine itself was immense and time-consuming to program. The reporter for *The New York Times* described it as having "some 40 panels nine feet high," and taking up almost all of the "30-by 60-foot room" within which it was housed.[6] Although the US Army and the Moore School continued to use ENIAC, its operations were not trouble free. In 1955, ENIAC was retired in favor of the advent of newer computers.

After World War II, we see the rise of supercomputers. For instance, the University of Illinois built the ordnance variable automatic computer (ORDVAC) in 1952 for the US Army's Ballistic Research Laboratory. It then created a duplicate machine named the Illinois automatic computer (ILLIAC) for the university's use. The ILLIAC, thus, "was the first automatic digital supercomputer built and owned by a university."[7] By doing so, scholars from across the university used it in their research including music composer Lejaren Hiller. It is in this postwar context, especially the 1960s and the 1970s, within which we begin to see historians wonder whether there might not be a place for computers in the process of producing historical knowledge.

Historians employed mathematics to analyze history long before computers made their appearance. For instance, Frank and Harriet Owsley used punch cards with a calculating machine in the 1940s to analyze federal census figures to study southern small family farms.[8] However, changes in computer technology in the 1960s and 1970s opened up new opportunities for historians to use this technology in historical analysis. In 1963, William Aydelotte's analysis of voting patterns in the British House of Commons in the 1840s became the first published historical work that used computerized research.[9]

Gradually a new subcategory of history emerged: quantitative history. Historians interested in questions of labor, elections and political behavior, demography, and other social and economic issues researched and analyzed numeric sets. It now looked possible to conduct statistical analysis that had been previously prohibitive because of the "laborious task of organization and tabulation" that "required a virtually prohibitive investment of time and energy."[10] In the early 1970s, the Inter-university Consortium for Political Research (ICPR) at the University of Michigan in Ann Arbor and the Family History Program at the Newberry Library in Chicago offered scholars training in computerized data analysis. In 1993, the Royal Swedish Academy of Sciences awarded the Nobel Prize in economics to Robert William Fogel and Douglass Cecil North for their work using quantitative methods to study economic history.[11] Social historians found quantitative methods particularly appealing for attempting to find sources that could give voice to the majority of people who did not leave manuscript materials that would have recorded their thoughts and feelings on events. Computers, social historians believed, could help them write history from the bottom up.

Computers changed the capacity of historians to analyze large sets of data. Nevertheless, as much as computers looked promising, there were also impediments to their widespread use in the historical profession. The highest hurdle was the absence of accessible training in computer programing for scholars of history. An almost equal barrier was funding. Early computer programming involved keypunching "thousands and often tens of thousands of data cards." Theodore K. Rabb estimated that between "keypunching, programming, and machine time," his study of the British elites in the early 1960s had cost over $10,000, of which he paid ninety percent.[12] The creation of the Statistical Package for Social Sciences (SPSS) in 1968 at Stanford helped humanities scholars by providing a standardized format to work with data. Still, most historians did not become quantitative ones. In comparison, the advent of the Internet has had a more far reaching effect on the historical profession.

Before we can begin a discussion about the creation of the Internet, we need to start with a conversation about ideas related to storing, retrieving, and sharing information. I am going to begin ours with Vannevar Bush. Bush was an electrical engineer who spent most of his academic career at the Massachusetts Institute of Technology. He was able to turn one of the electrical devices he created into a commercial success, out of which he established the Raytheon Company. His research was varied and among his interests was technology related to microfilm (a reduced photographic image on a film). In 1939, with war looming, Bush became the director for the National Advisory Committee for Aeronautics (now known as NACA). A short time later, he became the head of the Office of Scientific Research and Development (OSRD) for the federal government. The OSRD guided and coordinated the various research projects being developed by and between private and public entities (the military, universities, and industry). By 1945, Bush was a familiar and well-respected figure in the scientific community.

In 1945, Bush pushed an article "As We May Think," in *The Atlantic*, a journal of literary and cultural commentary aimed at highly educated audiences. In "As We May Think," Bush articulated an idea that should sound familiar to anyone who has used the World Wide Web. During the war, Bush witnessed scientists working in partnership. He noted that there was so much research produced in this period that it made it difficult at times to keep track of how different research agendas related to others. Bush wondered whether engineers could create a "machine of logic" to aid in issues of connection. Human brains, he argued, worked by making associations. Was there a way to create a machine to allow people the ability to "produce, store, and consult the record of the race" through links? He dubbed an imagined machine that could perform such a task the Memex.[13] While Bush did not invent the Internet or the World Wide Web, his work proved inspirational to some of those who did.

Who created the Internet? The federal government or private entrepreneurs? In public conversations, the answer to this question appears to depend upon whom you ask. A goal of this chapter is to demonstrate that the answer lies in the interactions between the public and private sectors.

The story of a tangible Internet begins with the development of the Advanced Research Projects Agency Network, commonly known as ARPANET. During World War II, two physicists who specialized in acoustics, Leo Beranek and J.C. Licklider, came into contact through their laboratory work at Harvard. This interaction became the foundation for a long-term professional relationship. After the war, Beranek moved to MIT and swayed MIT's Department of Engineering to secure an appointment for Licklider as well. After a few more years, Beranek became a cofounder of BBN (Bolt, Beranek, and Newman), a psychoacoustical consulting firm. In 1957, Beranek lured Licklider from his faculty position at MIT to BBN to help with "research about how machines could efficiently amplify human labor."[14] Three years later, Licklider convinced BBN to invest in state-of-the-art technology, a digital computer. It cost $30,000 (approximately a quarter of a million dollars in today's relative price). Licklider believed that digital computers could be programmed to facilitate "effective, cooperative association." For instance, creating the capacity for different people using different screens to simultaneously use one "mammoth central computer for word processing, number crunching, and information retrieval."[15]

In 1962, the US Department of Defense's Advanced Research Projects Agency (ARPA) hired Licklider to work at its Information Processing Techniques Office (IPTO). He remained there for two years. ARPA found his idea of networking especially attractive. Was there a way for researchers to work cooperatively using computers to share information across different sites? If someone could make it work, then ARPA would not have to buy each laboratory an expensive supercomputer.

In 1960, Paul Baran, of the RAND Corporation (a nonprofit think tank for solving public policy issues) had developed an idea for protecting information in the event of a nuclear attack.[16] He had proposed using the telephone communication system to send blocks of information over different lines, which would be reconstructed into a whole once they arrived at their terminus. He called these "message blocks."[17] His work was archived in the files of the US Air Force in an eleven-volume description. Lawrence Roberts, who was hired as IPTO's program manager in 1967, came upon Baran's work. Then, working with ideas from Donald Davies at the National Physical Laboratory in Great Britain, who coined the term "packet switching," and Leonard Kleinrock at the University of California, Los Angeles (UCLA), Roberts proposed that ARPA secure a contract to test out a "packet switching network."[18]

In 1968, ARPA awarded a combined contract to BBN, UCLA, Stanford Research Institute, the University of California at Santa Barbara, and the University of Utah. These schools, according to Beranek, were the most enthusiastic. They were also, except for BBN, all located in the west, which meant that they could avoid the expense of leasing cross-country telephone lines.[19] Each of the four sites would be a "node." Wes Clark from Washington University in St. Louis had come up with the word to describe a "network of identical, interconnected mini-computers."[20] Roberts took this idea and called these computers "Interface Message Processors" (IMPs). Instead of each supercomputer talking directly to each other, they would be hooked into a smaller node. This allowed the node to do "the difficult work of traffic management" leaving the supercomputer to spend its time on processing information.

Thus, the development of ARPANET fell between these various entities. The overall design, the hardware and software needs, getting the equipment to each site, installing it, and aiding in its operation were BBN's responsibility. Each IMP weighed about a half a ton and was the size of a 1960s refrigerator.[21] After everything had been installed, and internal trials run at both UCLA and Stanford, it was ready to test.

On October 29, 1969, 21-year-old Charles (Charley) Kline, a computer science major at UCLA, placed a call to Bill Duvall at Stanford.[22] While the two "were hooked up with a telephone headset," they attempted to have their respective computers speak to each other. In hindsight, Leonard Kleinrock believed they should "have prepared a wonderful message" in the tradition of Samuel Morse ("what hath God wrought") and Alexander Graham Bell ("come here, Watson, I need you"). Instead, the word they were trying to communicate was "L-O-G-I-N." Kline remembers typing the "L" and Duvall telling him "I got the L." Kline then typed "O," which Duvall also received. Kline typed "G," and Duvall's computer "had a bug, and it crashed." The first word over ARPANET became "L-O," which became interpreted as "ello," slang for hello. In sum, ARPANET was the result of a collaborative effort between the federal government, private enterprise, and universities.

By 1983, ARPANET had 562 nodes.[23] Its size prompted the federal government to divide it into two networks: MILNET (for the government) and ARPANET (for everyone else.) The government allowed commercial carriers to use its system as space for experimentation to figure out whether it would be useful in the private sector. It was. Soon, private corporations such as IBM and Bell began establishing networks. Private companies invested in fiber optic cables and the federal government helped subsidize these efforts. There was a long history of federal investment in supporting national systems of transportation and communication. For instance, the federal government subsidized the Central and Union Pacific's efforts to build a transcontinental railroad in the nineteenth century.

Vinton (Vint) Cerf, who had been a graduate student at UCLA and worked in Kleinrock's lab, and Bob Kahn, who had been at BBN, came up with the TCP/IP protocols for sharing information over different networks. Cerf explained the difference between ARPANET and the Internet: "ARPANET was built on the assumption that you could build a reliable underlying network. The Internet was based on the assumption that no network was necessarily reliable and you had to do end-to-end retransmissions to recover."[24] In May 1974, Cerf and Kahn published a paper, "A Protocol for Packet Network Intercommunication," in which they discussed "internetwork routing, accounting, and timeouts."[25] Cerf, with two graduate students, Yogen Dalal and Carl Sunshine, published a second paper in December of 1974, "Specification of Internet Transmission Control Program," which became the first time "Internet" was seen in print.[26] By 1989, ARPANET had become obsolete and the government retired it.[27]

Today, we typically access the Internet as individuals. You log into your desktop, laptop, or handheld device, which are all categorically personal computers. Although this has become many people's norm, it was not necessarily inevitable.

As ARPANET developed in the 1970s, so too did other types of networking strategies. The system developed at Dartmouth College, New Hampshire, between the late 1960s and early 1970s is one example. Undergraduate students, first at Dartmouth and then at colleges and other secondary schools mostly in the New England area, used the Kiewit network to access to the university's mainframe computer at the same time. "Time-sharing" was a major shift from the 1950s and 1960s when computers could only run one task at a time. This arrangement afforded thousands of students experience with computer programming, albeit in computer labs and not in their homes.[28]

In the 1970s, two other time-sharing networks in the Midwest provided numerous young people with a space to experiment and work collaboratively on developing computer programs. For example, the beloved *Oregon Trail* game was created by students and teachers in 1971 at a Minneapolis high school. However, at first it was a singular experiment. After the Minnesota Educational Computing Consortium (MECC) added the game to its digital library in 1974, thousands of students gained access to the program and started playing, even in their leisure time. *Oregon Trail* became a shared experience created by users together. In Illinois, the Programmed Logic for Automatic Teaching Operations (PLATO) network, which was hosted by the University of Illinois, provided a space for users to experiment with communication features such as instant messaging, bulletin boards, and electronic email.[29] These various networking developments (both ARPANET and time-sharing experiments) reveal to us the multiple avenues by which we have arrived at today's digital world. They also remind us that the World Wide Web and the Internet are not the same things.

The World Wide Web has become the dominant communication protocol for individually interfacing on the Internet. However, there were protocols created before and after the Web for personally collecting, storing, accessing, and sharing information on the Internet. One of these programs, for instance, was Gopher. Gopher was created in 1991 at the University of Minnesota, whose mascot is the Golden Gophers. Gopher allowed you to store materials in folders (and subfolders, and sub-subfolders, etc.), which appeared as text on the screen. The information could be shared between computer servers running Gopher, which tended to be academic institutions. In the 1990s, many students, staff, or faculty at universities across the nation became introduced to the Internet in their everyday lives in this way.[30]

Another vehicle for individually accessing the Internet in the 1990s was America Online, or AOL. Before 1989, AOL was Quantum Computer Services. It developed a partnership with three computer corporations, Commodore, Tandy, and Apple, to provide Internet access to their users. By the late 1980s, this amounted to approximately 75,000 people. AOL also wrote its program, Remote Automated Information Manager (RAINMAN), for creating content. In 1989, AOL opened up access to any person with a personal computer and dial-up modem.[31] It became one of three major companies to bring the Internet into people's homes in the 1990s. The line "you've got mail" still resonates with those who lived through this period.[32]

The World Wide Web was the brainchild of Tim Berners-Lee. Berners-Lee had an affinity for math. His parents were mathematicians, and in his autobiography he writes about how his mother and father were part of a team that helped program "the first commercial storied-program computer, the Manchester University 'Mark 1' in the 1950s." Berners-Lee became a physicist but was still interested in computers. In 1980, he took a position at CERN. (CERN was established in 1951 by UNESCO who adopted a resolution to create a European Council for Nuclear Research, which in French is Conseil Européen pour la Recherche Nucléaire. Today it is known as the European Laboratory for Particle Physics.) CERN employed Berners-Lee to consult on computer software.[33]

In hindsight, Berners-Lee's first impressions of CERN provide a window into how and why creating the World Wide Web made sense. First, the tour of the facilities brought him out onto a "catwalk, looking out and over what looked like a large, chaotic factory floor. This vast experimental hall was filled with smaller experiments, obscured by the concrete-block walls between them, hastily built to cut down on the radiation." Computers were not intermingled among the experiments. Instead, there was one control room within which there "were racks and racks of computing hardware, with no lighting except for the glow of the many indicator lamps and dials." Berners-Lee described the movement of the scientists and engineers from their stations to the computer room as a type of "pilgrimage." He explained that "most people at CERN did not have computer terminals in their offices; they had to come to a central facility, such as the terminal room next to the control room, to actually program a computer system." Berners-Lee described the disconnect: "The big challenge for contract programmers was to try to understand the systems both human and computer, that ran this fantastic playground. Most of the crucial information existed only in people's heads."[34]

Berners-Lee needed to figure out a way to remember who was who concerning their technological needs. He began writing a program to keep track of his casual conversations, which often included visuals. He recalled, "informal discussions at CERN would invariably be accompanied by diagrams of circles and arrows scribbled on napkins and envelopes, because it was a natural way to show relationships between people and equipment."[35] Berners-Lee began thinking about how people could access the central computer system with ease and, at the same time, retain their organization structure.

In the mid-1980s, Berners-Lee became aware of the existence of the Internet from a colleague who had worked in the United States. In the United States, various telecommunications companies were experimenting with and expanding the Internet. (In contrast, in Europe, the International Standards Organization was "pursuing a separate set of network protocols" of its design.) Berners-Lee was also familiar with the work of sociologist Theodor H. Nelson, who coined the term "hypertext" in the 1960s to describe nonlinear text. Nelson described hypertext as "nonsequential writing – text that branches and allows choices to the reader, best read at an interactive screen." He argued, "as popularly conceived [hypertext] is a series of text chunks by links which offer the reader different pathways."[36] Nelson also coined the term hypermedia to refer to nonlinear displays of sound, pictures, and various types of graphics. Last, Berners-Lee was acquainted with the work of Apple Computers, which introduced "HyperCard." The HyperCard program allowed nonprogrammers to create pages on a computer that could be grouped in a nonlinear fashion. All you had to do was point and click. All of these factors and ideas influenced Berners-Lee's thinking.

In 1989, Berners-Lee wrote a proposal to CERN for a "web of data that could be processed by machine." He believed that a hypertext database could reveal associations between people that they did not know existed. He asked readers to "imagine making a large three-dimensional model, with people represented by little spheres, and strings between people who have something in common at work." He then asked readers to "imagine picking up the structure and shaking it, until you make some sense of the tangle." The result he argued was one of possibilities: "Perhaps you see tightly knit groups in some places, and in some places weak areas of communication spanned by only a few people." This new "linked information system," he contended, offered the prospect "to see the real structure of the organization in which we work."[37]

At first, nothing happened with Berners-Lee's proposal. The next year he began creating a program on his computer. He called his browser World Wide Web. He created hypertext markup language (HTML) to create pages, which could be written, edited, and read on the browser. He came up with the concept for identifying each page with a unique address, which is called the uniform resource locator (URL). He came up with the protocol for transferring hypertext files, which is called http. A colleague of Berners-Lee got a computer and began writing pages, the two began sharing information first in CERN, and then they connected to the Internet.

While Berners-Lee was creating the World Wide Web, the National Center for Supercomputing Applications at the University of Illinois at Urbana-Champaign (UI) had begun to foster research into alternatives to Gopher. In 1993, a group of UI graduate students designed Mosaic. Unlike Gopher, Mosaic allowed the user to see both text and images at the same time. Berners-Lee met with the students and they discussed how to transform Mosaic into an editable browser. The university made the software available for free, and soon many downloaded the program. In the meantime, Berners-Lee returned to CERN and secured a declaration from it that the Web protocol he had created and the codes would be given to anyone to use. CERN would not ask for royalties. The Web would not become proprietary.

In 1994, a few former members of the working group who created Mosaic struck out on their own. They founded Netscape in Mountain View, California. For a time, Netscape dominated the Web browser market until Microsoft challenged it with the advent of Windows Explorer. In time other companies developed alternate browsers: Apple released Safari in 2003, the founders of Netscape released Firefox in 2005, and Google released Chrome in 2008. In December 1994, Berners-Lee and other like-minded individuals organized a consortium (the World Wide Web Consortium) to provide structure and allow for discussion and agreement on universal protocols for the Web. It continues to provide guidance.[38]

Today, historians use the World Wide Web for a variety of purposes, from a mechanism for teaching to a space to conduct research. When the Web first came on the scene in the early 1990s, "cyber-enthusiasts" hoped this new technology would lead "historians to rethink the ways that they research, write, present, and teach about the past." Another group, "techno-skeptics," promoted proceeding with caution.[39] Because HTML was easy to learn, many historians wrote their web pages in the beginning. However, over time computer software companies developed programs to create pages that were more sophisticated and made it easier to manage large sites. Most historians left computer coding to others or turned to centers, like the Roy Rosenzweig Center for History and New Media (CHNM), to develop applications for collecting, preserving, and presenting history on the Web. Universities turned to companies such as Blackboard Inc. and Instructure (Canvas) to supply learning management systems to use throughout their campuses.

In the beginning, more often than not, digital history projects focused on disseminating resources rather than fostering interaction. For instance, JSTOR (short for journal storage), was created in 1995 to provide university and college libraries with a digital archive of printed scholarly journals. The goal was to create greater access. This also freed each library from the ongoing expenses associated with housing library materials.[40] Most of these materials were considered secondary sources. The site's audience was scholars looking to place their research in conversation with their peers.

The Library of Congress began experimenting with digitalizing primary source materials and making them freely available for K-12 teachers in the early 1990s. At first, the Library of Congress placed these on CD-ROMs, but the rise of the Web offered new possibilities. Titled the American Memory Project, the Library of Congress's gateway to its digital resource proved popular with teachers, scholars, and the public. Within a decade, it placed over eight million items online, which cost $60 million.[41] Today the Library of Congress has merged the American Memory Project with its collections more generally, which can be accessed from its main website.

Creating sites for teaching was among the earliest uses of the Web by historians. In 1994, George Welling at the University of Groningen in the Netherlands created the website "From Revolution to Reconstruction," to "improve" the "computer skills" of students. Together they gathered primary sources, outlines, and other materials that fostered knowledge of US history.[42] Creating teaching sites also fostered institutional collaborations. In 1998, the CHNM at George Mason University and the American Social History Project at the City University of New York's Graduate Center produced "History Matters: The US Survey Course on the Web." They received funding from the W.K. Kellogg Foundation to bring the massive site online ("1,000 primary documents in text, image, audio; an annotated guide to more than 800 websites; model teaching assignments; sample syllabi; and moderated discussions about teaching with leading scholars"). More then a mere repository for materials, it offered visitors essays and other mechanisms for thinking about how to foster skills in historical thinking.[43]

Some historians attempted to use the Web as an experimental space. Edward Ayers and William Thomas published "The Valley of the Shadow: Two Communities in the American Civil War," as a model for nonlinear hypermedia history. The website is a digital archive that allows the user to engage in in-depth historical research (https://valley.lib.virginia.edu). Ayers and Thomas wrote an article "The Difference Slavery Made: A Close Analysis of Two American Communities," to challenge themselves and the historical community to apply digital tools to analyzing and communicating history. In particular, they attempted to write an essay using coded text. Readers can link to the sources (text and images) upon which Ayers and Thomas developed their analyses.

As the Web moved out of its infancy, Daniel J. Cohen explained, historians began to think about the "possibility of using the web not only to present the past but also to collect it."[44] The September 11 Digital Archive is one example of this conversion.[45] It was clear to all that the events on September 11, 2001, was going to be a transformative event in US history (although uncertain of how). Historians also knew that websites were temporary when compared to other print media. Authors abandoned their websites regularly. Also, websites, by design, were malleable. So how could you record people's impressions when they were in rapid motion?

While the events of September 11, 2001, were unique, the idea of collecting born-digital materials was not. The contested presidential election of 2000 had prompted the Library of Congress to work with a nonprofit organization called the Internet Archive to collect snapshots of websites to capture a diversity of opinions about the event as it unfolded. Hence, in 2001, the Internet Archive began "scanning the web just hours after the September 11 attacks." The Library of Congress then collaborated with the Internet Archive and launched a website on October 11, 2001. The goal was to "evaluate, select, collect, catalog, provide access to, and preserve digital materials for future generations." Within two months, the Library of Congress and Internet Archive had collected "nearly 30,000 websites and five terabytes of information."

The CHNM also set about creating a program to collect materials. In particular, the goal was to "collect – directly from their owners – those digital materials not available on the public Web; artifacts like email, digital photographs, word processing documents, and personal narratives." Three years later, CHNM had collected "more then 150,000 digital objects relating to the terrorist attacks, including more than 35,000 personal narratives and 20,000 digital images." To ensure the project's long-term sustainability, CHNM worked with the Library of Congress in 2003 to have the library formally acquire the September 11 Digital Archive.[46]

While the September 11 Digital Archive was hugely successful in its mission, other attempts to collect history online were not. In recounting their experience creating the Hurricane Digital Memory Bank in 2005, Sheila Brennan and T. Mills Kelly explained how this differed from creating the September 11 Digital Archive.

Figure 7.2 Acquiring the September 11 Digital Archive was a milestone in the history of the Library of Congress. *Source:* Jennifer Koslow.

In both cases, CHNM had designed websites that allowed "diverse audiences to be active participants in saving and shaping their own history." However, in the case of the hurricanes, the interface was relatively cumbersome. For instance, the website did not allow people to upload a batch of photographs. Moreover, many people were not ready to share their personal stories. Some people had lost trust in institutions following the disaster. Other survivors were still processing what had happened to them.[47] Ten years later, Sheila Brennan wrote about how the project allowed the creation of a unique collection. Displaced persons, and the communities who took them in, contributed in various ways to the project. Despite its limitations, the site was successful in creating a home for materials upon which scholars, journalists, and participants can draw their conclusions about the historical significance of Hurricanes Rita and Katrina.[48]

These early adventures into collecting, preserving, and interpreting history on the Web with and for public audiences provided historians with models. As the Web developed so has historians' use of it to teach, research, and have conversations with other scholars and the public about history. Some of this occurs behind paywalls, such as access to the rich research databases titled America's Historical Newspapers, 1690–1922, and ProQuest Congressional Publications. Some of it happens in public, such as the National Archives and the Library of Congress. In either case, historians continue to be inspired to use digital tools.

Theory

Daniel J. Cohen has argued that historians need to move from thinking about the Web as a noun to a verb. "Much of the problem here is conceptual," Cohen explains, "from the beginning of the Web historians have largely discussed *nouns* such as Web pages and websites, rather than verbs such as searching, sorting, gathering, and communicating." The question for historians is how can we use this technology as a method of communication and interaction rather than solely as a place of dissemination of information.[49]

In this section, we will examine how digital media have opportunities for practicing history with the public as well as limitations. To be able to think about why and how to use digital media, there must be some discussion about digital literacy. Hence, this section does provide some information about terms and digital tools. Still, students need to be aware that software and tools change rapidly. As a result, this is not a "how-to" guide. Instead, this is a conversation about how to think about the utility of digital tools for dissemination of, as well as interaction with, historical materials.

The first step for public historians to think about the benefits and drawbacks of digital media for collecting, preserving, and interpreting history with and for general audiences is to develop their digital literacy skills. Literacy typically refers to the ability to read and write. Digital literacy refers to a person's ability to use digital technology to create, communicate, and evaluate information. While the vocabulary of digital technology changes over time, the core concept remains the same. Literacy is the ability to "read" a particular set of knowledge.

Two words are essential to developing one's digital literacy: hypermedia and hypertext. Hypermedia refers to nonlinear displays of sound, pictures, and animation. Hypertext, a term coined by Theodor H. Nelson, refers to nonlinear displays of text. Hyperlinks connect ideas from one source of hypermedia or hypertext to another. Unlike a book, which traditionally includes text that is meant to be read in one sequential direction, hypermedia and hypertext allow the reader to choose their pathway through the material. Although the World Wide Web is not the only mechanism that allows a person to create, view, and read hypermedia and hypertext, it has become dominant.

Knowing how to read a web page is useful for developing digital literacy skills. A browser is software by which a web page is displayed. Examples of browsers in 2020 are Chrome, Firefox, Microsoft Edge, and Safari. These have not always been the dominant browsers, and in 20 years, there will probably be others. Browsers read HTML, which stands for hypertext markup language. HTML is a computer language that allows you to display text and images together in an interactive manner. (If you are curious to see what this looks like choose "view source" in your Web browser. An example of markup coding looks like this: **bold**.)

Every web page has a specific address. This is called the URL. The ability to decipher a URL is important because the Web address provides a wealth of information about a web page. Every URL is divided into a few basic parts. The first is protocol. What you will see on the Web is "http." Http stands for hypertext transfer protocol. Http is how computer servers communicate with Web browsers. The second part of an URL is the computer domain. This is where the service is located. The third part of the URL is the suffix. This tells you what type of organization is hosting the website. The most common hosts are a government (.gov), nonprofit organizations (.org), educational institutions (.edu), commercial organizations (.com), and networks (.net). The fourth part of a URL is typically a directory or subdirectory, which tells you where on the website the information you are accessing is stored.

The last aspect of the URL is the name of the file you are viewing. Filenames can end in several different kinds of suffixes. The most common are .html or .htm. You might also see .wav or .mp3, which stands for a sound file, .mov, which stands for a movie file, .php, which is a computer scripting language that can be read by a browser, and .exe, which is an executable program. If you are looking at the home page of a website, the name of the file might be hidden because it is index.

html or index.htm. Browsers omit this name to make the home page URL look more elegant.

If you happen to look at an image on the Web, you will see that it ends in either "jpg," "gif," or "png." These are all different file formats for a digital picture or graphic that a browser can read. You might also hear about "tiffs." A tiff is a file format that stores digital information at the highest quality. Archivists often use them for storage purposes. However, this also means that tiffs are large files. Consequently, tiffs are not a file format that can be read by a browser. (Although they are sometimes available for download.) In addition to familiarizing yourself with the different image suffixes, it is also useful to understand DPI, which stands for dots per inch. The higher the DPI means that the image contains more digital information. Most images can be seen reasonably well on a Web browser at a resolution of 75 DPI. However, if the author of the Web page wanted to print that same image at that same resolution in a book, it would be blurry. Traditional books need an image to be at least 300 DPI if not higher.

In addition to familiarizing yourself with the components of a URL, it is also important to understand what other types of digital media are available for engaging with and producing history. For instance, social media is a term applied to Web-based digital instruments of communication that allow for two-way interaction. Facebook, Twitter, Snapchat, and Instagram are all examples of social media. These are examples of proprietary software programs. In 2020, you do not have to pay to use them in the traditional sense. Instead, you pay by giving up a portion of your privacy.

Despite their limitations, proprietary social media platforms are extremely popular for fostering community engagement. Museums expect that visitors will show up with smartphones in their pockets and meld their virtual and real experiences into one. Where flash photography was forbidden, museums increasingly create spaces for people to take images of themselves and objects together. The idea of dividing visitors into digital or non-digital users is no longer an either or for museums; almost all visitors participate in both technological and non-technological opportunities to engage with material culture. While the jury is still out on whether taking a selfie at a museum is emotionally or intellectually transformative, it is clear that visitors desire space to join in these types of activities.[50]

Sometimes visitors use social media in unexpected ways. For instance, social media can be used to stage protests, such as the anti-opioid flash mob that appeared in 2018 at the Temple of Dendur in the Metropolitan Museum of Art in New York City. Its organizer, Nan Goldin, sought to draw attention to the influence of the Sackler family at the museum (the Sacklers owned Purdue Pharma).[51]

Wikis are another type of social media. A Wiki is a collaborative content management system. It allows a group of people to create, edit, and publish a web page or website. Wikipedia is an example of a very popular wiki. Similarly, a blog allows you to easily be the editor and publisher of a web page/website. (Examples of blogging programs available for free are Blogger and WordPress.) If you allow comments on your blog, you allow for interaction. Similarly, podcasting (downloadable audio recording) and vodcasting (downloadable video recording) enable individuals to create content and share it on the Internet.

Digital history scholars working in archives and museums have created open-source, free software to foster community engagement. Omeka, for instance, has become a standard in the field of public history. Described as a "next-generation web publishing platform for museums, historical societies, scholars, enthusiasts, and educators," Omeka facilitates the collection, preservation, and interpretation of history with and for public audiences. The program is designed to easily upload images, organize them into collections, and create Web exhibits.[52]

Crowdsourcing is another digital approach. It is a method for problem-solving. Businesses originally conceived of crowdsourcing as a means to connect with consumers and clients. The idea was to democratize innovation. Crowdsourcing can have various applications in history. For instance, the National Archives seeks "citizen archivists" to participate in transcription projects that would take any single individual a lifetime.[53]

These are all digital tools that can be adapted for collecting, preserving, and interpreting history with and for public audiences. Also, there are digital tools designed for historical research. There are citation management programs, such as Zotero and RefWorks, that allow scholars to keep track of their notes electronically. Note-taking, keeping track of where you obtained information and ideas on how you might use it, is not something new. However, these programs allow you to create links between notes to create digital relationships.

Museums also employ specialized programs to digitally manage their materials. For instance, PastPerfect is an industry standard. Besides its internal usage, the software allows museums to make their collections visible to the public. This allows multiple audiences to investigate material culture even if they cannot visit the museum in person. It also allows visitors to view materials not on public display. Revealing what was once hidden sometimes proves challenging for museums because it can raise issues about the true ownership of material culture. Questions about repatriation and compensation similar to those discussed in Chapter 3 on preserving historic sites and spaces have arisen within a museum context.[54]

Knowing about all of these different digital tools is important. Museums and historic sites increasingly use websites and social media to communicate with their audiences. Institutions need to consider how these different digital mechanisms can contribute to their institution's mission. Sometimes it might be to relay information about upcoming events. Sometimes it might be to gather information about interest. Either way, using social media is an investment of resources. Knowing the purpose of a connection can help public historians choose the best tool for their goals.

There are benefits and drawbacks to digitizing historical documents and artifacts. There are also pros and cons of using digital tools to engage with public audiences. It is the job of the public historian to weigh the advantages and disadvantages of collecting, preserving, and interpreting history digitally with and for general audiences.

A primary reason to digitize a document or artifact is the fragility of the original. Several different factors cause instability. Age, while it can be a consideration, is not the deciding one. Sometimes older objects are made from exceptionally durable materials. Paper is a great example. Medieval manuscripts are old, but because most were produced on vellum (also known as parchment), which was made in part from animal skin, they are incredibly stable. In the eighteenth century, people created a new papermaking process that used cotton and linen as its main ingredients. Called "rag paper," this new invention allowed for mass production even further. At the end of the nineteenth century, people replaced cotton with wood pulp. While this decreased the expense of paper production, it came at an archival cost. The high level of acidity in wood pulp translated into brittle paper. The result is that if you look at a newspaper from 1920, it is probably more fragile than one produced in 1820.

Other environmental dynamics besides chemical composition cause objects and texts to become vulnerable. Heat, humidity, and moisture can all cause deterioration (especially mold). These same conditions might create an attractive environment for insects. These are all excellent reasons to digitize material; digitization can preserve the material.

Another benefit to digitization is that it can increase access to the material. Archives are not always easy to reach. They are typically open during weekday business hours, which can prove difficult to those who do not have flexible schedules. Last, not everyone has an archive in their backyard. What a person might want to see could be several hours away. The beauty of digitizing is that people can look at the material when they want to access it. For instance, you can listen to podcasts or watch vodcasts on your own time. Videos allow you to experience a historical site, which may not be possible for many people. Moreover, if it is archival footage, you can visit a place that no longer exists.

A final benefit to digitization is that it can allow someone to look at the material in a new way. Zoom features can let you see details that might otherwise be hidden to the naked eye. If desired, enhancing visibility is a feature that needs to be forethought in creating a digitized image.

While equipment needs always change, it is useful to be aware of the basics. There are several options available for creating digital images. Persons might use a digital camera to take photographs at an archive for their personal use. In documenting a parade or other temporary event, a public historian might take digital pictures to be used in either an archive or exhibit. Libraries and archives invest in equipment that is more substantial: flatbed and other types of professional scanners. Scanners can range in price from under $100 to over $40,000 depending on what they will be used for and the quality of the image it can produce.

Digitizing images and then turning them into something of value for the public takes more than pressing a button. Public historians engaged in digital projects need to think about how to prioritize activities. It takes equipment, server space, time, and knowledge of how to write metadata. Metadata (information attached to an archival record) involves more than adding a name and a date to an image. It consists in being able to identify concepts and terms. Public historians have to think about how people might relate to the image and for what possible purposes it might be used. For example, a photograph of a gathering on the National Mall in Washington DC would be more useful to people if it was identified with a particular topic (protest march [if so what topic], folk festival, July 4 celebration, etc.). Before someone can catalog and describe artifacts and documents, they need to have done reading in relevant secondary sources to be able to make meaning of those materials. Thus, a disadvantage is that digitizing takes time and skill, to which an institution may or may not be able to devote resources.

Another disadvantage to digital media is that it may not reach all audiences equally. Not everyone has high-speed Internet access. Others might have physical disabilities for which digital media are unprepared to accommodate. Public historians need to be conscious of these differences and attentive to digital disadvantages in creating accessibility.

This discussion has focused on translating the physical into the virtual, but we need to also talk about materials that are born digital. Historians can use existing software and leverage it for their own needs. Wikis, blogs, and tweets function as mechanisms for fostering exchange. They can also be used to capture history. Another piece of software that can be used is a form. These can be added to websites for collecting stories. They are malleable, so they can be used to protect identities and to monitor authenticity. Forms can be used to allow the public to connect their personal stories with scholarship. They can also be used to give non-scholars a voice in producing history for public audiences. Another interactive tool is a poll builder, which allows you to ask your audience for feedback.

In sum, there is a myriad of advantages to digitizing material. It can increase accessibility. Using digital tools can also increase interactivity. At the same time, the disadvantages are that it can be costly. Technology can become obsolete. All technologies have life spans. It takes constant vigilance to keep abreast of changes in best practices for digitizing material and addressing born-digital materials. Last, sustainability is a significant issue. Digital projects need guidance both in their original conception and how to maintain them in perpetuity. Rosenzweig and Thelen identified this as "stewardship." Public historians can act as stewards, keeping up-to-date on changes in best practices and attempting to use digital medial to its best advantages.

Practice

1) Review two different online exhibits of history for (i) their ability to communicate an historical argument effectively on the home page and (ii) their ability to support that argument by the evidence they supply within their exhibit. (An exhibit is more than one web page. The site you review should explicitly identify itself as an exhibit.)

2) Take a historical speech and decide which words or phrases you would turn into hyperlinks. Explain your logic.

3) Follow a historian or a historical organization (the American Historical Association's Twitter handle is @AHAhistorians) on Twitter for at least a week. In what ways is Twitter useful or not for prompting conversations about history?

4) Visit a museum or historic site that also has a virtual exhibit of its materials or site. Compare and contrast your in person experience with your virtual one.

5) Work with a partner(s) to create a crowdsourcing project (for instance, finding all the monuments on campus, taking digital pictures, and putting them on a Wiki.)

6) Create a piece of digital history related to your family's history (using Omeka, WordPress, or Weebly, or another online tool.) The goal is to create a mini-exhibit that puts your family's history (or an aspect of it) into a historical context. You will need to do some digging in the archives to help you contextualize your family's history. For instance, if a relative passed through Ellis Island, use the passenger search function provided by the Statue of Liberty Ellis Island Foundation at www.libertyellisfoundation.org/passenger to see what ship they arrived on and whether they came alone or with family members. Look at a newspaper around the dates of their arrival to see what issues were being discussed. Find a secondary source that will help you understand the time and place your relatives arrived. If you need help, speak with your instructor or a librarian. Digitize your materials (photographs, 3D objects, textiles, etc.), create metadata for the objects you digitize, and then create a public presentation or exhibit of the materials.

Further Resources

- Beranek, Leon. "Roots of the Internet: A Personal History." *Massachusetts Historical Review* 2 (2000): 55–75.
- Berners-Lee, Tim. *Weaving the Web: The Original Design and Ultimate Destiny of the World Wide Web by its Inventor.* San Francisco, CA: Harper, 1999.
- Brennan, Sheila A., and T. Mills Kelly. "Why Collecting History Online is Web 1.5." (March 2009). Roy Rosenzweig Center for History and New Media. https://rrchnm.org/essay/why-collecting-history-online-is-web-1-5.
- Brennan, Sheila. "10 Years After Katrina, the Enduring Value of the Hurricane Digital Memory Bank," Roy Rosenzweig Center for History and New Media, https://rrchnm.org/news/10-after-katrina-the-enduring-value-of-the-hurricane-digital-memory-bank.
- Bush, Vannevar. "As We May Think." *The Atlantic.* www.theatlantic.com/magazine/archive/1945/07/as-we-may-think/303881.
- Ceruzzi, Paul E. *Computing: A Concise History.* Cambridge, MA: The MIT Press, 2012.
- Cohen, Daniel J. "History and the Second Decade of the Web." *Rethinking History* 8, no.2, (2004): 293–301. Roy Rosenzweig Center for History and New Media, https://rrchnm.org/essay/history-and-the-second-decade-of-the-web.
- Cohen, Daniel J., and Roy Rosenzweig. *Digital History: A Guide to Gathering, Preserving, and Presenting the Past on the Web.* Philadelphia, PA: University of Pennsylvania Press, 2006.
- Frana, Philip L. "Before the Web There Was Gopher." *IEEE Annals of the History of Computing* 26, no. 1 (January–March 2004): 20–27.
- Giannini, Tula, and Jonathan P. Bowen, eds. *Museums and Digital Culture: New Perspectives and Research.* Cham, Switzerland: Springer, 2019.
- Landow, George. *Hypertext: The Convergence of Contemporary Critical Theory and Technology.* Baltimore, MA: Johns Hopkins Press, 1992.
- Lukasik, Stephen. "Why the Arpanet Was Built." *IEEE Annals of the History of Computing* 33, no. 3 (March 2011): 10.
- Rankin, Joy Lisi. *A People's History of Computing in the United States.* Cambridge, MA: Harvard University Press, 2018.

References

1 Paul E. Ceruzzi, *Computing: A Concise History* (Cambridge, MA: The MIT Press, 2012): chap. 2.

2 David Alan Grier, "From the Editor's Desk," *IEEE Annals of the History of Computing* 26, no. 3 (July–September 2004): 2.

3 "Programming the ENIAC," Columbia University Computing History, www. columbia.edu/cu/computinghistory/eniac.html.
4 T.R. Kennedy Jr. "Electronic Computer Flashes Answers, May Speed Engineering," *New York Times*, February 15, 1946.
5 Ibid.
6 Ibid.
7 Rafal Ciolcosz, "The ILLIAC Computers: Product and Source of Innovation (and Controversy)," in *Engine of Illinois Innovation*, ed. Frederick E. Hoxie (Urbana, IL: University of Illinois Press, 2017): 197.
8 Robert P. Swierenga, "Computers and American history: The Impact of the 'New' Generation," *The Journal of American History* 60, no. 4 (March 1974): 1047.
9 Ibid., 1048.
10 Jerome M. Clubb and Howard Allen, "Computers and Historical Studies," *The Journal of American History* 54, no. 3 (December 1967): 602.
11 Claudia Goldin, "Cliometrics and the Nobel," *Journal of Economic Perspectives* 9, no. 2 (Spring 1995): 191.
12 Swierenga, "Computers and American History," 1065.
13 Vannevar Bush, "As We May Think," *The Atlantic*, www.theatlantic.com/ magazine/archive/1945/07/as-we-may-think/303881.
14 Leon Beranek, "Roots of the Internet: A Personal History," *Massachusetts Historical Review* 2 (2000): 57.
15 Ibid., 59.
16 Stephen Lukasik, "Why the Arpanet Was Built," *IEEE Annals of the History of Computing* 33, no. 3 (March 2011): 10.
17 Beranek, "Roots of the Internet," 63.
18 Ibid., 63.
19 Ibid., 66.
20 Ibid., 62.
21 Ibid., 70.
22 "40 Years Later, Looking Back at the Internet's Birth," www.npr.org/templates/ story/story.php?storyId=114376728.
23 Beranek, "Roots of the Internet," 72.
24 Charles Severance, "Vint Cerf: A Brief History of Packets," *Computer* 45, no. 12 (December 2012): 12.
25 Vinton Cerf and Robert Kahn, "A Protocol for Packet Network Intercommunication," *IEEE Transactions on Communications* 22, no. 5 (May 1974): 637.
26 Vinton Cerf, Yogen Dalal, and Carl Sunshine, "Specification of Internet Transmission Control Program," Internet Engineering Task Force, December 1974, https://tools.ietf.org/html/rfc675.
27 Beranek, "Roots of the Internet," 72.

28 Joy Lisi Rankin, *A People's History of Computing in the United States* (Cambridge, MA: Harvard University Press, 2018), 1–5, and chaps. 1 and 2.

29 Ibid., chaps. 5 and 7.

30 Philip L. Frana, "Before the Web There Was Gopher," *IEEE Annals of the History of Computing* 26, no. 1 (January–March 2004): 20–27.

31 Hector Postigo, "Emerging Sources of Labor on the Internet: The Case of America Online Volunteers," *IRSH* 48 (2003): 206–207.

32 David Gelles," Looking Beyond Troubled Past for Profits," *New York Times*, May 13, 2015.

33 Tim Berners-Lee, *Weaving the Web: The Original Design and Ultimate Destiny of the World Wide Web by its Inventor* (San Francisco, CA: Harper, 1999): 3–4.

34 Ibid., 8–9.

35 Ibid., 9.

36 Theodor H. Nelson quoted in George Landow, *Hypertext: The Convergence of Contemporary Critical Theory and Technology* (Baltimore, MD: Johns Hopkins Press, 1992): 3.

37 Berners-Lee, *Weaving the Web*, 21.

38 "W3C, Help and FAQ," World Wide Web Consortium (W3C), www.w3.org/Help.

39 Daniel J. Cohen and Roy Rosenzweig, *Digital History: A Guide to Gathering, Preserving, and Presenting the Past on the Web* (Philadelphia, PA: University of Pennsylvania Press, 2006), 1–2.

40 "JSTOR: Mission and History," https://about.jstor.org/mission-history.

41 Cohen and Rosenzweig, *Digital History*, 26; "Digital Collections," Library of Congress, www.loc.gov/collections.

42 Cohen and Rosenzweig, *Digital History*, 19; "American History: From Revolution to Reconstruction and Beyond," www.let.rug.nl/usa/.

43 Cohen and Rosenzweig, *Digital History*, 46–47; "The U.S. Survey Course on the Web," History Matters, http://historymatters.gmu.edu.

44 Daniel J. Cohen, "History and the Second Decade of the Web," *Rethinking History* 8, no.2, (2004): 293–301, Roy Rosenzweig Center for History and New Media, https://rrchnm.org/essay/history-and-the-second-decade-of-the-web.

45 "Saving the Histories of September 11, 2001," The September 11 Digital Archive, http://911digitalarchive.org.

46 Cohen and Rosenzweig, *Digital History*, 184–187.

47 Sheila A. Brennan and T. Mills Kelly, "Why Collecting History Online is Web 1.5," (March 2009), Roy Rosenzweig Center for History and New Media, https://rrchnm.org/essay/why-collecting-history-online-is-web-1-5.

48 Sheila Brennan, "10 Years After Katrina, The Enduring Value of the Hurricane Digital Memory Bank," Roy Rosenzweig Center for History and New Media, https://rrchnm.org/news/10-after-katrina-the-enduring-value-of-the-hurricane-digital-memory-bank.

49 Daniel J. Cohen, "History and the Second Decade of the Web," *Rethinking History* 8, no.2, (2004): 293–301, Roy Rosenzweig Center for History and New Media, https://rrchnm.org/essay/history-and-the-second-decade-of-the-web.

50 Tula Giannini and Jonathan P. Bowen, " Museums, Art, Identity, and the Digital Ecosystem: A Paradigm Shift," in *Museums and Digital Culture: New Perspectives and Research*, eds. Tula Giannini and Jonathan P. Bowen (Cambridge, UK: Springer, 2019), 64 and 88.

51 Ibid.

52 "Omeka," Roy Rosenzweig Center for History and New Media, https://rrchnm.org/omekaplatform.

53 "Citizen Archivist Dashboard," National Archives, www.archives.gov/citizen-archivist/registerandgetstarted.

54 Tula Giannini, "Contested Space: Activism and Protest," in *Museums and Digital Culture*, 101–102.

8

Practicing Ethical Public History

Public engagement with history at sites, museums, and archives continues to increase in the twenty-first century. In general, the public trusts cultural institutions to enhance their historical knowledge but is sometimes quite skeptical about the choices Public Historians make in presenting the past. This chapter investigates how Public Historians can practice responsible conduct of research and creativity when they are collecting, preserving, and interpreting history with and for public audiences.

According to the American Historical Association's *Statement on Standards of Professional Conduct*, "by practicing their craft with integrity, historians acquire a reputation for trustworthiness that is arguably their single most precious professional asset."[1] The issue of trust is essential for Public Historians when they strive to share authority and inquiry with public audiences. These concepts are fundamental to a Public Historians' ability to make history meaningful to general audiences.[2] Sharing authority also raises complicated issues of how to realize sharing responsibility without abdicating accountability. Sharing authority and inquiry takes on various meanings depending upon the situation. The National Council on Public History's *Code of Ethics* offers Public Historians a means to think about their varied responsibilities to the public, employers or clients, the profession and colleagues, and themselves.[3] Integrity, independence, respect, and self-reflection all play a role in the professionalism of Public Historians.

Through this chapter, you will learn about the variety of ethical issues that arise in attempting to share authority and inquiry in museums, archives, and historic sites. These are the most common locales of employment for Public Historians. Each field has its own set of ethics upon which it relies and which comes with its own set of histories. Thus, you will learn about best practices as crafted and defined by the leading professional organizations whose members work in these types of institutions: the American Alliance of Museums, the International

Public History: An Introduction from Theory to Application, First Edition. Jennifer Lisa Koslow.
© 2021 by John Wiley & Sons, Inc. Published 2021 by John Wiley & Sons, Inc.

Council of Museums, the Society for American Archivists, the National Alliance of Preservation Commissions, and the Oral History Association.

This chapter differs from others in the book in that the history of the development of ethical codes is directly related to theory. In some cases, the adoption of an ethical code is quite recent. Therefore, dividing the two into separate sections on history and theory would only prove redundant. Instead, history and theory are presented together in this chapter. Within this streamlined approach, this section of the chapter covers four topics: museums, archives, historic preservation, and oral history. The reason for this separation is that each of these areas has a distinct code of ethics and/or a statement of best practices. A Public Historian needs to be aware of and reference all codes that are related to the work they do in addition to that of the historical profession.

History and Theory

Tereza Cristina Scheiner, the director of the School of Museology, Federal University of the State of Rio de Janeiro (UNIRIO) in Brazil, describes the diversity of roles museums play in our current society:

> The museum is today, among other things, a communication agency and a temple for cultural consumption; a political arena for special interest groups and a place for discovery; an intellectual ground for research and for the manifestation of the human genius.[4]

As the American Alliance of Museums states, the "root value" common to all museums is their "commitment to serving people, both present and future generations."[5] It is because museums are "grounded in the tradition of public service" and function as "public trusts" that adherence to professional ethics are critical.[6]

Everyday ethics – distinguishing between right and wrong – is not necessarily the same thing as professional ethics. As respected museologist Gary Edson explains, professional ethics is about learned activities, not intuition.[7] Hence, he suggests that the best method for preparing museum workers is to provide them with a set of principles, which they can then apply to the myriad of sticky situations they will face working in the field. Museum workers need to know how to formulate a plan.

Museum workers have been talking about the issue of ethics for a long time. In 1925, the American Association of Museums (now the American Alliance of Museums, AAM) adopted a *Code of Ethics for Museum Workers*.[8] It guided museum workers for over 50 years. However, as the profession changed in the late twentieth century so did professional ethics. As Kenneth Hudson – an influential twentieth-century museologist – articulated in 1998, "the most fundamental change that has affected museums during the [past] half century . . . is the now almost universal conviction that they exist to serve the public." He explained the contrast:

> The old-style museum felt itself under no such obligation. It existed, it had a building, it had collections and a staff to look after them. It was reasonably adequately financed, and its visitors, usually not numerous, came to look, to wonder and to admire what was set before them.

The crucial difference, Hudson argued, was that visitors in there "were in no sense partners in the enterprise. The museum's prime responsibility was to its collections, not its visitors." As a consequence of these developments, the *Code of Ethics* needed to be revised.[9]

The AAM began to rewrite its Code in 1987 and completed the process in 1993. Seven years later, in 2000, it was amended again.[10] The core notion that "the commitment to serving people, both present and future generations" has remained central to the document. In its revised iteration the Code also captured new expectations about the role of a museum in a pluralistic society.[11] The Code speaks to the specific topics of governance, collections, and programs. The AAM also recommends that individual nonprofit museums that are members of AAM adopt an institutional code of ethics following the values outlined in AAM's document.

Museum workers in the United States were not alone in codifying their professional activities and attitudes. Codes were adopted in New Zealand in 1977, Canada and Israel in 1979, Australia in 1982, and Great Britain in 1983.[12] In 1986, the International Council of Museums (ICOM) – a public interest organization formed in 1946 by and for museum professionals around the world – produced a Code that has been subsequently adopted by several different nations.[13] It "presents a minimum standard for museums" in a global context.

There are eight basic principles to ICOM's *Code of Ethics for Museums*, which all museum professionals should be cognizant of in their work (FYI: there are additional codes of ethics which the professional societies of conservators and registrars have also adopted related to their specific professions):[14]

1) "Museums preserve, interpret and promote the natural and cultural inheritance of humanity." In actualizing this principle, ICOM notes that in taking on this responsibility the governing body of a museum is accountable for seeing that the "human, physical and financial resources" are "made available for that purpose."
2) "Museums that maintain collections hold them in trust for the benefit of society and its development." In donning stewardship for the public, ICOM notes that museums "have a special position in law and are protected by international legislation." In respecting the law, museum workers need to consider

issues of "rightful ownership, permanence, documentation, accessibility, and responsible disposal."

3) "Museums hold primary evidence for establishing and furthering knowledge."
4) "Museums provide opportunities for the appreciation, understanding and management of the natural and cultural heritage." In elaborating on this code, ICOM directs museum workers to think about their role as educators in partnership with the communities they serve.
5) "Museums hold resources that provide opportunities for other public services and benefits." As this code suggests, museum workers should not be discouraged from collaborating with other civic organizations. However, ICOM points out that these engagements "should be organized in such a way that they do not compromise the museum's stated mission."
6) "Museums work in close collaboration with the communities from which their collections originate as well as those they serve." As ICOM makes clear, museum workers need to be mindful of the fact that material culture often holds definite meanings for those communities from which the artifacts were derived. The museum needs to be responsive to these ideas in its policies.
7) "Museums operate in a legal manner." Museum workers need to consider all levels of law: local, national, and international, in their actions and policies.
8) "Museums operate in a professional manner."

These principles provide museum workers with a basic framework within which to consider specific questions.

In the late twentieth century, several special issues about cultural property arose. Some questions were related to the cultural heritage of Native peoples and antiquities. Other issues were related to art that was acquired during the Holocaust. Determining to whom cultural capital belongs is no easy question. For instance, should the British Museum give back the Elgin Marbles?

While serving as the British ambassador to the Ottoman Empire in the early nineteenth century, Thomas Bruce, the Earl of Elgin, believed that the sculptures and friezes that adorned the Parthenon Temple in Athens, Greece, were in jeopardy. It had suffered numerous mishaps over the centuries, including suffering significant structural damage in the late seventeenth century during a bombing. At the turn of the nineteenth century, tourists and looters were continually taking pieces. Hence, Elgin made an agreement with the Turks, who controlled the territory, to remove the remaining sculptures and send them to the British Museum in London, where they have remained ever since. In the late twentieth century, the Greek government formally contested the notion that the Turks, as occupiers, ever had the authority to approve the removal of these cultural objects and began seeking their repatriation. The British government disagrees. The issue remains a point of contention.

Answering the question of the Elgin Marbles and similar questions elicits impassioned debate. There are also legal issues that need to be considered. The Hague Convention for the Protection of Cultural Property in the Event of Armed Conflict, 1954, and subsequent UNESCO Conventions regarding Cultural Property and The Native American Graves Protection and Repatriation Act (NAGPRA), 1990, assist in weighing different claims in the twenty-first century.

In the aftermath of extensive aerial bombing during World War II, there was international support to adopt a treaty designed to protect the world's cultural heritage. The result was the 1954 Hague Convention for the Protection of Cultural Property in the Event of Armed Conflict. In signing the treaty, member states agreed that "damage to cultural property belonging to any people whatsoever means damage to the cultural heritage of all mankind, since each people makes its contribution to the culture of the world." The treaty referenced previous Conventions of the Hague that occurred before World War I (1899 and 1907) and the Washington Pact of April 15, 1935, as precedents for protecting cultural property. Clauses within these previous pacts discussed respecting the integrity of cultural property. Many no longer supported the idea that cultural capital could be taken as part of the "spoils of war." The 1954 treaty was different from these previous conventions in that it focused solely on cultural property.[15]

However, the nature of armed conflicts changed again in the postwar period. A second protocol to the Convention was added in 1999 in reaction to the "acts of barbarism committed against cultural heritage during numerous conflicts that took place at the end of the 1980s and the beginning of the 1990s." This protocol addressed intrastate conflicts. In particular, attempts by one group to destroy the cultural heritage of another "with the intent of humiliating the target group by taking away its past, culture, and heritage."[16] When conflict arises, and in anticipation of battle, member states of the United Nations agree to use these treaties to respect and protect cultural property.

In the United States, the NAGPRA of 1990 was born out of Native American activism in the 1970s and 1980s.[17] The Act recognized ownership rights of Native peoples of cultural materials that had been excavated or discovered on federal and tribal land. The law required federal agencies and museums to make an inventory of their relevant holdings, provide a summary, and work with Indian tribes and Native Hawaiian organizations to return items. Native Americans, through their governing bodies, could also relinquish control over cultural properties if they so desired. Since the law's passage, more than 50,000 sets of human remains, 1.4 million funerary objects, and 14,000 cultural items have been returned to Native peoples.[18]

While the law itself seems simple, anthropologists, archaeologists, historians, and tribal leaders attest to the complicated nature of complying with the law. Consultations with Native American tribes do not necessarily yield an agreement on what and how cultural artifacts can and should be repatriated.[19] Different tribes have different financial resources to aid in the process. Divisions within tribes also shape Native peoples experiences with NAGPRA.[20] Last, while nothing in the law specifically refers to repatriation as a "healing" process, this has been one unexpected result. While not universal, for some Native Americans repatriation provides some closure to the wrongs of the past.[21]

International and federal law provide museum workers with guidance over questions of ownership and dispossession of cultural property. However, what is legal is not always the same as what is ethical. One way forward is to consider Professor of Philosophy Karen J. Warren's suggestions. Instead of framing the debate about "possession," she suggests we focus on stewardship. Instead of attempting to create hierarchies of competing interests, we could generate consensus over materials that cannot be "owned."[22] There is no single answer for twenty-first-century museum workers. They need to be aware of the various possible routes to anticipate and address these types of issues as they arise.

Archives are not just spaces for historians. Archives are created to serve communities in the present in multiple ways. Record keeping is paramount in a democracy; archival records provide evidence and foster accountability. Issues of electronic management of records, censorship, whistleblowing, and intellectual property are more than practical problems. These matters provoke ethical questions for archivists. Many of the issues for museum professionals at large also hold for archivists and, hence, archivists should be familiar with the ICOM Code.

However, the Society of American Archivists (SAA) developed its own *Code of Ethics* in 2005 and updated it in 2012. The organization's governing body also adopted a statement of *Core Values of Archivists* in 2011. These two documents help archivists develop a sense of what they should "believe" about their professional role and how they should behave in that role.[23]

The question of trust is as vital for archivists as it is for museum workers. As the SAA explains, "the behaviors and characteristics outlined in this Code of Ethics should serve as aspirational principles for an archivist to consider as they strive to create trusted archival institutions." Trust is also one of the seven areas the SAA specifically identified as a critical concern. The other six areas are professional relationships, judgment, authenticity, security and protection, and access and use. Within these areas, the SAA Code uses the verbs to cooperate, collaborate, document, ensure, protect, recognize, encourage, and promote to describe an archivist's relationship to materials and society. The SAA reminds archivists that they are duty-bound to act as "advocates for documentary collections and cultural objects under their care." At the same time, archivists also must "ensure that those materials entrusted to their care will be accessible over time as evidence of human activity and social organization." Sometimes those two charges can conflict. The Code is offered to help archivists "navigate the complex situations and issues that can arise in the course of their work."[24]

Archivists can use these principles to guide their work in public and private sector jobs, but sometimes it is not very easy to apply these tenets. Take, for instance, the famous case of the Thurgood Marshall papers. Supreme Court Justice Marshall decided to donate his papers to the Library of Congress upon his death. He desired immediate public access to the materials and signed a deed of gift agreement with the Library of Congress that indicated as such. The agreement stated: "Thereafter the collection shall be made available to the public at the discretion of the Library." It also noted that the papers should be open to "researchers or scholars engaged in serious research." Among the first to ask to see the papers were journalists, which added to the controversy.[25]

In 1993, when the Library of Congress opened the papers to the public, Chief Justice William Rehnquist and some members of Marshall's family raised objections. Rehnquist wrote a letter to the Librarian of Congress describing the Library's decision to provide immediate and unrestricted access to the materials as "bad judgment." He argued that the immediate opening of the papers to the public hindered the ability of the US Supreme Court to function. He claimed it threatened "the Court's long tradition of confidentiality in its deliberations." He intimated that no other justices would leave their papers to the Library of Congress if the policy remained unchanged. The case did not go to court, but the issue of the archivist's choice to open the records, how to interpret "discretion" and "serious research" remained controversial questions. The SAA supported the decision of the Library of Congress but encouraged the institution to adopt less ambiguous language in any future deeds of gift.[26]

Historic preservationists arrive at their chosen career through several different avenues. Some are archaeologists, some are architects, some are urban planners, and some are historians. Depending on a person's professional affiliation, they might adhere to different codes of professional ethics.

In 1966, Congress passed the National Historic Preservation Act. It provides a framework within which individuals and local and state governments can protect historic properties. Local communities, through their governments, created various civic commissions – landmark, historic preservation, and architectural review boards – to implement the new law.

The National Alliance of Preservation Commissions (NAPC) was formed in 1983 to act as a clearinghouse of information and to advocate for preservation commission efforts. In 2006, it developed a *Code of Ethics* that provides a set of principles for commissioners to follow. It is a reminder to all commissioners that they are, in fact, public servants and need to act accordingly.

The NAPC divided the Code into three main categories. The first is responsibility to the community: "The most effective historic preservation takes place locally, and all preservation commissioners and staff should remember that it is their duty, as public servants, to advance the greater good of the community." The second category is for commissioners to respect their responsibility to the profession. In this category, the NAPC acknowledges the unique nature of historic preservation as a career choice:

Preservation commissioners and staff are drawn from many disciplines and backgrounds. The common thread that joins them is their interest and commitment to preserving heritage resources in their communities. A multi-disciplinary profession has developed over the years from the historic preservation movement, and commissioners and staff should advance the best interests of this profession in the context of their commission work.

The last category is standards of professional conduct:

As public servants, commissioners and staff are expected to conduct themselves in accordance with the law. These standards set forth both a baseline for such legal conduct as well as aspirational goals for ethical behavior that may require a conscientious effort to attain.

Within each category, the code elaborates even further on each principle.

Historic preservationists come from a variety of disciplines. The NAPC's *Code of Ethics* provides guidelines, just as the AAM and SAA do for museum workers and archivists. While the details are different because of the nature of the work, all three organizations stress the importance of viewing one's work as public service. In doing so, it provides direction for conducting principled practices.

Ethics in oral history overlaps with many of these other topics. In particular, what is legal is not always ethical. Although the Oral History Association has not drafted a code of ethics, it does have a *Statement on Ethics*. Also, ethical concerns are embedded in its *Statement of Best Practices*. The history of oral history and best practices are covered in depth in Chapter 6, Recording Memory as History. This section will focus on the problems of ethics.

Questions about the ethical obligations of an interview-historian in constructing an oral history have been central to the development of the field of oral history since its articulation as a distinct methodology in the 1950s.[27] Some of those same concerns still permeate discussions about the ethics of process and product. Should oral historians build intimate rapports or keep an objective distance from narrators? Should oral historians work to interview people amid a crisis or wait? Can an interview cause personal, political, or psychological harm? The Oral History Association's *Statement on Ethics* notes, "everyone involved in oral history work, from interviewers and narrators to archivists and researchers, becomes part of a web of mutual responsibility working to ensure that the narrator's perspective, dignity, privacy, and safety are respected."[28] This "work" includes that of preparation and communication before the interview, the interview itself, the preservation of the conversation and its access to the public, and, last, the use of oral sources.

An additional aspect that keeps morphing is the issue of whether Institutional Review Boards (IRBs) should be reviewing oral histories. (IRBs can most often be found at universities.) Best practices today for oral histories demand that inter-view-historians ask and receive consent from their narrators. Originally, IRBs developed to evaluate the merits of biomedical research with human subjects at institutions receiving federal funds. In the 1980s, IRBs expanded their areas of purview to include the social sciences and humanities. However, according to oral historians, oral histories functioned very differently than biomedical research. For instance, IRBs typically demanded that human subjects be identified with pseudonyms to protect identities. However, this practice was at odds with the entire purpose of oral history, which is to record a specific narrator's memories of an event. Researchers are also required by IRBs to submit their questions before they conduct the research. However, in the case of oral history, researchers tailor the questions to each narrator during the interview. Overall, the goal of producing generalizable knowledge from a medical research study is different than the pur-pose of creating individualized knowledge from oral history.

In the late 1990s, the Oral History Association joined with the American Historical Association and the Organization of American Historians to work with the federal Office for Human Research Protection (OHRP) to create more explicit guidelines for IRBs about oral history projects. Specifically, the three organiza-tions lobbied to make oral histories exempt from review.[29] The OHRP agreed to a certain extent. In 2003, the OHRP determined that most oral histories were exempt. In 2015, the US Department of Health and Human Services recom-mended excluding oral history from review by IRBs. It did so based on the fact that the Oral History Association has a *Statement on Ethics* and informed consent is an established best practice.[30] As with museum workers, archivists, and historic preservationists, what is ethical is not always legal.

Perhaps the most significant conflict between what is ethical and what is legal for oral historians is what to do when a historian-interviewer encounters evidence of a crime. In March of 2011, authorities in Great Britain asked Boston College to turn over materials from its oral history program. In the late 1990s, the conflict in Northern Ireland looked to be concluding, and as part of an oral history project, two interviewers tried to capture the memories of those who had participated. These oral histories were to be kept closed until the interviewee's deaths. The interviewers assured the interviewees that the contents would be kept confidential.[31] One of the interviewees died in 2008. He had said in his interview that he would not have spoken to the interviewer without the condition of it being closed: "I think a lot of the stuff I'm saying here, I'm saying it on trust, because I have a trust in you. I have never, ever, ever admitted to being a member of the

IRA – never – and I've just done it here." Unfortunately for oral historians, the law says that they must abide by court orders.[32] There is no doctor–patient or attorney–client confidentiality type of protection for oral history.

Not all ethical dilemmas for oral historians rise to this level. For instance, Selma Thomas, a US-based filmmaker who often creates and installs exhibits for museums, recounted a more routine ethical question. She was interviewing an important figure in the National Association for Stock Car Auto Racing (NASCAR) racing history. In describing his background, he mentioned how his childhood had been difficult. His mother died when he was seven, and he began hanging around the local racetrack where race car drivers and owners began taking care of him. At the age of 11, his father kicked him out of the family's home. The young boy found employment at a local junkyard, and his new boss provided him with an old car to use as a living space. The interviewee shared information that provided enough background for people to understand his history but did not share any other intimate details about this time in his life. Thomas asked herself whether "on behalf of the public record" did she "have the right to press him?" In the end, she decided no. She acknowledged the fact that "not all informants share all their memories." Furthermore, pressing the interviewee on what were very private memories did not advance the purpose of the interview, which was to gather memories related to the history of race car driving.[33]

Whether you are working in a museum, archives, historic site, or engaging in the practice of oral history, you are entrusted with collecting, preserving, and interpreting history. Doing so is a public service. Being entrusted with protecting and advocating for historical resources involves questions of ethics. Knowing what different professional organizations have to say about the ideas and behaviors expected of experts in their fields is vitally important for anyone contemplating a career in public history.

Practice

In this practice section, five scenarios relate to working in a museum, archive, historic preservation, and oral history. Sometimes there is an overlap between these types of activities and institutions. As you answer a scenario, consult the relevant code of ethics for that profession and/or institution.

Scenario 1: You are an education coordinator for a state museum, and an intern has been assigned to work with you by the director. You and the intern write out a proposal that outlines the different kinds of jobs the intern will be performing. The intern will work on the reorganization of a collection of Greek vases by doing a condition assessment and rehousing materials where appropriate. The intern will also create materials for K-12 educators based on the collection. Nothing in the contract agreement with the intern specifies that the intern will give tours. One day you are shorthanded, and you ask the intern to provide a tour for a school group of middle school age, which the intern is excited to do. The exhibit they will visit is about Ancient Rome and contains artifacts in the form of statues and pottery. Afterward, you ask the intern how it went, and they tell you it went well. A few weeks later, you receive a letter from the teacher complaining that the intern discussed at length a piece of pottery that showed nude men. The teacher felt it was inappropriate for his school group. The teacher demands that the museum remove the piece from the display and fire the intern. You ask the intern about the tour. She tells you that she described a piece of pottery that depicted Hercules fighting a lion. She believed it would be one of the Roman Myths the students would know. She also talked about the pottery techniques the Romans used to make the vase and for what purposes the Romans might have used the vessel.

Questions to Consider

Was it ethical for the education director to ask the intern to conduct the tour? Was the tour given in an ethically appropriate manner? Should the education director respond to the teacher and if so, how?

Scenario 2: You are the director of a historic house museum in Florida, and you have decided to revamp an exhibit that is in the dining room of the house. The house's history extended back to the 1820s and remained in one family's possession until they created a foundation to turn it into a museum in the 1980s. There is no mission statement for the museum. However, when you took the job you were told that the foundation wanted the museum to promote cultural understanding of the region's history as well as to preserve the history of the family. The family initially made money in cotton and later turned the estate into a quail hunting plantation. You have a tremendous amount of information about the items the family owned and less about the men and women who worked in the house.

Questions to Consider

Are there issues of minorities and women that you need to consider as you revamp the exhibit?
If you redo the display in this room, will you redo any of the other displays?
How will you think about issues of invisibility and stereotyping?

Scenario 3: You are the director of a small museum and archives that is housed inside a liberal arts college. Its mission is to preserve, collect, and interpret material culture about that institution. You are the institution's archivist as well as its museum director. One day the student volunteer at the front reception desk calls you to the lobby to speak with someone who has come to donate materials. You arrive in the lobby, and all you see is a big box and the receptionist. He tells you that the donor said she was in a hurry and left. He did not get her name or a contact number. You open the box, and there is no information inside as to who the owner was. It contains some old college yearbooks that you don't have, a ballpoint pen with the school's name on it, some baseball cards, old photographs that are unidentified and don't appear to be on campus grounds, and a fraternity paddle that seems to have dried blood on it and looks like it was made out of ivory. As an aside, you believe that fraternities on campus promote philanthropy.

Questions to Consider

Do you bring the materials up to your office?
Do you keep all of the items?
What if it turns out the baseball cards are worth money?
Do you have the blood on the paddle analyzed?
Can you put any of the items on display?
If you put the fraternity paddle on display, how would you interpret it?

Scenario 4: You are an architect who serves on a local historic preservation committee for a small town. It has come to your attention that a community organization (an art gallery) is trying to sell one of its properties upon which is one of the oldest homes in the town. You go to speak with their director and she tells you that the organization is experiencing financial difficulties. They made some bad financial decisions and need to sell the property to remain afloat. If they can't sell the property with the old house on it, they believe they might be able to sell it if they demolish the house. The director tells you that the old house needs significant work to make it habitable, but she has not been in contact with any contractors who regularly do historic preservation work in the community. As an architect, your own company provides just that kind of assistance. As a thank you for coming to talk, the director of the arts organization offers you two free passes to an upcoming event, for which the tickets are $100 apiece.

Questions to Consider

Do you offer your company's services to assess the historic house?
What do you tell the other members of the historic preservation committee?

Scenario 5: Twenty years ago, as a graduate student, you interviewed 25 older women about their experiences giving birth in a public hospital. In each of their interviews the interviewees verbally agreed to donate their oral histories to your university's oral history center. However, you did not prepare a written agreement. One of the interviewees requested in her interview that her name be withheld until after her death. First, she discussed giving birth. She then decided to discuss her experience having an illegal abortion in the 1940s. You go through the normal process of transcription, and she does not cross this part out. Once the transcript is complete, you give her a copy of the transcript of the oral history for her to keep. The transcript was released under "anonymous." She has now died, and the archive has switched "anonymous" to the person's name. An upset family member contacted you after having searched the internet and found a link to the transcript. They ask that you destroy the oral history.

Questions to Consider

Should you abide by the family's wishes?
Can you conceive of any alternatives to destroying the oral history that the family
  might find acceptable?

Further Resources

- American Alliance of Museums, *Code of Ethics*, https://www.aam-us.org/programs/ethics-standards-and-professional-practices/code-of-ethics-for-museums.
- American Historical Association, *Statement on Standards of Professional Conduct*, www.historians.org/jobs-and-professional-development/statements-standards-and-guidelines-of-the-discipline/statement-on-standards-of-professional-conduct.
- Burton, Antoinette. *Archive Stories: Facts, Fictions, and the Writing of History.* Durham, NC: Duke University Press, 2006.

- Colwell, Chip. "Can Repatriation Heal the Wounds of History." *The Public Historian* 41, no.1 (February 2019): 90–110.
- Cox, Richard J. *Ethics, Accountability, and Recordkeeping in a Dangerous World.* London: Facet Publishing, 2007.
- Cumo, James. *Whose Culture? The Promise of Museums and the Debate over Antiquities.* Princeton, NJ: Princeton University Press, 2009.
- Edson, Gary. *Museum Ethics.* New York, NY: Routledge, 1997.
- Fine-Dare, Kathleen S. "Disciplinary Renewal Out of National Disgrace: Native American Graves Protection and Repatriation Act Compliance in the Academy." *Radical History Review* 68 (1997): 25–53.
- International Council of Museums, *Code of Ethics for Museums,* https://icom.museum/en/activities/standards-guidelines/code-of-ethics.
- Lavine, Steven D. *Exhibiting Cultures: The Poetics and Politics of Museum Display.* Washington, DC: Smithsonian Books, 1991.
- Marstine, Janet C. *The Routledge Companion to Museum Ethics: Redefining Ethics for the Twenty-First Century Museum.* New York, NY: Routledge, 2011.
- National Alliance of Preservation Commissions, *Code of Ethics for Commissioners and Staff,* www.okhistory.org/shpo/clgs/ethics.pdf.
- National Council on Public History, *Code of Ethics and Professional Conduct,* https://ncph.org/about/governance-committees/code-of-ethics-and-professional-conduct.
- Neuenschwander, John A. *A Guide to Oral History and the Law.* New York, NY: Oxford University Press, 2009.
- Oral History Association, *Statement on Ethics,* www.oralhistory.org/oha-statement-on-ethics.
- Oral History Association, *Principles and Best Practices for Oral History,* adopted October 2009, www.oralhistory.org/do-oral-history/principles-and-practices.
- Page, Max. *Giving Preservation a History: Histories of Historic Preservation in the United States.* New York, NY: Routledge, 2003.
- "Roundtable: Curating History in Museums." *The Public Historian* 14, no. 3 (Summer 1992).
- "Roundtable: Ethics in Practice." *The Public Historian* 28, no. 1 (Winter 2006).
- "Roundtable: Ethics and Public History." *The Public Historian* 8, no. 1 (January 1986).
- "Roundtable: History After the Enola Gay." *The Journal of American History* 82, no. 3 (December 1995).
- Sheftel, Anna, and Stacey Zembrzycki. "Who's Afraid of Oral History? Fifty Years of Debates and Anxiety about Ethics." *Oral History Review* 43, no. 2 (2016): 338–366.

- Shopes, Linda. *Human Subjects and Institutional Review Boards*, Oral History Association, www.oralhistory.org/do-oral-history/oral-history-and-irb-review.
- Society of American Archivists, *Core Values Statement and Code of Ethics for Archivists*, www2.archivists.org/statements/saa-core-values-statement-and-code-of-ethics.
- Society of American Archivists, *Standards & Best Practices Resource Guide*, www2.archivists.org/groups/museum-archives-section/standards-best-practices-resource-guide.
- Sullivan, Robert. "Evaluating the Ethics and Consciences of Museums." In *Reinventing the Museum*, edited by Gail Anderson, Lanham, MD: Alta Mira Press, 2004.
- Thomas, Selma. "Private Memory in a Public Space: Oral History and Museums." In *Oral History and Public Memories*, edited by Paula Hamilton and Linda Shopes, Philadelphia, PA: Temple University Press, 2008.
- Warren, Karen J. "A Philosophical Perspective on the Ethics and Resolution of Cultural Properties Issues." In *Reinventing the Museum*, edited by Gail Anderson, Lanham, MD: Alta Mira Press, 2004.
- Weil, Stephen E. *Making Museums Matter*. Washington, DC: Smithsonian Institute, 2002.

References

1 American Historical Association, "Statement on Standards of Professional Conduct," www.historians.org/jobs-and-professional-development/statements-standards-and-guidelines-of-the-discipline/statement-on-standards-of-professional-conduct.

2 Katharine T. Corbett and Howard S. (Dick) Miller, "A Shared Inquiry into Shared Inquiry," *The Public Historian* 28, no. 1 (2006): 15–38.

3 National Council on Public History, "NCPH Code of Ethics and Professional Conduct," https://ncph.org/about/governance-committees/code-of-ethics-and-professional-conduct.

4 Tereza Cristina Scheiner, "Ethics and the Environment," in *Museum Ethics*, ed. Gary Edson (New York, NY: Routledge, 1997), 180.

5 AAM, "Code of Ethics," www.aam-us.org/programs/ethics-standards-and-professional-practices/code-of-ethics-for-museums.

6 Ibid.

7 Gary Edson, " Ethics and the Profession," in *Museum Ethics*, ed. Gary Edson (New York, NY: Routledge, 1997), 32.

8 The American Association of Museums, "Code of Ethics for Museum Workers (1925)," http://ethics.iit.edu/codes/AAMu%201925.pdf.

9 Kenneth Hudson quoted in Stephen E. Weil, *Making Museums Matter* (Washington, DC: Smithsonian Institute, 2002), 30–31.

10 Edson, "Ethics," 10 and 13.

11 AAM, "Code of Ethics," https://www.aam-us.org/programs/ethics-standards-and-professional-practices/code-of-ethics-for-museums/. The very first articulation of this idea in 1925 stated, "The life of the museum worker, whether he be a humble laborer or a responsible trustee, is essentially one of service." http://ethics.iit.edu/codes/AAMu%201925.pdf.

12 Edson, "Ethics," 13 and 14.

13 Edson, "Ethics," 14. ICOM's Code has been updated twice since 1986, once in 2001 and again in 2004. While much of the content builds on earlier versions, the format was revised based on the most current practices.

14 ICOM, "Code of Ethics for Museums," https://icom.museum/wp-content/uploads/2018/07/ICOM-code-En-web.pdf.

15 UNESCO, "Convention for the Protection of Cultural Property in the Event of Armed Conflict with Regulations for the Execution of the Convention 1954," http://portal.unesco.org/en/ev.php-URL_ID=13637&URL_DO=DO_TOPIC&URL_SECTION=201.html.

16 UNESCO, "Information Kit," http://www.unesco.org/new/fileadmin/MULTIMEDIA/HQ/CLT/pdf/1954Convention-InfoKit-EN-Fina-webl_02.pdf.

17 Kathleen S. Fine-Dare, "Disciplinary Renewal Out of National Disgrace: Native American Graves Protection and Repatriation Act Compliance in the Academy," *Radical History Review* 68 (1997): 25–26.

18 Chip Colwell, "Can Repatriation Heal the Wounds of History," *The Public Historian* 41, no. 1 (February 2019): 90.

19 Fine-Dare, "Disciplinary Renewal," 36–37.

20 Ibid.

21 Colwell, "Can Repatriation Heal the Wounds of History," 92–94.

22 Karen J. Warren, "A Philosophical Perspective on the Ethics and Resolution of Cultural Properties Issues," in *Reinventing the Museum*, ed. Gail Anderson, (Lanham, MD: Alta Mira Press, 2004): 320.

23 Society of American Archivists, "SAA Core Values Statement and Code of Ethics," www2.archivists.org/statements/saa-core-values-statement-and-code-of-ethics.

24 Ibid.

25 John A. Neuenschwander, *A Guide to Oral History and the Law* (New York, NY: Oxford University Press, 2009), 4–5; Randall C. Jimerson, "Ethical Concerns for Archivists," *The Public Historian* 28, no. 1 (2006): 87–89.

26 Neuenschwander, *A Guide,* 4–5; Jimerson, "Ethical Concerns for Archivists," 87–89.

27 Anna Sheftel and Stacey Zembrzycki, "Who's Afraid of Oral History? Fifty Years of Debates and Anxiety about Ethics," *Oral History Review* 43 no. 2 (2016): 338–366.

28 Oral History Association, "OHA Statement on Ethics," www.oralhistory.org/oha-statement-on-ethics.

29 Mary Larson, "Steering Clear of the Rocks: A Look at the Current State of Oral History Ethics in the Digital Age," *Oral History Review* 40, no. 1 (March 2013): 36–39.

30 Oral History Association, "Information about IRBs," www.oralhistory.org/information-about-irbs.

31 Jim Dwyer, "Secret Archive of Ulster Troubles Faces Subpoena," *New York Times,* May 13, 2011, www.nytimes.com/2011/05/13/world/europe/13ireland.html.

32 Neuenschwander, *A Guide*, 24–25 and 109–110.

33 Selma Thomas, "Private Memory in a Public Space: Oral History and Museums," in *Oral History and Public Memories*, ed. Paula Hamilton and Linda Shopes (Philadelphia, PA: Temple University Press, 2008): 98–100.

Index

Page numbers in *italics* refer to Figures

Public History: An Introduction from Theory to Application, First Edition. Jennifer Lisa Koslow.
© 2021 by John Wiley & Sons, Inc. Published 2021 by John Wiley & Sons, Inc.

Carnegie Institution   99
Carson, Dr. Clayborne   128
Carter, President Jimmy   124
Casey, Lt. Col. Thomas Lincoln
   121
Center for History and New Media
   (CHNM)   170–173
Cerf, Vinton (Vint)   166
CERN   168, 169
Certified Local Government (CLG)
   Program   87
Charleston Library Society   18
Chatelain, Verne   5–6
Cheney, Lynne   37
citation management programs   176
civil rights   7, 31, 33–34
   Haymarket tragedy   119
Civil Rights Act (1964)   31
Civil War   5, 37, 64, 65, 171
   Jefferson's home   81–82
   monuments ad statues   114, 121
   oral history   141
   see also Confederacy
Civilian Conservation Corps   5
Clark, Wes   165
Clark, William   20
Clarke, John Henrik   32
class   19, 22, 30, 34, 43
   Haymarket monument   116, 119
Cleveland, President Grover   145
Cleveland Museum of Art   29
Clinton, President Bill   127, 150
Coca-Cola Museum (Atlanta)
   45, *46*
Cohen, Daniel J.   171, 173
Colonial Dames of America   70
Colonial Williamsburg   30, 69–70, *71*,
   71–72, 75
Columbia Oral History Research
   Office   145–146, 148, 149, 152

Commission of Fine Arts   122, 124,
   127, 130
Committee on Public
   Information (CPI)   3
Commodore   167
communism   115
community archives   93
computers   161, *162*, 162–173
Confederacy   65, 81, 85, 97
   Jefferson's home   81–82
   monuments and statues   113–115,
   131, 132
Connor, R. D. W.   102
constructivism   44
Cook, James   23
Cooks, Bridget R.   32
Coolidge, President Calvin   100
Corbett, Katharine T.   10
Correll, John T.   40–41
Corse, Carita Doggett   141
Crabtree, Charlotte   37–38
Crouch, Tom   38
crowdsourcing   176
cultural heritage   59, 69, 80, 85, 87
   ethics   188–189
Cultural Property   188, 189, 190
Cunningham, Ann Pamela   60, 62, *63*,
   63–65, 81
Cunningham, Louisa   62

d

Dalal, Yogen   166
Daley, Mayor Richard M.   117, 119
Darwin, Charles   24
Daughters of the American
   Revolution   5, 65, 99, 100
Daughters of the Confederacy   65
Davies, Donald   165
de la Garza, Luis Alberto Campos   106
Degan, Frank   116
Degan, Mathias   116, 118